WAITING FOR PEACE
THE JOURNALS & CORRESPONDENCE
OF A WORLD WAR II MEDIC

WAITING *for* PEACE

THE JOURNALS & CORRESPONDENCE
OF A WORLD WAR II MEDIC

COMPILED AND EDITED BY
KAREN BERKEY HUNTSBERGER

LUMINARE PRESS
WWW.LUMINAREPRESS.COM

Printed in the United States of America
Cover Design by Claire Flint

Luminare Press
467 W 17th Ave
Eugene, OR 97401
www.luminarepress.com

LCCN: 2015902784
ISBN: 978-1-937303-47-1

Dedicated to my mother,
Martha Barrett Berkey,
who knew this should be a book
and to Dad and Buster,
who lived the story.

TABLE OF CONTENTS

CHAPTER ONE – PRELUDE TO SERVICE 7

CHAPTER TWO – EMBARKATION 29

CHAPTER THREE – FRANCE! 41

CHAPTER FOUR – EN ROUTE TO THE FRONT 57

CHAPTER FIVE – DECEMBER 1944 85

CHAPTER SIX – WOUNDED AND WORRIED 109

CHAPTER SEVEN – RELIEF 119

CHAPTER EIGHT – FEBRUARY 1945 145

CHAPTER NINE – MARCH 1945 167

CHAPTER TEN – THE FINAL PUSH 191

CHAPTER ELEVEN – IT'S OVER 233

CHAPTER TWELVE – LOOKING BACK AND MOVING
    FORWARD 265

CHAPTER THIRTEEN – JULY 1945 293

CHAPTER FOURTEEN – AUGUST 1945 315

CHAPTER FIFTEEN – SEPTEMBER 1945 341

CHAPTER SIXTEEN – WAITING TO GO HOME 353

EPILOGUE 364

WHO'S WHO – FURTHER INFORMATION 365

BIBLIOGRAPHY 371

ACKNOWLEDGMENTS 381

Dragon teeth stood gray and stolid,

In among them he crept and bled.

Smart enough that he should've been scared,

Knew why, and how he bitterly cared.

Now all there was, was Pfalz gray sky,

to see the end of a futile try.

And he, whose person had belied,

Lived and fought and so slowly died.

—Richard Berkey 1945

PREFACE

My father never talked about the war and I never asked. More than twenty years after he passed away, I still have so many questions. I am grateful for the extraordinary opportunity to combine these journals, letters, and photos into a single narrative. I have come to know my father, his siblings, and his parents in a way that would not have been possible otherwise.

From 1939 to 1945 over 12 million United States citizens served in World War II. 400,000 were killed, 670,000 were wounded, and 73,000 went missing in action. More than 40 nations were involved and more than 60 million people were killed worldwide.

These figures are staggering. They do not include the millions who suffered far from the battlefield from the loss or wounding of a family member or loved one, people who suffered displacement or loss of their homes and their livelihoods, and children who were sent out of harm's way. The statistics do not speak of the millions who contributed to the war machine by working in a multitude of needed industries. They manufactured aircraft, ships, tanks, military vehicles, munitions, garments, and medical supplies. They worked in agriculture, food processing, lumber, rubber, and the media industries that supplied propaganda and educational material. Virtually every American's life was affected, from the man serving on the front lines to the grandmother sitting at home knitting bandages.

This book is about one young man's war experience. He was a combat medic. The stories here come from his journals, the letters he sent home, and the letters sent to him. They also come from his family—from two brothers and a sister in the Navy, from a sister away at college, from a youngest sister and parents at home, and from friends scattered by the forces of war. Together these journals and letters tell a story of people behaving dutifully, unselfishly, and honorably in a world out of control. Through this book, I hope that readers will connect with the people who lived the story, and through their experiences, to every soldier who served.

Karen Berkey Huntsberger

June 24, 2014

WHO'S WHO

FAMILY

Richard J. Berkey – Combat Medic

Lennie Martin Berkey (Mother) – Richard's mother

James G. Berkey (Dad or Daddy) – Richard's father

Jonas Berkey – Richard's older brother

Lucy Berkey – Richard's oldest sister

Virginia Berkey – Richard's younger sister

David Berkey – Richard's youngest brother

Eleanor Berkey – Richard's youngest sister

Mildred Berkey – Jonas Berkey's wife

FRIENDS

(Frank E.) Buster Crockett (Crockey) – Richard's best friend from childhood

Harold Bush (Dee) – Richard's high school and college friend

Claude and Eska Bush – Dee's parents

Edgar DeJean (DeJean) – Richard's high school and college friend

Maurice E. Berkey (Junior) – Richard's cousin

Eugene Rodman (Rodman) – Richard's high school friend

Julia – Richard's high school and college friend

68TH ARMORED INFANTRY BATTALION MEDICAL DETACHMENT

Norman Eliasson (Eli) – Aid Station/Field Hospital Tech

Allan Goldstein (Goldie) – B Company Medic

Glenn Scott (Scotty) – C Company Medic

Captain Miller – Company Dentist

Captain Battenfeld – Commander of the 68th Armored Infantry Battalion Medical Detachment

68TH ARMORED INFANTRY BATTALION C COMPANY

There were 251 members of C Company upon arrival in France. As a medic attached to C Company, Richard was responsible for caring for the men of the 3rd Platoon with appropriate medical treatment on and off the battlefield. Some of these men became his friends.

WORLD WAR II COMBAT MEDIC DUTIES

A combat medic's job was to get the wounded off the battlefield as quickly as possible. Medics were unarmed and risked their lives every time they came to the aid of a wounded man. When they reached the wounded, they had to quickly assess the injuries, stop bleeding, apply a tourniquet if necessary, sometimes give morphine for pain, and get the patient out of harm's way.

A wounded soldier had an 85% chance of survival if treated within an hour of being injured. If the soldier was mobile, he and the medic ran, walked, or crawled out of range of gunfire. If the soldier was "walking wounded," he would then make his way to a casualty collection point alone, and the medic would stay at the front line to treat other casualties. If the injured man was not ambulatory, litter bearers retrieved him as soon as possible. The red or white crosses on medics' helmets and armbands were supposed to protect them from enemy fire, but enemy soldiers often could not see the crosses or did not care.

Each medic carried a small bag with these basic supplies: scissors, safety pins, iodine swabs, burn-injury set, gauze bandages, eye dressing, tourniquet, litter carrying straps, emergency medical tags (tied to patients' clothing), pencil, various medications (laxative, quinine, glycyrrhiza and opium compound, analgesics, ipecac and opium powder, apomorphine hydrochloride, atropine sulfate, cocaine hydrochloride, morphine sulfate, hydroglycerin, strychnine sulfate, morphine tartrate syrettes, sulfadiazine, sulfanilamide), hypodermic needles, thermometer, adhesive, plasters, smelling salts, surgical knife, forceps, suture silk, and compressed cotton for earplugs.

EVACUATION OF WOUNDED DURING WORLD WAR II

Injured soldiers traveled from the casualty collection point by jeep or ambulance 1-3 miles behind the line of battle to the forward aid station. At the aid station a physician removed the temporary bandaging, made a diagnosis, and gave the soldier blood plasma and morphine as needed. If surgery was necessary, the patient was rushed to a clearing company far in the rear, where surgery would be performed. When able to travel, the casualty would be moved by ambulance to an evacuation hospital in a safe city. Sometimes the ambulance would take the casualty to a hospital train that delivered patients to the evacuation hospital. —Ed.

68th Armored Infantry Battalion Organization (AIB)	
Headquarters Company	*Service Company*
169 men Commanding officers and staff	73 men Technical support, communications, vehicle maintenance, food, and supplies

Company A Rifle Company 251 men Infantry—on the battlefield	*Company B* Rifle Company 251 men Infantry—on the battlefield	*Company C* Rifle Company 251 men Infantry—on the battlefield

Medical Detachment
36 men, divided into Aid Station Squad,
Litter Bearer Squad, and Company Aid Squad
4 combat medics were assigned to each Rifle Company

This chart is very basic for the sake of clarifying
the larger divisions of the 68th AIB

The majority of the text focuses on Richard's year overseas in France and Germany. Chapter One presents background material to help readers understand how Richard came to be a combat medic. —Ed.

CHAPTER ONE
PRELUDE TO SERVICE

December 9, 1941, two days after Pearl Harbor was bombed

Mother to Richard, pre-med student at Indiana University (IU)

Dear Richard,

I started a letter to you yesterday but in the excitement of war news and everything I did not get very far. We had a cold house, too, most of the day, for the furnace had been smoking again and Daddy and David cleaned it out. You are probably glad you escaped the job this time.

We have been thinking a lot about you boys and this terrible situation. It looks as if we are in for a bad time of it. We heard this morning over the radio that the students at Illinois U were all out putting on a demonstration last night, and we wondered if IU was doing the same.

Patriotism is fine but I do hate to hear people trying to arouse racial hatred. I heard a congressman say, "Let's exterminate those war-mad Jap devils from the face of the earth." There may be a group of leaders who do deserve to be wiped out but most of the Jap soldiers are boys just like you, with homes and families and ambitions of their own, and it isn't their fault they are made to fight. Why can't the poor old earth just learn to exterminate *War*?

This is the week when all the clubs have their Christmas parties but nobody seems to be in much of a mood for them. I did not go to Study Club this afternoon but will go to Bethany Circle tomorrow. I am to have devotions and the subject is the usual Christmas one of "Peace." You can imagine how hard it will be this time.

Yesterday afternoon we made a popcorn Christmas tree decorated with red berries. We saved it until noon today but David couldn't wait any longer and dug in.

I really must do something about Christmas shopping before long. I haven't been to town yet, except to the parade week before last and I got only a few little things then. Here comes Daddy, so I must stop and warm up supper.

With Love,

Mother

From Richard's Journal, Indiana University[1]

August 8, 1942

War bad. Haven't got draft papers yet.

NOTICE TO REGISTRANT
TO APPEAR FOR
PHYSICAL EXAMINATION
August 28 , 19 42
(Date of mailing)

You are directed to report for physical examination by the local board examiner at the time and place designated below:

Dr. J. L. Mitchell - Salem, Indiana
(Place of examination)

at 3:30 p.m., on September 2 , 19 42

This examination will be of a preliminary nature, for the purpose of disclosing only *obvious* physical defects, and will not finally determine your acceptance or rejection by the armed forces.

If you are so far from your local board area that reporting for the above physical examination will constitute a hardship, you may submit a request to your local board for reference to another local board for preliminary physical examination. Your request must include the following information:

1. The reasons for your request for reference to another local board.
2. The designation (name and location) of the local board having jurisdiction over the area in which you are now located.

Failure to comply with this notice will result in your being declared a delinquent and subjected to the penalties provided by law.

D. S. S. Form 201
(Rev. 4-1-42)
Member-Clerk of Local Board.

October 14, 1942

Draft of 18-19 year olds likely to be soon.

---

1   Richard was the second generation of his family to attend IU. His mother graduated in June 1917, with an AB degree, cum laude, in journalism. This was a significant achievement for a woman, especially during World War I. —Ed.

October 22, 1942

Got letter from draft board and insurance company, made replies.

November 16, 1942

Did not go to any classes. I talked to Dean of Men and obtained Official Complete Withdrawal due to military reasons from IU, effective Nov. 13 (last Friday).

November 23, 1942

Packed all my belongings in car this morning. Bid all and Bloomington adieu, thus my last day at old IU.

From Richard's Journal, at home waiting to enter the Army

November 26-30, 1942

These days were spent doing what I wanted to do, messing around with the automobiles, hunting rabbits and quail, doing a little work now and then for my father and Mr. Bush and whoever else. Nothing seems to be very exciting around here, but only quiet and just plain wonderful, as only one's home should be. Just as I dream that someday I may have a wife and quiet peaceful home.

December 5-9, 1942

It's very nice to be able to stay home at times like these while our neighbors' boys are giving their lives so that places like little Salem may live on and flourish in peace and happiness. These days were also spent enjoying life as it really should be and as some day after I get out of the Army, it's going to be, first work and then play and relaxation. Some of these days when it's rainy and things are rather gloomy I try to cheer myself up, but all in vain. I get disgusted at a small task I'm trying to do, and I swear and curse myself and the task at hand. And then at night in my prayer at bedtime, I forgive myself.

January 1, 1943

What this year holds for me is of course unknown, but what this year holds for this good earth and its people is a much *greater* unknown because it is easy to foresee that with this terrible war, many human lives must be shed all in foolishness. If only the great military leaders, those merciless murderers, could spend a few hours with me just walking around and observing these wonderful things in and around Salem and Washington County—hunting wild game, helping farmers and townspeople with their work, and eating a good hearty meal. Oh! But how they would surely lay down their arms and enjoy the wonders of this world, nature always at her loveliest.

January 6, 1943

Got papers for Army—report 16th at Louisville.

January 16, 1943

Got up at 6:30. Went on Army bus to Louisville to physical exam for Army. Passed, with limited service, one hell of a day taking an examination, feel like hell tonight.

January 23, 1943

Got up at 6:00, ate and came to Fort Benjamin Harrison on bus with other guys. Sat around in barracks all afternoon and messed around. Didn't do anything and still got civilian clothes. This Army looks as if it's going to be fun at least while here.

January 30, 1943

Got up at 5:00. At last, my name is on the shipping list! Left Fort Benjamin Harrison at noon and arrived in Danville, Kentucky, at 10:00 tonight. Got admitted, etc. Another boy and I made trip alone to Darnell General Hospital, which is about 4 ½ miles from Danville. It's really a swell place, modern and nice looking, a swell Army post.

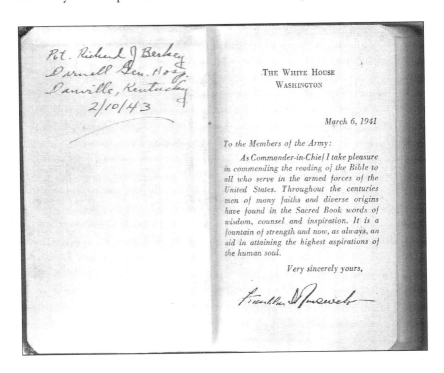

February 14, 1943

This is strictly an Army hospital for Army men who have become mentally sick while in service. Some are actually insane and others alcoholics and dopers, here for rest and treatment. This ward, D-1, has no bed patients, all suicide watch.

February 24, 1943

Wrote some letters tonight. Got a letter from Jonas today,[2] and he has completed his submarine-chasing schooling at Miami and is awaiting assignment to a boat. He said he was absorbing the Southern sun. He'll probably see some action soon and I hope and pray he comes through all right. I want all our boys to be safe, wherever they're in action. But, of course, although we want it to be, it can't possibly happen that all will come back home alive and safe. Many will end up in places like this hospital.

May 17, 1943

Found out today that for sure I go to Ohio State Friday for reclassification and assignment to ASTP.[3]

May 21, 1943

Six of us left at 4:30 a.m. for Ohio State, arrived here at 4 bells, some fun. Put in the dorms at the stadium. Will start refresher college courses soon, psych, math, military, etc.

---

2   Richard's oldest brother.
3   Richard was accepted for the Army Specialized Training Program (ASTP), which sent over 200,000 soldiers to 227 colleges throughout the U.S., where they took accelerated courses in foreign languages, medicine, engineering, psychology, dentistry, physical education, and military studies. Their standard workweek was fifty-nine hours long. The program ended by April 1944 as these troops were needed as replacements in Europe and the Pacific. The ASTP did allow many young men to attend college for the first time and encouraged them to pursue a college education when their military service ended. Soldiers were selected for the program based on their inherent ability instead of their socioeconomic status. Keefer, Louis E., "The Army Specialized Training Program In World War II," http://www.pierce-evans.org/ASTP%20in%20WWII.htm (Jan. 1, 2014).

August 19, 1943

Lucy joined the WAVES and is considered a seaman.[4] She will go to Hunter College, NY, to take her "boot" training. Four of us are in the service now.

December 13, 1943

Started new term today and what a bitch! Looks like we are going to be plenty busy this next twelve weeks with physics, recreation, history, English, military, geography, and math. Some schedule!

January 25, 1944

I've been in the Army one year now. Heard on radio this morning that ASTP was soon going to be disbanded. I hope so, I'm getting tired of going to school. Had history and math exams, study hall, and wrote letters.

February 27, 1944

Hitchhiked home to see Lucy on leave from WAVES in DC.

---

4   WAVES: Women Accepted for Volunteer Emergency Service. Part of the U.S. Navy, the WAVES program was created in August 1942 due to the need for more military personnel. At first, WAVES served only in the continental U.S., but later in the war many were sent to Hawaii. By the end of the war there were over 80,000 enlisted WAVES and 8,000 officers. —Ed.

Richard's ASTP Photo

Front row L-R: Jean Berkey (cousin), Lucy Berkey, Richard, Virginia Berkey, Mildred Berkey; Back row L-R: Martha Neal (cousin), Eleanor Berkey, February 28, 1944. Courtesy of Geneva Head

Richard and Lucy, February 28, 1944. Courtesy of Geneva Head

WAITING *for* PEACE

Richard and Lucy with their parents, February 28, 1944.
Courtesy of Geneva Head

February 29, 1944

Payday and Graduation Day! Classes and tonight had closing exercises in Wilson with a big speech, chorus, talks, etc. Got a certificate for 3 terms.

March 9, 1944

Got Big ASTP Diploma at 7 bells this morn, packed barracks bags, shipped out tonight at 6 bells, marched to station, big troop train, rode to Louisville, then to Nashville and Camp Campbell. Got here at noon, assigned temporarily to 501st Armored Field Artillery Battalion for reclassification.

Army Specialized Training Program

The ARMY *of the* UNITED STATES *hereby certifies that*

Private Richard J. Berkey, 35694330

has completed satisfactorily the course of study in

BASIC ENGINEERING

pursued at UNIVERSITY OF CINCINNATI

His training was completed on 4 March 1944 . *The record of his performance is available, on request by appropriate authority, for the purpose of determining his academic credit.*

BY ORDER OF THE SECRETARY OF WAR:

Registrar FOR CERTIFYING CERTIFICATION

W.E. DUVALL
Colonel, C.AC   COMMANDANT

March 11, 1944

This morn got classified and assigned to 84th Medical Battalion, 14th Armored Division. Buster Crockett (68th AIB, First Cook) came over this afternoon. Great reunion! First guy from Salem I've met since in Army. Went over to his mess hall and ate some pie he made (pumpkin). It was sure good, just like his mother makes. Sure swell to see him.

Buster Crockett and Richard Berkey, c. 1940.
Photographer unknown

Buster Crockett, 1944. Photo courtesy of Lynn Manship

KAREN BERKEY HUNTSBERGER

March 25, 1944

KP,[5] first time since been in Army, 14 months, but wasn't tough. Went to a show tonight, have pretty good shows here every night, not very satisfied with first impression of this outfit—entirely too much *chicken.*

April 2, 1944

Jonas made lieutenant last month and David got Seaman 1st Class, also Lucy.

April 27, 1944

Volunteered for infantry. Out in field today, clearing platoon procedure, signed furlough papers for May 1-10, and best of all, signed transfer to infantry.

June 2, 1944

On guard again this morn, tower guard over at stockade. Lots of trees and birds around. I counted 18 different kinds of birds when on guard. Crockey and I took off for home about noon and got there at 10 bells tonight. Nice to be home again!

June 6, 1944

D-Day! The much-awaited day. Allies invade France between Le Havre and Cherbourg successfully. Was on guard in prison ward in State Hospital (2:00 a.m.) when I heard the news. I listened to the radio all day, that's all that was on radio.

July 1, 1944

Today I am a godfather!! Frank Richard Crockett, IV, born at 7 a.m.—weight 7.5 pounds.[6]

---

5   KP: Kitchen Patrol. —Ed.
6   Buster Crockett's first child. —Ed.

Courtesy of the Salem Leader

July 6, 1944

Went out today with B Company—got up at 3 bells—went on actual combat firing problem. It was hot. I ate lots of blackberries and fired an M-1.

August 2, 1944

Assisted on a major surgery and a few emergency minor surgeries. I worked 11 hours and had a swell time on a major hernia this morn.

August 23, 1944

On range all day. Fired expert on both carbine and M-1.[7] Got 175 on carbine and 181 on M-1. I'm worn out tonight. Crockey came down and we went to the PX for ice cream.[8]

August 24, 1944

Went thru 2 combat courses this morn, street fighting and close combat. This afternoon laid out equipment for inspection and got glasses for gas mask.

---

7   Richard learned to hunt as a boy. He was already an expert marksman when he was drafted. —Ed.
8   PX: Post Exchange. The PX was like a small grocery and provided soldiers with American products when they were stationed away from home. Typical items sold at the PX included cigarettes, candy, gum, and toilet items. Cooke, James, "Chewing Gum, Candy Bars and Beer: The Army PX in World War II," *49th Parallel*, http://www.49thparallel.bham.ac.uk/back/issue26/Gomez-Gali-steo_review.pdf (Jan. 26, 2014).

August 31, 1944

Last day at hospital. Took off about 3:00. I'm mighty glad to get this school over with. Buster was down a while. Got 17-day furlough this afternoon at 4 bells. Missed this evening's train, so I caught the 2:12 in the morning.

September 19, 1944

Made will, power of attorney, and voted. Got things ready to go back. Last day of furlough. Saw a few friends before catching the 5:30 Monon train to Louisville.[9] Caught train in Louisville at 1:30 a.m., arrived back at camp at 2:30.

September 30, 1944

Got pass to go home. Won 25 bucks in crap game. Buster and I took off for home. Hit Clarksville and had a steak dinner and all. Caught train to New Albany, then hitchhiked to Borden. Walked from Borden to Blue River. Got a ride, dropped Buster off at Pekin, then home at 7:45.

October 1, 1944

New preacher at home. We had a big dinner. Saw Crockey's boy, Frank Richard. He is really growing, 3 months and 14 pounds. Drove around a little after dinner. Writing now at 3:00 p.m. This is all for this diary. Am enclosing in an envelope for Dad to put in the vault. The war is just beginning for me.

October 1, 1944 (new diary)

Hit the Monon, Crockey and I. It was rough to say goodbye to Mother and Dad. Got Crockey and myself rather intoxicated in Louisville, then got train to Clarksville.

---

9   The Monon, also known as the Chicago, Indianapolis, and Louisville Railroad, existed from 1897-1971. —Ed.

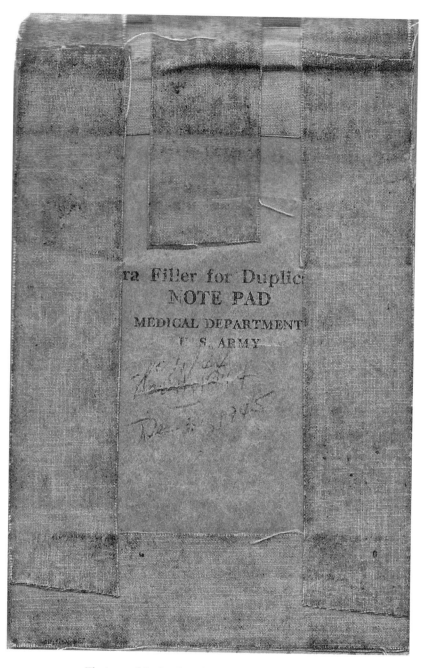

The journal Richard used during his year in Europe.
Actual dimensions are 3 5/8 x 5 3/4 x 5/8 inch

October 2, 1944

Sad sack today, just mooned around at dispensary. Saw Crockey a while tonight. I'm still sad, wrote letter home.

October 3, 1944

Dad to Richard

Dear Son,

Just to let you know that I brought the large envelope containing your things down to the office and put it in the vault. Yesterday Mother received word that little Tommy Wyman has the polio and is now in Riley Hospital. We received the tinted photo of Lucy. Good luck.

Your Dad,

James G. Berkey

October 4, 1944

Mother to Richard

Dear Richard,

We received your short epistle this morning and were glad to hear that you were still able to consume ice cream. It was so hot here this afternoon that Eleanor got a quart of Williams Grocery's Purity Made and it was swell. I have been cleaning around, washing windows, taking down screens, etc., all day.

We had a letter from Mildred. She looks for Jonas any day. His mail is being forwarded to their address and is piling up. She got a letter from a boy who had left Jonas' ship telling where all have been—about everyplace but Australia and New Zealand.

Your cousin Tommy is in Riley Hospital for infantile paralysis but it was a very light case and he will be home in three weeks. Following a fever I told you about, his leg was affected, but they say it is a weakness and not a real paralysis.

It's bedtime so I won't write much. Come again if you can. I have new sorghum and we'll have pancakes.

Lots of Love,

Mother

October 6, 1944

Richard's Journal

On train now. Breakfast in Knoxville, supper going through Blue Ridge.

October 7, 1944

Breakfast in Washington while watching the Potomac, cocoa while crossing the Susquehanna, dinner in Baltimore, supper in New York City while gazing at Statue of Liberty, New York skyline, and Empire State Building. We arrive at Camp Shanks, NY.[10]

October 8, 1944

Slept most of morning. Ran out of cigarette papers yesterday so had Cyphert or rather Martinez get me some more from PX tonight. Improvised a pipe out of a vaccine container and an eyedropper tube with cotton as a filter. Tasted like any damn pipe. Listened to Cards take Browns 2-0 this afternoon to make series 3-2 Cards. Lost 3 bucks and all my change in a crap game and am now completely broke except for a few odd pennies. Shufrin owes me 10 but he went broke in game, too. Goldstein got hot and won about 30 in one roll.

---

10   Camp Shanks was the largest Port of Embarkation in the United States. Over 1.3 million soldiers departed from this 2,040-acre base along the Hudson River. It was nicknamed "Last Stop, U.S.A." In 1942, the government informed 130 families that they had two weeks to move out of their homes and vacate their farmland. The land was converted in just three months and contained more than 2,500 buildings. At the end of the war, the families were able to purchase their land back from the government at the same price. Levine, David, "Remembering Camp Shanks," *Hudson Valley Magazine*, http://www.hvmag.com/Hudson-Valley-Magazine/September-2010/Remembering-Camp-Shanks/ (Jan. 20, 2014).

Checked inserts, got equipment, etc. Got a glance of Crockey this morn. Got typhus shot and physical. Felt bad all day.

Mother to Richard

Dear Richard,

We got your change of address card yesterday so suppose you've already gone east. You have just missed Jonas. He is already at Jeffersonville and called us last night. Mildred had gone to Vincennes and he had not yet been able to reach her by phone, so I don't know just when they will get up here.

If at all possible, you know we'd love to have you come to see Jonas—fly, maybe—but we know it isn't likely to be possible. If you are sailing at once, we wish you the very best luck. Our love and prayers are with you always.

Mother

October 9, 1944

Richard's Journal

Got letter from Mother today and Jonas is home—at last. Thank God for his safe return.

October 11, 1944

Richard's Journal

Played poker and shot dice most of afternoon and evening, won some and then went broke, as usual, broke completely. Ha! Saw Crockey a minute tonight in PX drinking a beer, had a few myself, ice cream, candy, etc. Lots of big games going on and plenty of excitement tonight, especially in the latrine. Chow isn't bad here, in fact quite good. Still smoking Duke's Mixture although did buy some Prince Albert this evening. Big headlines, battlefront is Aachen, surrounded, doing okay there I guess. The Navy is within 200 miles of Japan.

October 12, 1944

Final packing, cleaning up and messing around, lay around most of day. Went to PX and beer garden tonight. Saw Crockey in beer garden. Got some candy to take with me in aid kits then took a nice cold freezing shower.

Richard to Folks

Dear Folks,

Received Mother's two letters some time ago. Glad to hear that Jonas made it home okay. Say hello for me. How many days did he get? Haven't seen much of Buster lately, although I did merely say hello to him last evening. Am okay.

Love,

Richard

Gene Rodman to Richard

Evenin' Richard,

I received your letter right in the middle of a tactical blackout maneuver so I attempted to wade through your news by means of a blackout flashlight. Yes, it was great—I only suffered with moderate eyestrain. I received that letter on the first week of an extended five-week maneuver spent in Louisiana, Texas, and Mississippi. Three weeks are under our belts already and we are now taking a week's breather back in camp. Next week we move out to Mississippi for 17 more days with the 63rd Division. It sounds kind of rugged on the 63rd. We are going to actually support the infantry with live ammunition. Would you feel safe with 25 pounds of TNT whistling over your head? Well, with the 96th doing the firing, anyone can feel safe!!

Say, old man, what's this I hear about you being ready to go overseas? Is that right? Just between you and me, I may be seeing you at the POE.[11] We are alerted already and all we got to do after the maneuver is to furlough all the guys who haven't had a furlough in the last six months. We seem to be pretty hot and expect to spend New Year's Day on a boat.

Drop me a line whenever you can. And if you ever get to Burma, look me up. I'll be there in a foxhole somewhere—and brother it'll be *deep*!

Take care,

Rod

---

11   POE: Point of embarkation. —Ed.

CHAPTER TWO
EMBARKATION

October 13, 1944

Richard's Journal

Great day today and a lucky one also, up at 5:00, breakfast in Italian PW mess hall.[12] Strapped on full field pack and off to train to ferry on 23rd St. to Pier #10 to transport.[13] Loaded on ship, the *LeJeune* at 1:30.[14] Sack lunch en route on ferry and Red Cross coffee, doughnuts, and candy at pier. Hit that gangplank at 1:30 sharp and one hell of an ordeal, very crowded quarters, but clean. Bunks are so close together you can barely get in and there's equipment everywhere it can be stashed. Told there are over 4,000 of us on this ship. Messed around till about 6:00 and had good chow. Sauerkraut and franks, potatoes, slaw, chocolate pudding, and bread with peach preserves. Long wait for food.

---

12 PW: Prisoner of War. —Ed.

13 Full field pack: Soldiers carried all their belongings in this pack, which could weigh up to 90 pounds fully loaded. Straps were included to attach a bedroll and a tent shelter-half. —Ed.

14 The *LeJeune* was originally constructed as a luxury liner of the German commercial fleet. Early in the war, Germany used the *LeJeune* to supply its submarine fleet. The ship avoided contact with the British, escaping in 1941 to the port of Santos, Brazil. Aware that the ship would be impounded by the government of Brazil, the crew sabotaged the engines but didn't sink the ship. The U.S. Navy bought the ship from the Brazilian government in 1943, installed a small diesel engine in it, and brought it to the Norfolk Naval Shipyard in 1943. Refitting the ship for a troop transport took most of a year. As a troop transport, the ship housed 281 officers and 4,385 enlisted men. Priolo, Gary P., "Service Ship Photo Archive," *NavSource Online*, http://www.navsource.org/archives/09/22/22074.htm (Jan. 3, 2015).

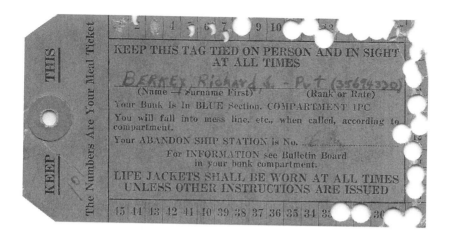

Mother to Richard

Dear Richard,

It is a beautiful Friday afternoon and I'm sitting with my hat and coat on, waiting for Jonas and Mildred to come back from town to take me to Martinsburg. I suppose Jonas is being held up by people who want to talk to him.[15] He had to go to the bank to turn some money into traveler's checks.

Jonas is fine, so far. I hope he doesn't get malaria while here. He is slim but has such an appetite that he will surely gain quickly. He got so tired of all the dehydrated and canned foods on board ship and at receiving stations that he was not eating much. Now he enjoys raw tomatoes with salt, roasting ears, lettuce, and all kinds of fresh stuff. Last night he and Mildred got supper after we came from the farm and you should have seen his centerpiece of fruits and vegetables and his combination of yellow peaches, raisins, and celery leaves![16]

---

15 Richard's oldest brother, Jonas, had joined the Navy in January 1942. —Ed.

16 The Berkey farm was situated on a mostly wooded piece of land with a creek 11 miles southeast of Salem, a 30-minute drive from town down country roads. —Ed.

KAREN BERKEY HUNTSBERGER

Friday night. We're back from Martinsburg, saw all the photos, and got two bushels of apples. Tonight Daddy took Jonas to Lions Club and Mildred and I went to the show to see *Snow White and the Seven Dwarfs*.

Well, I want to start at the beginning and tell you about Jonas. He was at the receiving station at Guadalcanal when he wrote last. He got a ride on an aircraft carrier but had to sleep on the hangar deck as the officers' quarters were full. He stopped at Hawaii, which he said was just like getting home, Honolulu being like any American city. He came to San Diego, where he got a free plane ride to Albuquerque. Then he took a train to Kansas City and paid his way on a plane to Indianapolis and then to Louisville. I think I told you in my other letter that Mildred was away at Vincennes. She was visiting Elmira and June Howard and they had gone out to the airport, or flying field, and did not get in until nearly midnight. When Mildred finally talked to Jonas, she wanted to come right away, so her friends took her to Shoals and Jonas, after two hours sleep, started out to meet her there. He had left his luggage at a Louisville hotel so they went there, and had a flat tire on the bridge at 5:30 in the morning. They went over to Mildred's parents that afternoon and had supper there. They started here soon afterward, expecting to get here at 8:00, but it was 10:00, because they had another flat tire between Galena and Greenville.

Jonas hasn't had breakfast since he has been here, but sleeps until nearly noon every day. He hasn't changed a bit but argues and teases and wrestles like always. He answers questions until he must get very tired of them. He was based first in Panama, where he and other officers had a house and the screens were broken, causing his malaria. He was first in the hospital there. He was then based at New Caledonia, then Fiji, then Guadalcanal.

He was in the hospital in Espirito Santos in the New Hebrides and at the hospital at Suva in the Fijis. Once they were alongside the SS *Dixie* and took him on when sick. He said the overdoses of quinine were the worst. The second time he had malaria he was sick three weeks. They were pouring 60 grams of quinine a day down his throat and he was nauseated day and night—couldn't sleep, couldn't eat, and couldn't read because his eyes wouldn't focus. After he took an Atabrine pill every day he had lighter attacks, but he won't take it now.[17]

He has visited every island of any importance in the South Pacific but Australia and New Zealand, but has never encountered a sub. He has convoyed lots of ships and done patrol duty to keep subs out of harbors. At one time they carried equipment for a landing crew of 10 men, but the tents and stuff rotted and they threw it all overboard. They carried an awful lot of ammunition—a big magazine full, 20 feet long, 9 feet wide, and 9 feet deep—besides lockers full of ammunition for the small arms—rifles, pistols, and machine guns. He said one thing that happened that was never in the papers was the destruction of a big ammunition dump at Guadalcanal last December. It got on fire and exploded for 18 hours, destroying between $1 million and $1.5 million dollars' worth, setting the war back at least three months. No loss of life, or very little. He thinks the war won't be over for at least another two years.

Jonas and Mildred are going to the football game at Indiana University tomorrow with Virginia and her roommate. Lucy is coming next Thursday for a four-day emergency furlough to see Jonas.

Crocketts got a letter from Buster a couple of days ago. We thought we would hear from you, too. Mattie is being so careful about saying nothing that it is amusing. Commendable, however.

This morning Ida got five letters from Junior, in the midst of the mess.[18] He was already cold—said his feet were cold, but the

---

17 Atabrine was used as an antimalarial in World War II with toxic side effects. —Ed.

18 Ida was Richard's aunt, mother of his cousin, Junior (Maurice). —Ed.

tent was warmer than it had been because of a stove captured from the Germans.

I certainly do wish you were here tonight, and tomorrow night, and the next. Well, I didn't get my wish but I also wish you a safe journey, and safety in the months ahead. I know you will be useful and I'm happy to think you will be helping to save lives.

With much Love,

Mother

October 14, 1944

Richard's Journal

Sailed today at 4 bells. Out on deck and watched the last bits of NY disappear. The last bit of land I saw was a long ridge. Ate a big supper tonight and as boat began to rock, so did I. So I went to bed right away, as long as in bed okay, but get out and stand up and dizzy as a fruit. Lots already sick and in the latrine throwing up. So I stay in sack.

October 15, 1944

Really a sad sack today, up three times and sick entire day, went to chow (chicken dinner) but couldn't eat. Waiting in line with the boat rocking made me sicker. Moved watch up ½ hour.

October 16, 1944

Sea rather rough today so stayed in bed most of time. Went up on deck once, saw Crockey finally sitting out on edge of deck taking it all in. He doesn't get sick and eats like a horse. Takes a long time to serve everyone, so we only get 2 meals a day at 0700 and 1700. Feel terrible tonight, would like to shower, etc., but just can't make it. Moved watch up another half hour. Don't know yet where we are headed.

October 17, 1944

Got up at 0600 and took a shower, but got sick before I got done. Got up again at 1000 and went up on deck and remained rest of day. I feel so much better on deck—the stench down in the hold is incredible at times. Takes so long to get a shower, I think some guys are skipping it altogether. Sea smoother and feel better. Lt. Lorimer got me four oranges and so I ate them and surprisingly enough, I kept them down. Saw Crockey and talked to him a long time this afternoon. We watched the other boats in convoy and talked about various things,[19] home and Frank Richard, of course. Kinda rainy out today, no sun visible. Was able to eat some tonight—carrot salad, vegetable soup, beef, bread, Coke, potatoes, strawberry jam. Sure did enjoy a bite of each, after having eaten very little of anything since Sunday. Latest war info is that Hungary quits, Rommel dead, and in Western Theater, Formosa bombed and aflame. How the days drag. Moved watch up ½ hour.

October 18, 1944

Feel better today. Ate prunes for breakfast and oranges and soup for supper. Talked to Buster a long time out on deck this morning and slept this afternoon. Red Cross passed out kits today. Got one from Rison, Arkansas, Cleveland County Red Cross. Contained writing tablet and envelope, pencil, package cigarettes, deck of cards, assorted mint candy, a book, and sewing kit—very nice.

Mother to Richard

Dear Richard,

---

19   An armored division usually had 35 ships in the convoy. This convoy was small, with just 18 ships total. The men were on the *Santa Rosa,* which was a former South American cruise ship; the *LeJeune,* formerly the German *Windhuk;* the *James Parker,* formerly the liner *Panama;* and the submarine *Sea Robin,* which was brand new. The fourteen other ships carried equipment, but no trucks, peeps, half-tracks, or tanks were on these ships. Captain Joseph Carter, *The History of the 14th Armored Division,* (Atlanta: Albert Love Enterprises, 1947), Chapter V p. 1, Chapter VII p. 17.

We got your short letter Saturday and were glad to have a word from you and know you were still in this country. It may be otherwise by this time. You ask how many days Jonas got and I realized that I never did tell you exactly. He got 18 days + 4 days "proceed" time plus 4 days travel time. He landed in San Diego October 1 and will have to report in Miami on October 28. Fortunately Jonas has kept well and has not had an attack of malaria yet.

It has frosted now and some of the garden stuff is ruined. The leaves are brilliant. Daddy and I rode over here to this meeting in Scottsburg with a Mr. Allen from Washington, Indiana, and it was a beautiful drive. It is very warm during the day but cold at night. We are going to have a fried chicken dinner now. Yum Yum! Wish I could send you a piece.

Love,

Mother

October 19, 1944

Richard's Journal

Spent most of day on deck with Buster playing 500 rummy and cassino. Ate half of breakfast and about all of supper. Feel much better except for dizziness. Lots of rain, snow, and wind today. Stuffy as hell in this hole—wow! does it stink down here at night. By a ventilator, which helps a bit.[20]

October 20, 1944

Seven days on boat, 6 days at sea, a very pleasant day. Ate the 2 meals without much trouble and sat out on deck in the sun and

---

20   The assorted smells on the ship were so strong that even a "strong man would be sick" (Carter). Soldiers complained about the smell of each other, the hot air, the smell of oil from the engine rooms, and the constant odors of cooking. The only respite from this was on deck and that was only as the weather allowed. Captain Joseph Carter, *The History of the 14th Armored Division*, (Atlanta: Albert Love Enterprises, 1947), Chapter V p.1, Chapter VII p.17.

fresh air and read and talked. Read the entire book *Fast Company* by Marco Page that I received in Red Cross kit. Talked to Buster and Mert Finger quite a while before we came in tonight at 6:45 because it was dark. Reported over loudspeaker system this afternoon that MacArthur and troops landed on small isle in Central Philippines, thus MacArthur makes his word come true that he would return some day to the Philippines. Hot and stuffy as hell in this hole tonight, as usual. Hope we soon reach our destination. Of course, all types of rumors as to where we will and when we will.

October 21, 1944

On deck this morning, Buster and I saw some small bat-like birds shimmying over water. Surely land somewhere within a few hundred miles. Builds the morale anyway. Went to church service in bow this morning at 11:30 and stayed until 3:00. Saw a few bouts of boxing and a variety program and got slightly sunburned, also. Pretty warm today. This evening after chow, while out in the stern, saw a ship go by. Everyone became quite excited, first ship other than convoy we had seen since starting. Read *Saturday Evening Post* of 14 Oct this evening and ship's news. Aachen falls and MacArthur's landing on Leyte in Philippines came as a complete surprise to Japs. They expected one on Mindanao or south someplace.

October 22, 1944

Indeed a derelict day. I'm lazy, sleepy, and about half goofy. A wind has come up and is rather uncomfortable on deck so slept some this afternoon. Rumor from sailors that we passed the Azores last night. Fried chicken for supper and an all around good meal. Little sleep any more.

October 23, 1944

On deck a while this morning. Cool wind, so came down and played cards. Read some and slept. Out on deck this evening, sea very rough but amazingly beautiful. Saw a couple of airplanes go past. Morale around seems to be still very high but much more of this and . . . I think we are going the longest and also the slowest route to wherever we are going.

October 24, 1944

Sea rough and windy today. Played cards with Crockey tonight down in the hold. Too cool to spend much time on deck, moved watch up ½ hour for 10th time, now on London time. Can't sleep lately.

October 25, 1944

The most wonderful day I've spent for many a day! Rose early, shaved, and had breakfast of beans, cornbread, rice, and a couple pears. Then up on deck at 8:40 and LAND! Wow—how nice to see land again. On the left side (port) the cliffs of Spain shone brilliantly in the morning sun and on the right (starboard) rose the magnificent hills of Tangier and Spanish Morocco. Indeed a beautiful sight after so many drab days of misery without sight of land. Slowly we slipped toward the mine-swept Strait of Gibraltar. On the port side shone brilliantly the chalky cliffs of Spain and the white houses of the villages. And on the left the amazing gray mountains of Morocco—then the big moment! About 9:30 I sighted the sturdy Rock of Gibraltar standing out in the sea in all its imperturbable glory! And on the right, the gray and rolling cliffs of Hercules. How beautiful were these enormous gray cliffs in the morning sun. Indeed a thrill—how inspiring! How unique Gibraltar! Looking back at the big rock gives one a feeling of security similar to that of a child held in its mother's arms. The concrete "water" slabs on the east side are interesting. Coursers darting around in the air and corvettes and dolphins darting around in the water. Yes the water, how calm, blue green and so serene. This morning was the most exciting in scenery I've ever witnessed. Now on the right rose up the towns of Ceuta and then Tétouan with the Spanish cliffs fading to the left. How wonderful. This afternoon was spent roaming the decks in the brilliantly warm Mediterranean sun. Face slightly sunburned. Watched a few boxing matches in the bow with Buster, then played euchre in the hold an hour or so before a supper of mashed potatoes, soup, beef stew, green mango slaw, black eyed peas, peaches, and cocoa. Then up on deck to see the most beautiful sunset. Almost as good as at home, purple clouds visible over the rocky coast of Morocco, a half moon directly above, Mars and the evening star, the Big Dipper over the partial coast of Spain, lightning and sea to the east. Finally had to go in at 7:30. Beautiful moon on the water, deep red sunset a few minutes before.

October 26, 1944

Announced by the skipper of ship at 11:30 that we are destined for ports in Southern France, where rumor had us going anyway. The sea is becoming rough and this evening I had to lie down to keep from feeding the fish. What a transition from yesterday. This ol' boat is really tossin' tonight.

October 27, 1944

Sick all day. The water is so rough that the adjoining transports appear to be submerged at times. Announced this morning that we are going to Marseille and will arrive in the morning. Threw up breakfast but managed to keep supper down. Given day's K rations.[21] Boy is it rough tonight.

---

21   K rations were portable food for troops. Packages were waterproofed and all contained cigarettes. The breakfast K ration had canned meat, biscuits, a cereal bar, ground coffee, a fruit bar, water-purification tablets, sugar tabs, a can opener, toilet paper, and a wooden spoon. Lunch K rations contained canned cheese, biscuits, a candy bar, gum, assorted beverage powders, sugar tabs, salt tabs, matches, can opener, and spoon. The dinner ration had canned meat, biscuits, bouillon, gum, confections, coffee, sugar, can opener, and a spoon. Meant to be temporary food, K rations were often the troops' only food for weeks at a time in battle conditions. The rations didn't provide much food and the men grew very tired of them., "Army Operational Rations – Historical Background," *US Army Quartermaster Foundation,* http://www.qmfound.com/army_rations_ historical_background.htm#The%20K%20Ration (Jan. 21, 2014).

KAREN BERKEY HUNTSBERGER

October 28, 1944

Unit History[22]

Medical Detachment—3 officers and 33 enlisted men arrived at Marseille, France, from NY, at 1600 hours.

Richard's Journal

Everything happens to me on Saturday! Ha! Arrived in harbor of Marseille and anchored at 3 bells after quite a hectic night and morning on the roughest and windiest sea ever, and how! Regardless of how rough and unpleasant the old Mediterranean has been, it nevertheless has been extremely beautiful. Looked like a great field of ice and blowing snow in the morning sun. Too sick to eat breakfast but sure had an appetite for supper of sweet potatoes, soup, Vienna sausages, fresh tomatoes, grape jam, fruit salad, and pudding. Watched the sunset and the moon come up in the harbor, extremely touching. Still a strong wind however. 'Tis really a thrill to view Marseille, so beautiful, the white shale cliffs and all. Watched the lights before coming in tonight.

---

22   Entries labeled as "Unit History" are derived from a number of U.S. Army archived reports. These include After Action Reports, S-3 Periodic Reports, Unit Histories, and Daily Journals. Morning reports were filled out daily by each company and are the only records that still exist down to the company level. The morning reports list those who were killed, wounded, or missing in action, incoming or outgoing soldiers, promotions, demotions, and those going to a hospital, for training, or on leave for rest. The morning reports are extremely important as they give the exact location of each company. Morning Reports also could include a "Record of Events" showing troop movement and the action the company saw that day. The report always contained a "Strength Count" showing the number of officers and enlisted men on a daily basis. *Note: Unit History entries are not included in the text for days when no changes were reported (i.e., the Company did not move or no one was wounded/sick). In addition, the men listed as wounded, missing, killed, or sick are only from C Company and not from the entire 68th Armored Infantry Battalion. —Ed.*

CHAPTER THREE
FRANCE!

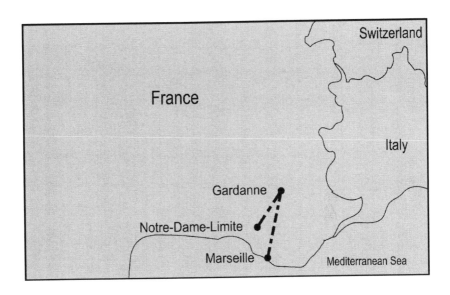

October 29, 1944

Unit History

Medical Detachment—33 enlisted men and 3 officers disembarked at Port of Marseille, France, at 1600 hours. Proceeded from Port of Marseille on 10 mile road march and arrived at bivouac area, Delta Base Station, at 2000 hours.

Richard's Journal

Up on deck a while in a strong wind and then below to prepare for the debarkation. Waited around all day and finally piled off at 4:05. Hit the gravel pier, with full field pack, and long drawers,[23] to say as so many soldiers before said, "Lafayette, we are here again!"

---

23   Long drawers: long underwear. —Ed.

Marched through the pier seeing much devastation, up through the hills of Marseille's slums with a big blister on the ball of my left foot. God only knows how it got there with that 90-pound full field pack. And so we marched some three odd hours to a staging area, how gruesome. Arrived at the staging area, Septèmes-les-Vallons, tired, hungry, footsore and weary in the white sticky mud of the French Riviera. Ate a K ration heated over the fire and pitched a tent with Slim Steinmann and spent a cold, miserable, rainy night on the side of a striking French hill, where a few weeks before the lousy Nazis were driven closer to their impenetrable Fatherland, the Bastards!

Thank God for this Lord's Day and the *assured* answer to my prayers that peace will someday be somewhere, if only in heaven.

October 30, 1944

Didn't have to awake early this morn, but I did arise, frozen, cold, sore, stiff, and indeed not at all glad to be fighting the battle a degraded medic must struggle thru to help the afflicted. Built a fire, ate K ration for breakfast and C ration for dinner and supper.[24] Just sat round all day and tried to keep comfortable. Cold and rainy tonight. I find we have another enemy, the thieving and conniving French low class bums, beggars and bastards. Yesterday we walked thru Marseille and they welcomed us with outstretched arms to receive our candy, cigarettes, and any darn thing, butts and all, the low down dirty half-breeds. If we are fighting for them, then to hell with it all. I'm looking forward to the good 'ol U.S.A. Got duffel bags and extra blankets this morning so tonight have a more comfortable sack, cold however and rainy. The French here are indeed a peculiar

---

24   The daily C ration for a soldier was three cans of B units, three cans of C units, and one accessory pack. C units contained variations of meat and beans such as: meat and vegie stew, spaghetti and meat, pork and rice, pork and beans, ham and lima beans, or chicken and veggies. B units varied and contained biscuits, compressed cereal, raisins or candy-coated peanuts, powdered coffee, sugar, powdered juice, cocoa powder, candies, jam, and caramels. Accessory packs contained matches, toilet paper, chewing gum, a can opener, water purification tablets, and nine cigarettes. Streeter, Timothy, "U.S. Army Field Rations," http://www.usarmymodels.com/ARTICLES/Rations/crations.html (Jan. 21, 2014).

race, plenty mixed and plenty rugged. Sat around fire till midnight with the boys and then to sack.

October 31, 1944

No pay today—ha! Ate C rations, not much sleep, cold and rainy. Sat around and heard rumors about French and all. Got mail! Two letters from Mother and one from Rodman. Mother told me all about Jonas at home. Buster was down and we exchanged letters, rumors, and whatnot. Sat round fire most of day, hit sack tonight, rain and all, but think did sleep for a change. Halloween, a candle but no pumpkin. And so to bed.

Mother to Richard

Dearest Boy,

We are still waiting to hear from you. I think we started looking for a letter too soon. It has now been 19 days since you left, and most families don't hear for three weeks or a month. They haven't heard from Lee Edward Smith for over a month. Elmo Colglazier's got word that Jack has been slightly wounded. I'm sorry I didn't get a letter written all last week. This morning we got two letters from David, there being in one a check for $100. He says he is fine but still misses fresh food so much.

Jonas and Mildred left here a week ago tonight. They arrived in Florida on Friday at noon. We don't have their address yet. Jonas gained several pounds while he was here and looked much rested. He slept until nearly noon most of the time. Lucy got back to Washington, DC, okay a week ago yesterday morning but was train sick again. We took her to Mitchell on Sunday to catch the train. The Crocketts have their four-room housecar done and are going to live in it.[25] Aunt Fannie says they are going to sell their home. I don't think they should.

Love,

Mother

---

25   Housecar: Early term for a travel trailer equipped with beds, kitchen, and bathroom. —Ed.

November 1, 1944

Unit History

Pvt. Richard Berkey, Pvt. Kenneth Hazelton, Pvt. Leon Ladd, and Pvt. Francis Steinmann promoted to Private First Class (Pfc.).

Richard's Journal

Cold and rainy this morn, hard to climb out of sack and build fire, got first hot meal this morning. Two hot cakes, jam, and coffee, not bad, seconds for dinner and supper but still hungry. Made Pfc. today. Ha! Just lay round all day. Helped Bopp and Beiner with supplies this morn, no mail today. Wrote three letters home tonight and 2 to friends, first letters I've written for about a month since I left Camp Campbell. Moon out tonight and warmer, rained every day since we have been here on the white mud hillside. And so to bed—11:30.

Richard to Folks

Dear Folks,

Received two letters from Mother yesterday and am finally getting around to writing tonight after quite a duration of time. Arrived here very safely although the boat ride wasn't exactly enjoyable. I'm referring to my being seasick, which was indeed an experience, quite comical but not so very likable. But at present I am indeed a true "chowhound" and am having more fun than a barrel of monkeys.[26] Was glad to learn all about Jonas and would also like to know what he said about David. Buster was over a while ago and we exchanged letters, rumors, etc.

Love,

Richard

---

26   Due to censorship, soldiers were very restricted about what they could include in letters. They could not state their location in case letters accidentally came into enemy hands. Soldiers also tried to reassure their families that they were fine, whether they were or not. —Ed.

Richard to Dad

Dear Dad,

Arrived overseas safely, feel fine (now) and am enjoying myself, and hope you are also (feeling fine, I mean). Was seasick on the boat and lost a lot of weight, but am now again consuming rations quite consistently. Would like to be home enjoying apples, pumpkin pie, etc., especially Mother's good food and then maybe do some rabbit hunting. I hope you go, or did I expend or expel the entirety of the ammunition? Ha! How's the new secretary? Okay? Hope Lucy got home while Jonas was there. Received your letter and thanks for putting my valuables away. Hope to hear from you.

Your son,

Richard

Richard to Mother

Dear Mother,

Was glad to hear about the boxes coming this way. In fact, I'm eager to receive them. I've been hearing lots about boxes (other than Christmas ones) being sent to men overseas. I understand that there must be a request letter available before you can send anything. There are some things I'd *like* to have, but none that would cause you any trouble in purchasing and sending. The main items are soap (laundry or otherwise), toothpaste and brush, airmail stamps, razor blades (double edge), and naturally anything to eat that is all right to mail.

Thanks for your swell letters. I've received two so far.

Much Love,

Richard

November 2, 1944

Richard's Journal

Up this morning at 6:45, built fire, warmed up and had chow, sat round entire day. Rained again, as usual but this afternoon rather fair weather. Still camped on the hillside here and not doing anything. The French people around here are evidently of the poorer classes with small farms, unique carriages, cars, and vehicles. The houses all seem to have a reddish white appearance, red tile roofs and smooth mud sides, the vegetation has a semi-tropical appearance, evergreens. People are poorly dressed and all carry some sort of container or sack with them, slung over shoulder, etc. Many bicycles and lots of converted charcoal and steam operated automobiles. We were warned about two things—German teller mines and French drivers. [27]

November 3, 1944

Pretty chilly this morning and heavy dew as usual. Don't feel so hot today. Sat around this morning and slept this afternoon. Buster came down tonight and we talked a long time. He usually always comes down a couple times during the day and we bat the breeze. Cigarettes are rough around here, sell for 50 francs a pack which means a buck in American dough. Soldiers are trading damn near anything (chewing gum, cigarettes, candy, etc.) for the sour wine and cognac. I can't drink vinegar and that's about what the stuff tastes like, or sour cider. Most of the boys are getting along very well. Think if I can scrape up some dough I'll go to Marseille some of these days before we leave here. Hear it's a rough town.

---

27   As the name suggests ("teller" is the German word for dish or plate) the mines were plate-shaped. Containing little more than 5.5 kilograms of TNT and a fuse activation pressure of approximately 200 pounds, the teller mine was capable of blasting the tracks off of any World War II era tank or destroying a lightly armored vehicle. Because of its rather high operating pressure, the teller mine would only be set off by a vehicle or heavy object passing over the mine. Deighton, Len, *Blitzkrieg*, (New York: Alfred A. Knopf, 1979).

November 4, 1944

Up at 6:45, built a fire and got a little exercise, ran around fire, and jumped rope. Went up to 43rd General Hospital about 10 miles from here this morning to be a blood donor. About 30 of us went in a truck—Cyphert, Kerr, Skillman, and myself from medics. Sat in lab all morning waiting for turn, had swell chow, breaded Spam, macaroni and cheese, peas and carrots, peaches and jam, went back for seconds. First meal I've had enough to eat for a long time. They got enough blood for today so gave us a towel and got to take a swell shower. Um, um, was it nice. First bath for two weeks. Went back in truck to camp, beautiful scenery, southern end of Alps. This hospital was taken over by Germans, then Americans, with all sorts of people around the place. Chow at Service Company and then saw a movie, *Pin-Up Girl*, not bad! Betty Grable and Martha Raye. Sat around fire till 12:00 and then hit sack, lots drunk tonight.

November 5, 1944

Up at 6:30, made fire outside and in corporal's tent, chopped wood, all to get warmed up. Cold night and much noise outside, not much sleep. Went to hospital again this morning. Gave a pint of blood and got 495 francs and lost it in a crap game 5 minutes after I returned here to camp. Ha! Had a good meal at hospital and also this evening. Had Vienna sausages and seemed to miss out on the Sunday chicken, which usually isn't too good. Really a swell day today, but pretty cool this evening. Crockey dropped around a few minutes this evening, sat round fire tonight and shot the bull. Feel rather weak this evening so hit the sack, most of boys gone to Marseille, Aix-en-Provence, Notre-Dame-Limite or Septèmes-les-Vallons tonight. Drew 3 ambulances, 2 weapons carriers, and a peep today.[28]

November 6, 1944

Being that it's Monday I did a little washing this morning, a few hankies, sox, a towel, and T-shirts. Used the last hankie Mother did for me this morning. Had plenty of chow today for the first time, got

---

28   World War II U.S. armored divisions called the jeep a "peep." —Ed.

more seconds for dinner than I could eat. Had Vienna sausages for the last 5 meals, plus some beef for dinner, and swell tasting butter beans. Slept from noon till 4 bells. Really a pleasant day, no clouds and sunny. Some of the boys lost a new weapons carrier that only yesterday we had drawn. Sellen, the driver, is a sad sack today. At least I'm glad I lost all my dough or I'd probably be in on it. Crockey down by fire tonight and talked a while, chilly tonight and I don't feel too well. Writing this by candlelight in tent.

November 7, 1944

Election Day! Looks like another Roosevelt victory, and I well know it is since I'm writing this in the Red Cross in downtown Marseille on Thursday night (7:00 p.m.) while waiting for Buster to show up. Washed this morning and messed around as usual again. The most beautiful red sunset I've ever seen, indeed rare. Sat around fire and got a few early election returns on radio in CP.[29] Wrote letters tonight. Am assigned to C Company as aid man (3rd Platoon) and will be with them when we move out. Scotty and Mude also are aid men and I think we got a swell combination to really fix and patch old C Company up.

Richard to Dad

Dear Dad,

How's things on the west side public square? Rather frosty these days, I expect. I also imagine the trees are very beautiful. I would enjoy seeing them at the farm.

The money I said was being sent to the Building and Loan will be sent to you instead. So you may do with it as you like. It is indeed officially signed over to you, as of yesterday.

I see that today is Election Day—hope things turn out as you hope for, or since I did happen to vote also, I hope they turn out as I voted. Am feeling okay and getting enough to eat.

---

29   Command post. —Ed.

Bye,

Richard

Richard to Folks

Dear Folks,

Thought I'd better get to writing a line or so before this week passes as quickly as last.

Have as yet received only three letters, two from Mother dated the 14th and 20th of October and one from Rodman, who is probably home on furlough now. He says his folks live in town now, on Hackberry Street. Buster usually drops down every day and we have a few words. Last night he got to talking about grade school days and all the trouble he was always getting into among other things. The mail service seems to be messed up here. Some fellas got regular mail faster than airmail today. So I decided, as did another, that probably at present regular mail goes as well as any, however you may not get this before Christmas.

Love,

Richard

November 8, 1944

Richard's Journal

It's a profound fact that Roosevelt is again elected, am anxious to learn about Washington County and all, since I did happen to vote about September 19 for the first time. Messed around all day as usual. Went up to C Company with Scotty and Mude and got the lowdown on things. Also packed a few things and got my junk in order to move out sometime. Broke down and went to Marseille tonight and what a time. Went in an ambulance with some of the boys. Sold 2 packages Duke's Mixture for 20 francs up at Red Cross after putting vehicle in parking lot.[30] Had a flat beer on the way. Flaharity, Anderson, Hazelton, Sowell, and Cyphert in bunch. Then went and saw a rare show put on by 2 women for 50 francs. Then we buzzed around and sold a carton of cigarettes for 500 francs (10 bucks). Got a Tom Collins (sour) and a shot of sweet wine. Went up to another restaurant and then back to "flop" house where it cost me 150 francs and 25 in tips. Wasn't any good, but satisfied nevertheless. Rushed back to parking lot at 10:30 and rode to camp.

November 9, 1944

Messed around this morning and did nothing much in general except read a *Coronet* magazine a little. Went to Gardanne about 5 miles north of here with Sellen, Haggerty, and Shufrin and took a shower in a factory, returned at 3:00. Messed around and took off to Marseille. Hit the Red Cross first and met Crockey and Burke the B Company cook from Ohio. We messed around and drank a glass or two of beer and then I got lost trying to find the "Shaker" bar over by the opera house. Finally found it and had a couple rounds of sweet wine, very good. Then we messed around and weather was so cold we hitched a ride back to camp.

Edgar DeJean to Richard

Dear Richard,

This is my first experience in writing an overseas letter so excuse it if the censor obliterates fractions of my endeavor. It seems that we missed you by one weekend while you were home on furlough. We were sorry we didn't get to see you. Not only did we have the bad luck of missing you, but we also didn't get to see Jonas while he was there.

Graduation is only 40 days off and I still have enough details to finish up for at least six months work. I met my senior requirements about a month ago so that is not a worry anymore. I still

---

30 Loose tobacco mix for rolled cigarettes, usually made from the least desirable tobacco. —Ed.

have to pass finals and then my state boards are more thorns in my side. These past six years seem short although at times I've wondered if this graduation could really be such a future event.

We took our final type examinations of officer candidates last Thursday. This will probably surprise you as much as it did me—as yet they refuse to accept me. Of all those puny, under-weight, undernourished students, I'm one who can't pass the physical. I think I'll surely pass but if they don't give me some reassurance soon, I'll begin to worry. I've signed waivers on it but they claim even that may not let me in. Well, will wait and hope.

I trust you are still with a mobile surgical unit. Met a fellow last weekend who is with one as an instructor here at Fort Benjamin Harrison. He seems to like it fine.

The baby grows daily—"he" is quite the one, of course he may turn out to be a girl, but we are entitled to our hopes I guess. Elly even goes so far as to criticize my occasional very mild outbreaks of profanity by informing me that I must watch my language in front of the baby.

Certainly is a good thing that I don't have an addiction for nicotine due to the fact that there don't seem to be any "weeds" in this country. Al and Billy, the couple upstairs, had a 9 lb. 13 oz. boy last week and he (Al) gave me a cigar. I, against my better judgment, smoked the darn thing. It was Sunday before I could see one object where one should exist. Up until then there were always at least two.

Write soon, sooner than we did. We hope to be more prompt with our correspondence from now on. Guess I better go find an airmail stamp and rush down to the nearest plane to see that it goes out. Be careful—be seein' ya.

As always,

Ed and Elly

Mother to Richard

Dear Richard,

In three more days it will be a month since we've heard from you. It surely won't be much longer until we get a letter, although some say they don't hear for five or six weeks. Of course they didn't hear from Lee Henry Norris for six months because the dumb kid just didn't write! The Smiths finally heard from Lee Edward but it was a letter written while he was still on the water; however, Eleanor Churchman Smith got a letter from the wife of one of Lee Edward's buddies and he said they had landed in France. There is naturally now a lot of anxiety about the boys. Elmo and Mary Colglazier got word that Jack has been slightly wounded and Charlene Newlon has heard that Dale is seriously wounded. I see in the paper that Freeman Hinds, Jr. was also slightly wounded and got a Purple Heart but he was able to write home about it. Mary Colglazier said Marie's husband was in France and was wanting more food than was given him. He wanted more powdered coffee and more bouillon cubes for hot drinks. If you find you need anything, do write us what it is. And if you just *want* something you don't really need, tell us about that, too. Are you going to have enough warm socks?

Election day came and went. We voted about four o'clock. Anna Sullivan said the votes of our four absent children were all in the boxes. As far as the national election is concerned, I guess they were lost, but the county went Republican, except in a few cases.

Today I am sending the photographs of you Indiana University children in service to the alumni magazine. Maybe they'll get in sometime in the next year! I had a letter from Secretary Heighway saying he wanted them.

We got another letter from Jonas. They had not found an apartment and were afraid they never would. They were still at the small hotel, the Leona, and haven't even unpacked the heavy trunk they took. Jonas' course was to begin this last Monday,

November 6. He said it was an advanced course and might be tougher than before. Daddy says to be sure to write us as often as possible and tell us all you can. Eleanor has just come in from school. They have their swell new band uniforms, but haven't worn them yet. The poinsettias are beginning to get red.

Lots of Love,

Mother

November 10, 1944

Richard's Journal

Up late (7:00) chow, windy as hell. Went up to C Company a while and listened to about 5 minutes of a map reading class and then back down to tent and read a while and tried to keep warm. Ate dinner and then went on an hour and a half road march. Very beautiful scenery. There is a big mountain of rock about 8 miles north of here and 'tis always beautiful. Returned from road march and ate chow and took off for Marseille again. Beautiful red sunset again. Went to Red Cross and got a haircut, tonic, and massage for 40 francs. Finished up in dark after barber blew a fuse on massage machine. Went downstairs and had cup of coffee and then outside and sold 6 packs of cigarettes for 300 francs and took off down main drag. Had a sorta street carnival, same as home. Drank 3 beers in a nearby bar and then went to "Shaker." Bought a map of Marseille for 4 francs and a language book for 20 francs. Had a few shots of wine, was joined by my Jewish buddies, Tec 5 Goldstein and Pvt. Jarow. Talked to guy that owned the joint. He told us about the Germans and FFI.[31] He was a member of the FFI and said he got a few of them but not enough, etc. Took off at 10:00 for MP parking lot, waited

---

31   The French Forces of the Interior were often called "French Freedom Fighters." French resistance fighters in the later stages of World War II, FFI soldiers became regular French Army troops by October 1944, when most of France had been liberated from Germany. Renouard, Jean-Pierre, *My Stripes Were Earned in Hell: A French Resistance Fighter's Memoir of Survival in a Nazi Prison Camp,* (New York: Rowman & Littlefield Publishers, Inc., 2012).

till 11:00 for ambulance, and then to camp. Got good and warm in the command post and wrote this.

November 11, 1944

France! ARMISTICE DAY! New Diary Book—took shower this morn. In Gardanne about 6 or 7 miles north of here in an old factory of some sort, not bad at all but water was extremely soft. Gardanne is a very nice little town with the usual sycamore lanes through the center of town. Returned to camp area at 0100 and naturally thought of 26 years ago. Messed around this afternoon. Finally after supper I got the urge to do my laundry and did so and dried by the fire. Had blackout and saw bomb flashes toward Marseille. Reported observation planes bombed east Marseille.

About 9:30 went with Haggerty, Red Kerr, Sowell, and Ladd to a French home in Notre-Dame-Limite outside Septèmes-les-Vallons. Very unique house. Andre, wife, and very beautiful daughter. Had 3-course supper, potato soup, stewed rabbit, and then some kind of potato dish with plenty of garlic and red pepper, later had stewed chestnuts. Haggerty left and we remained till 12:30 trying to talk out of the book! Drank the sour wine and danced a little with the only daughter. Had a swell time and quite an experience. Returned to camp and messed around awhile and finally to bed at 2:00.

November 12, 1944

Very cold late supper and went to church with Mude across the road, where division chaplain had a peep and portable organ. Had a baptism, Sgt. Hendries, B Company. We had a very nice and sincere service. Tore down tent and packed things this afternoon in prep for moving out in the morning. Made bedroll, "Slim" Steinmann helped and then had chow at both C and Service Companies, chicken. Took equipment to 3rd Platoon C Company mortar squad half-track.[32] Crawled in sack about 11:30. Have been here exactly two weeks now

---

32   Half-track: military vehicle with regular wheels on the front and caterpillar tracks on the back wheels. These vehicles provided greater maneuverability over bad terrain, ice, and snow. —Ed.

and have had it very easy. Am now prepared to move up and hope for the best. A letter from Julia today, first letter from her over here. She has not as yet received any of my letters, so I presume they haven't received my letters at home. Julia started her letter with "Dearest Richard." I was quite thrilled. Can't seem to quite figure her out, but yet I do, indeed a swell gal, one that anyone would be proud of. I think of her quite a lot and just keep trying to figure out what the heck she thinks of me. Well, so much for that. But I guess 'tis a natural thing to reason and think. I'm in the war now and must do my job, however meager, but yet one must think of returning to those he loves in order to remain in a sober state of mind. Must indeed stop this meandering and go to bed.

Mother to Richard

Dear Richard,

I don't usually like V-mail so much, but no two letters were ever more welcome than the ones we received from you today.[33] It was exactly a month since you had written from an eastern port. It's too bad you were so seasick but you have had the great experience of crossing the ocean. Also, from what you say, your appetite was not affected very long!

Eleanor took the post office key, "just in case," when she went to town, and came back with your letters and one from David. Aunt Fannie came up to hear the letters, and Bonnie Crockett

---

33   Victory Mail (V-mail) used special stationery, which was a combined letter and envelope. V-mail messages were reduced to thumbnail sized images on microfilm in the U.S., saving valuable cargo space on ships. The microfilm images were enlarged upon arrival at their destination, copied on special paper, and delivered to soldiers. The final product was a miniature image of the original letter and resembled a photograph. Most people didn't like V-mail because they didn't want strangers reading their letters, but their use increased greatly as the war went on. A 16mm reel of microfilm could contain 18,000 letters. V-mail went by air and, at its best, reduced the point-to-point delivery time to one week. "V-Mail," *National Postal Museum*, http://postalmuseum.si.edu/exhibits/past/the-art-of-cards-and-letters/mail-call/v-mail.html (Jan. 24, 2014).

came by, so we sent the letters down there.[34] They have not heard from Buster but probably will tomorrow.

You asked what Jonas said about David. He is in the center of a 10-mile beachhead, the only point we hold on Bougainville. There are 20,000 Japs on the island but they are not dangerous as they are cut off from supplies of arms and ammunition. There is a large active volcano on the island, which shows up plainly in the pictures. Jonas said David's mustache was a great big conductor type. His health and attitude were good and he was sure he was not going to do anything that would hurt him. David was the only person Jonas found that he knew, all the time he was overseas.

We'll be thinking about you all the time and watching the papers. I hope you can be very useful and yet safe.

Lots of Love,

Mother

---

34   Bonnie was Buster Crockett's sister. —Ed.

CHAPTER FOUR

EN ROUTE TO THE FRONT

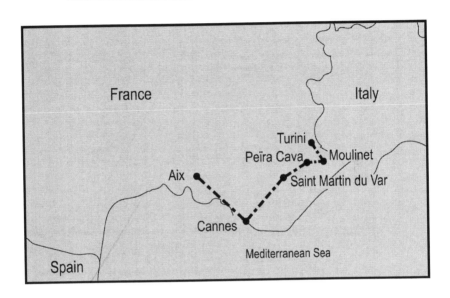

November 13, 1944

Unit History[35]

C Company—243 enlisted men and 6 officers left Delta Base Station, Marseille, on 128 mile mounted motor march at 0450 hours. Arrived St. Martin-du-Var, closed in bivouac area at 1520 hours. Morale good.

Richard's Journal

Up at three, hot coffee and moved out at five, pretty cold in half-track. Up to Aix-en-Provence then over to Cannes. North to Nice and

---

35   Richard was now attached to C Company with the 3rd Platoon. These were the men he cared for when they were sick or wounded. —Ed.

to bivouac area somewhere near front. Am writing this while lying on my bedroll (7:10) with a small candle as my aid. We are bedded down in an old bombed factory deep in the Maritime Alps, 1/8 mile north of St. Martin-du-Var—indeed scenic. Cannes looks like an American city and of course the blue green Mediterranean is indeed beautiful. Cannes wasn't torn up too much. Saw shore installations and pillboxes, burned vehicles on side of road, signs of artillery and small arms fire. The snow-capped peaks of the Alps above the bird's eye view of Cannes was extremely swell. Ate a C ration for dinner in the outskirts of Cannes, bought a bottle of wine for 40 francs. Ate a dinner K ration this evening and hot coffee. Nice and dry inside this building and not windy but quite warm. Scenic and tropical vegetation, oranges, lemon trees, vineyards, etc. I assume we're near Italian border, not far from Monte Carlo or Monaco. Think I'll get some needed sleep.

November 14, 1944

Had the most wonderful experience I've as yet encountered since being one of Uncle Sam's GIs, etc. I've always wanted to climb a mountain and that very thing I did this aft. Nine of us from the 3rd Platoon started and 3 finally reached the top, Platoon Sgt. Ross and Squad Leader Billhymer and myself. We started at 1:15 and reached the top at 3:00. Very rough climbing but very beautiful scenery. We got black from brushing against burned brush, probably caused from by artillery fire. We could see Nice on the Mediterranean toward the west and only mountains elsewhere, except a passage way toward the northeast, the only way to the very near front (reported 15 mi). We started down at 3:15 and came down the most treacherous places, indeed a few times we were in places where it seemed most impossible to go either up or down or even move at all. Many times I wondered if we would even return to the camp below, which looked so near yet so far away. It took almost an hour to scale the wall downward and to reach more pleasant terrain directly above an old mine shaft. From there we slid down on a sorta landslide and had much fun. We got back to camp at 4:30. Indeed an experience, although no great climb (est. 1000 feet), but quite rough and extremely treacherous. I can truthfully say I was thrilled to the point where I indeed became alarmed or scared. Chow was swell and I even got seconds. Rained after chow. Lit a candle and Erwin, Donahue, and myself played cards, 500 rummy. Erwin finally won one game after two hours. Quite cool so hit sack at 1:30. The mountains cut off much of the wind and it is quite warm in daytime and chilly at night. I've seen Buster around now and then, good spirits as usual. Great life, this Army.

November 15, 1944

Indeed a useless day spent doing absolutely nothing. Rather chilly all day but very clear and sunny. Sun came over mountain about 10 and disappeared about 5. Some went up to front today and came back tonight loaded with lots of rumors. A and B Companies moved out today and we are supposed to leave in the morn. Stood around fire awhile and got warmed up so guess I'll go to bed (7:30).

November 16, 1944

Unit History

Left St. Martin-du-Var at 0700 hours on mounted march of 26 miles. Arrived at Peïra Cava, France, at 1100 hours. Closed in bivouac area. Roads good—morale high.

Richard's Journal

We were up at 5:00, chow, packed up and took off at 7:00 in half-tracks for the *front*. All morning we wound up and up through the mountainside amid the snow covered peaks of the Maritime Alps. Got stuck in the snow a couple of times and finally at 11:00 arrived at our "rest area," which appeared to be quite a modern resort, the name of which I'm at this time unfamiliar, since we moved away immediately. We packed guns, ammo and rations and blankets on mules and the 3rd Platoon took off through the mountains for the front a little after noon. Ate a K ration dinner on the way. We went thru snow a while and then down, down into the valley, winding this way and that. Down in the valley the temp was quite warm and the walking was quite enough to keep us warm. I tracked along behind the 3rd, finally about 3 bells we arrived at this town of Moulinet, only a week ago captured from the Germans. A group of 509th paratroopers held the place and we relieved them. They were rugged looking boys, have been all over hell, I guess, Africa, Anzio (Italy), D-Day in Southern France and here. They were exceedingly anxious to go. One grizzled corporal stayed to show us around and take some of the boys on a patrol. We all got rooms in this hotel building. I got one with Erwin on the 2nd floor, east side, a little veranda and there is a snowcapped peak above, to the left, supposed "no man's land!"[36] We had a warm meal of some kind of 10-in-1 rations the paratroopers had left so off to bed we went at about 9 bells on nice innerspring mattresses.[37] Who'd believe that, at the front on innersprings. Some day!

November 17, 1944

The corporal took some of the boys on a recon patrol and returned soon after 12. The mule train came in at 11 and brought supplies, plus Major Townsend, our battalion executive officer, who is a West Pointer and quite the stuff, he thinks. The sun comes up about 10 and leaves at 3, gets light at 7 and dark at 5. All the boys are having a great time rummaging around the building, but always aware of booby traps, which are quite a menace. All are enjoying themselves and digging up everything imaginable. A few civilians have returned here and are quite a problem to keep away from our own booby traps.

---

36   No man's land: common term used to describe the area between the two opposing armies. —Ed.

37   The 10-in-1 ration contained enough food to feed three daily meals to ten soldiers. Contents were similar to K rations, but breakfast and dinner were packaged together for cooking at the beginning and end of each day. The lunch portion was like a snack to be handed out to men on the move. Streeter, Timothy, "U.S. Army Field Rations: The 10-in-1," *Modeling the U.S. Army in WW II*, http://www.usarmymodels.com/ARTICLES/Rations/10in1rations.html (Jan. 23, 2014).

Not used to sleeping on innersprings and so didn't sleep too well last night, then again maybe I've the fear of the Jerries' artillery, which we didn't get or just the excitement of events in general.[38] A civilian brought us in some pears and Sgt. Ross and myself went up the road about a half hour towards no man's land and got a helmet full of chestnuts, which the cook baked for us and they were quite good. The paratrooper corporal left and so did the major so we are on our own.

The paratroopers said that the Germans don't recognize the Geneva cross here and that I should remove mine.[39] So, I guess I'll wait for orders. I talked to their medic and he carried an aid kit full of grenades and was their best BAR man - ha![40] No wonder, he was from Indiana (Clinton, I think). Talked to the lieutenant over the phone at 9:00.

Mother to Richard

Dear Richard,

Here I sit writing letters in the morning! I have your package ready to mail and want to write something with it. I'm just sending the toilet articles this time, for I don't think food should be in the same perfume package. Send another request for food right away!

I was downtown Wednesday afternoon and saw Helen.[41] She was in the ten-cent store buying blue ribbon just then but she said she had been buying the warm socks and candles that Buster wanted. They had had two letters from Buster, written November 2 and 3, and she said they *certainly were* glad to get them!

---

38   Jerries: slang for Germans, mostly used in reference to soldiers. —Ed.
39   The Geneva cross is the classic Red Cross symbol placed on medics' clothing and helmets, ambulances, field hospitals, and other humanitarian vehicles and equipment. The accepted convention, not followed by all soldiers, was not to fire upon people, buildings, and vehicles displaying the Geneva cross. —Ed.
40   Browning Automatic Rifle. —Ed
41   Buster Crockett's wife. —Ed.

There was an article in the Times this week saying that request packages have been getting to the Army very slowly. It seems that the rush of Christmas packages delayed them. I am putting your airmail stamps with this letter so that you can get them more quickly.[42] I've also been reading about the hail, snow, and mud in those parts, and I do feel sorry for the infantry. Maybe you can ride in the Medical Corps trucks, but poor Buster! Do you sleep in tents at night or just in sleeping bags or something—maybe foxholes? Let us know what you can of your setup.

It is getting plenty cold here but has not snowed yet. We never did get our popcorn gathered at the farm. It rains or is cold and windy every Thursday and Sunday when we could go.

The Smiths finally heard from Lee Edward Tuesday morning but a censor had cut out portions of his letter with scissors.[43] He said he was seeing nothing but bombed cities and dead Germans. He had been driving a jeep for an officer before they left here.

Eleanor goes to school an hour early almost every morning. The swell new band uniforms are here and they are going to have a band concert next Tuesday night and also play for a ballgame the next night. She says the uniforms are navy blue with gold braid and buttons and gold plumes on hats. The old band uniforms were 15 years old, but these cost $1,500 and a lot of people have contributed.

---

42 The constant moving of soldiers made delivery of mail very difficult. Unless you sent mail to soldiers via airmail, it went by ship, adding weeks to the delivery time. An airmail stamp for a regular letter cost 6 cents in 1944. —Ed.

43 Censorship was handled by an officer in each unit. The censor, whose job was considered unimportant, inked over or cut out any information that might reveal a soldier's location or how strong the troops were. Most soldiers avoided having their letters censored by writing about food and the weather. And most wanted to reassure their families that they were fine. This censorship practice ended with World War II. Fox, Myron, "Censorship," *PBS.org*, http://www.pbs.org/wgbh/americanexperience/features/general-article/warletters-censorship/ (March 27, 2014).

We haven't had any letters from the other kids this week. Virginia will be coming home next Thursday, I guess, but will have to go to Indianapolis on Saturday for a wedding.

I must close and mail this.

With much Love,

Mother

November 18, 1944

Richard's Journal

Mail today, one from Mother, Imy, the church, and rebel Tom Collins written in French, too. Met the mule train and got a litter and wheels, 7 units of plasma, bandages, ASH, APC, boric acid, etc.[44] Was glad to get the plasma which I might be able to use. Also, got a splint set. Didn't do much this afternoon. Patrol came back okay, no casualties as yet. About 8:00 tonight had quite a scare. One of the guards fired a couple rounds at what he thought was a man and everyone rushed around in the dark getting to his post but nothing else happened. One more guard did fire a round or two later on. Moved across the hall on the west side of building where I can see the square. Have a window blacked out and can have a light, finally got to bed about 10. Erwin on guard so probably not much sleep tonight.

Virginia to Richard

Dearest Richard,

Heard from Mother that you arrived okay so I'm writing a note tonight while I have a little extra time. Midterms are over and I read the schedule for finals this morning. Naturally, I have three straight on one day. Then Christmas and one more semester—that makes me happy. I mean if I make it and get the A.B. Have to pass the English Comprehensive in the spring.

---

44   APC contained acetylsalicylic acid, phenacetin and caffeine, used for colds and headaches. —Ed.

What a week this has been! Ernie Pyle came back on Monday.[45] They had a big thing just before noon and awarded him a Dr. of Humane Letters degree—made it up. Funny. Pyle's old cronies were there to crack off about all the old gallivantings and campus dirt. You see, Pyle didn't graduate. Apparently not such a brain—and they laughed about how to get a degree—just get your picture in *Life, Time, Fortune,* etc.

I got an application blank for entrance to Yale School of Nursing. Don't know if this is going to work out but I want it to. I get so mixed up trying to plan my life.

I'll admit I'd love to get married but haven't found a man. So guess the best thing is to proceed toward my aspirations. I may end up a medical missionary. Would you like to join me?

Ever since you left, I have fairly ached to be there by your side working to save people's lives. I think of you often and wish it over and over. You think I'm crazy, but I'm not. I mean it—I feel it. That's why I've got to get into something practical. Only drawback with Yale is the folks hate for me to go so far. Laugh—probably end up at Indianapolis!

Well, darlin', must get some shut-eye. Take care of yourself and be good.

Lots and lots of love!

Virginia

---

45   Ernie Pyle, born in 1900, was a famous battlefield reporter during World War II in Europe and the Pacific. He had attended Indiana University, but did not graduate. On April 18, 1945, less than five months after the evening with his cronies described here, Pyle was riding in a jeep with three other officers on Ie Shima Island, west of Okinawa. When fired upon, they scrambled for cover. Pyle raised his head and was killed instantly by a bullet that hit his left temple. "Ernie Pyle," *Indiana University School of Journalism,* http://journalism.indiana.edu/resources/erniepyle/ (Jan. 23, 2014).

November 19, 1944

Richard's Journal

Am writing this in the Hotel de Paris in Moulinet, France, Sunday morning, 9:15, Nov. 19, 1944, while sitting in a chair in most "spacious" room overlooking the town square, while at the other side 100 yards away is a monument dedicated to those who gave lives in the last war. 1914-1918 it is inscribed, plus helmet, victory palms, and sheath of rods and axe, etc. I've found some French ink in the vestibule of the hotel, which is now our most exclusive dining hall.

Richard's Journal, on Sunday evening

Might as well write up to now for today. Our first combat patrol went out at 7:30 this morning with 15 men. I hope they all return. Had bread, bacon, eggs, and coffee for breakfast. The cook is okay, can't spell his name, Von Japnis or something, crazy as heck anyway. My feet and hands are cold so think I'll stop and get warmed up a bit. I might finish when I know what happens.

Rearranged aid kits on veranda and while doing so the Jerries threw a few shells on yon mountainside so I finished up in my room. The mule train came without any mules, just some boys dropped over from Peïra Cava to say hello or else for the walk—oh yeah! Had chow and then Platoon Sgt. Ross and I went up the way to gather a basket of apples. Upon return I rummaged through an old closet down the hall and found various interesting books and whatnot. So now I have a library in my room, a couple of medical books and the rest French, German, and English school books. I hope to master this French some day. Found a skeleton arrangement in one of the medical books so I taped it on the door beside the Red Cross I improvised. About 4:00 (chow time) I went up the hill to bring in an outpost with Sgt. Ross. On the way back I gathered some very nice quinces and got a couple big persimmons, also a few grapes. Mother would sure like to have all the quinces around here to can with her apples, make preserves, etc. Dark about 5, so to room and shot the baloney awhile with roomie

Erwin and Bernstein from across the hall. Something upset a couple of booby traps between 7 and 10 and so had everyone running around like chickens with their heads off.

Mother to Richard

Dear Richard,

It is a dreary, rainy afternoon with nothing to do but write letters. Chiefly I want to tell you about Dale Rigdon. I think I told you he was seriously wounded and they heard from him twice last week. The first letter he wrote three days after his accident. He said he couldn't tell them where he was or what had happened but he was being moved and hoped he could later. He said he wrote as soon as possible, hoping his letter would reach Charlene before the official notification, so that she wouldn't worry. She felt better, even from that letter, because she knew he could see to write. She had said she could stand anything better than hearing it was his eyes. In a few days another letter came. He said his legs were full of holes made by shrapnel but no bones were broken. He owed his life to five of his buddies he will never forget. They made a stretcher of blankets and carried him back under heavy fire to the medics. He said the medics were the unsung heroes of this war and were marvelous—said they never even looked around for cover but worked right on. Dale is in a 14-story modern hospital in Paris, most of the doctors being from Chicago. I have no idea where you are, but I know the boys sometimes get to go to Paris for weekends so I thought you might sometime get to look up Dale. One never knows.

Mrs. Amanda Owens, who always asks about you, says she would be so glad if you would write her a message of some kind, as she has never had any mail from overseas and would like to keep it. Roy Clark has gone to Boston to see the commissioning of the USS *Scribner* on which Leroy will sail. I've ordered a duck for Thanksgiving from Mrs. Clipp—dressed and delivered for $2.

Lots of Love,
Mother

November 20, 1944
Unit History

16-20 Nov 1944 on the front lines in Battalion Reserve. One platoon occupying the town of Moulinet, France. Remainder of company billeted in Peïra Cava. Patrols operating daily. Medical Detachment treated 3 battle casualties, evacuating 2 men and retaining one in infirmary. Dispensary was inspected by Lt. Colonel Edwards (Battalion Commander), installations and activities found in good order.

Richard's Journal

Up at the most un-Army like hour of 8:00 a.m., rainy and clouds very low, had breakfast of cooked cereal that tasted like cardboard, C rations and biscuits and coffee. Went up with Sgt. Ross (rebel from Virginia—ha) to an outpost and gathered some more quinces, pears, apples, and above all some flowers for my room. Got some nice pink, red, and yellow flowers, put them in gallon can and placed them on the table in front of the window, also a dish of fruit. So now our room looks very home-like. On the dresser is a large washbowl, 2 oil lamps, ashtray, a couple hand grenades—one acting as a bookend and a can of green paint as the other. Have my map taped above on the wall beside a picture of a praying priest with a cross in his hand.

Also have a small table for medical supplies, etc. Then a little bed table with a nice silk covering, also have nice silk, white curtains, in the other corner the bed and then a table in the other corner with a squared white and blue cover for packs, etc. Floor is hexagonal red tile, ceiling white, and brown striped posy wallpaper. Ah ha! And how—no place like home.

Met mule train at 11 after washing and shaving. Got some paregoric, bismuth, and subnitrate pills for the GIs (diarrhea).[46] A few of the boys including myself have been bothered, due I guess, to change in diet. Also got some (DDT) insecticide powder for delousing, etc. Capt. Hess came down with mule train.[47] Says B Company up to the north has had some casualties, a Sgt. Peterson killed by own machine gun, didn't know him I don't think. Stroman got mortar fire, knew him, from 2nd Platoon same as Buster, hope Buster is okay. B Company has had other casualties too, I hear. Haven't seen Buster for quite some time now, about a week I guess.

Afternoon chow of turkey and peas combined (from cans) and a few C rations. I went rummaging around in the modern bar and hotel next door, now indeed a mess after shelling that I assume drove the Germans out. Collected quite a few very interesting stamps. Am writing this at 3:00 and am getting cold again so will finish at bedtime. Had a little excitement after chow (about dark). A couple of jeeps loaded down with Americans and FFI men ran into one of our booby traps of white phosphorus grenades, so I got my first business besides minor cuts, etc. One fellow had the side of his face burned pretty bad and the rest had small speckle burns here and there. Patched them up with boric acid and sulpha and sent them back to an aid station. First evidence of FFI in this sector. Every night seems to afford some excitement of some kind, all because of our booby traps. Getting another combat patrol going in morning, don't guess I'll get to go. Got in an 81 mm mortar that will play heck with the Jerries fort.[48]

---

46   Paregoric was a household remedy used primarily for diarrhea and as a cough expectorant. Bismuth was used as an antacid and subnitrate was used for upset stomach and diarrhea. —Ed.
47   Captain Hess was the Company Commander. —Ed.
48   An 81 mm mortar was the largest weapon in the arsenal of a U.S. World War II infantry battalion. —Ed.

November 21, 1944

Had three booby traps go off at about 4 this morn and everyone got on the alert. Got up for about an hour but nothing happened so back to bed and up at 7:20 in time to see patrol off and gave them a box of morphine. Had chow of dried eggs, corned beef—had seconds, in fact. Spent first part of morning cleaning up room, making bed, and sweeping around a bit. Took a sponge bath and then about 11:00 Scotty came down and gave me the latest dope on things up in Peïra Cava, nothing much new. Can take Red Crosses off helmet, carry a concealed weapon, and wear armbands only. Gathered a few chestnuts up the street and then did some laundry and wrote Folks a letter for Scotty to take back this evening. Very beautiful day and very comfortable. Patrol came back the middle of afternoon and reported contact with the enemy. The sniper thinks he got a Jerry, we hope, no casualties, only a guy got his hand skinned on the mortar. Had chow at 3:30, then messed around till dark doing nothing in particular. Blacked out room and read some in the books I found in the closet a couple days ago. Found an English-French book with selections from English poets and authors—Milton, Browning, Dickens, etc. Read till about 8:00 and Erwin went on guard so here I sit thinking about going to bed probably only to arise soon at the ever familiar echo of a booby trap. Think I'll eat a quince and hit the hay. Picked a few nice white and yellow chrysanthemums and have them in a wine glass I acquired in the downstairs bar sitting on my table. Tried to study a little French tonight also.

Richard to Folks

Dear Folks,

Can now tell you that I'm in France and have visited Marseille. Am feeling fine and have plenty to eat, and it's not bad at that. Haven't seen Buster for quite some time now. I hear that Carroll Moore is in France now.[49] Received Mother's letter of the 31st a couple of days ago, expect that you have heard from me by now. Received a letter from David that took over a month. These French people are something, indeed unique from what I've been used to.

Write!

Love,

Richard

November 22, 1944

Unit History

Pfc. William Greene was killed in action at 2315 hours 21 Nov 44 while on a repair patrol between Peïra Cava and Turini, France. The patrol's mission was to provide security for the wire party. Lt. Paul Dixon, wounded in action, vicinity of Peïra Cava as of 18 Nov 44, not hospitalized.

Richard's Journal

Combat life, and how. Up at 7:30 and messed around the entire day. Getting on my nerves. Had chow of C rations at 8, cleaned up room. Messed around in another hotel across the way and found some interesting stamps and post cards. Road is now open to peeps from Sospel so we got our fruit rations by vehicle both this morning and afternoon. Got some medical supplies Scotty sent, boric acid, gauze, iodine, and wound tablets for all the men. More C rations for noon meal. Went up to the orchard by the outpost and gathered some

---

49   Buster Crockett's cousin. —Ed.

persimmons for my room, my supply of apples was practically nil. Some of the boys found what was formerly the mayor's automobile, a yellow junky-looking affair, both truck and auto, so they have it running and spent practically all afternoon playing around with it. One boy found a bicycle and has it in good running order, even took a spin on it myself. More C rations chow, also have cooked apples about every meal and mashed potatoes now and then when the boys run across them in an old cellar, etc. Blacked out room and looked thru a French science book. I find it a good way to learn French since there are lots of pictures in it.

November 23, 1944

Sent out a combat patrol this morn. Cleaned up room and then had the intentions of gathering some apples but never did. Strayed off around town awhile and then went thru an old hotel and started my stamp collecting again, found some very interesting ones.

Had chow, a few pieces of beef, slice of bread, and cup of cocoa. Capt. Miller, Swientko, Scotty, and Cyphert dropped in and had chow. We went up to the 81 mm position, put jeep in tunnel, and looked at German fort and barracks we are trying to take. I stayed up at position and came back with the boys in the old car and walked part of way back and got some chestnuts. Patrol came in at about 2:00 and so we had supper at three, indeed a good meal of steak, mashed potatoes and gravy, applesauce, coffee and bread and got seconds. So got my fill, quite a transition from dinner. Took my bandage scissors and cut around stamps for awhile and find I have two envelopes full all ready and still have some more to get. The ration jeep brought the *Stars & Stripes*, Mon. and Tues. papers. First news for a long time.

Patton outflanked Metz, and Patch took Belfast.[50] Seems to be a general drive up with lots of snow and wind, I guess. Yanks still cleaning up on Leyte in Philippines. Has been cold all day and my feet are pretty cold this evening so to bed is the solution I guess.

November 24, 1944

Spent an hour grinding down an old knife I found on an old grindstone I also found. Went rummaging around in the school (ecole) on the opposite side of the square. Found a German entrenching tool which just fits my carrier so I took possession, since I broke the handle of mine back in Marseille. Found some interesting things in the school, appears to be a grade and high combined. Found a very good centigrade thermometer, some nice big maps, plenty of books, and even 3 American short story magazines dated about 1927. Had a very good turkey dinner with mashed potatoes, cabbage (cooked), carrots, onions, bread, and coffee. Received 2 nice dressed turkeys in the rations yesterday evening. Spent the first part of the afternoon collecting stamps in the hotel adjoining the school, found some more interesting ones. Combat patrol came back with no casualties. Scotty and Swientko came down in the jeep and brought another litter, litter rack, and my pay—yes! Finally got paid—amounted to 950 francs (figure it out for yourself, Mr. Berkey).

The Frenchies came carting along a body in a sack that they wanted hauled down the road. I took a peek in the sack and indeed what a mess. They said the Germans killed "it" before they left, so one can use his own imagination as to how it looked—and smelled.

Had chow of good ham this evening and it tasted swell. Have a sick boy tonight and am giving him medicine (paregoric and bis-

---

50   Lt. Colonel Alexander Patch commanded the 7th Army in which Richard served during the invasion of Southern France, and he continued to lead them during the May 1945 attack on the Siegfried Line. Born in 1889, Patch died of pneumonia just a few months after the war was over. He had previously served as a soldier in World War I and was better known for commanding U.S. Army and Marine Corps forces during the World War II Guadalcanal invasion. Wyant, William, *Sandy Patch: a Biography of Lt. Gen. Alexander M. Patch,* (New York: Praeger, 1991).

muth) for stomach cramps on the hour, give him the last one in a few minutes and then to bed.

November 25, 1944

Unit History

Tec 5 Howard Terry, exhaustion, transferred to unknown hospital. Left Peïra Cava 0700 hours to relieve B Company 68th AIB at Turini, France. One platoon remained at Moulinet.

Richard's Journal

Wrote letters to Folks, Tom Collins, "the rebel from South Carolina" (Georgetown), which I received a V-mail from (also in French) (former Cincy ASTP boy), and a letter to Rodman. After the letter writing ordeal Bernstein, a young kid from Omaha, Nebraska, and myself took a stroll up the mountainside to the orchard and gathered huge quantities of apples, pears and quince. We returned in time for chow, naturally.

The entire afternoon was spent in making a book from the stamps I've been collecting and a stamp book I also found. Acquired some flour from the kitchen and a little water made a nice sticky goo. I found that out after spilling about half of it on my pants. I pasted the stamps in haphazardly but finally got finished by 4. Am indeed proud of my book as I surveyed the results a while ago. This evening was taken up by more letter writing, indeed an unusual letter day. Wrote to David and Virginia and Martha Jean and Imy. Was going to write to Lucy but just can't remember all of her long drawn out address. The boys have the old car in ship-shape these days, acquired a few more tires, etc. Packed my musette bag and collected junk, ready to move out in the morn I hear.[51]

---

51   Musette bag: small bag made of canvas with a shoulder strap, to be used during hiking and marching. —Ed.

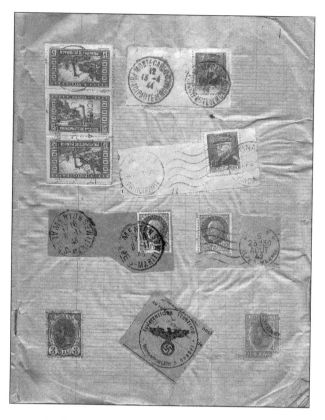

Richard's stamp book—24 pages, 281 stamps from 6 countries: France, Germany, Italy, Romania, Monaco, and Morocco

Richard to Folks

Dear Folks,

Have managed to acquire a few airmail stamps off a guy, and so will put one to use. This letter may reach you before the one I wrote a day or so ago. Was going to write Lucy this morning but find I have misplaced her address and can't seem to remember it in its entirety.

I received the church newsletter and would be most grateful if you'd inform them of change of address. Am having lots of fun trying to pick up this French language. I have acquired various books on the subject, so am proceeding okay. I find it quite easy to get straight, except those verbs and idioms. Have not as yet received any papers. We get the Army newspaper *Stars & Stripes* here and that affords the only means of news acquisition. We received a couple of them a few days ago, first news we've had for what seemed ages. Mail seems to be very slow, I expect due to lack of transportation facilities in the Theatre. Am still OK and feeling fine, chow good as expected.

Love,

Richard

November 26, 1944

Unit History

20 enlisted men promoted to Pfc. (Private First Class). One platoon rejoined Company from Moulinet at 1300 hours setting up positions at Turini, France.

Richard's Journal

Moving day again. Up at 7:30, chow, finished packing things, and moved out at nine up the long trail back to Peïra Cava. We are supposed to replace 2nd Platoon B Company at Turini (Buster's Platoon and my old one—ha!). Likewise they are to relieve us. Turini is north of Moulinet and the hot spot where B Company has had a number of casualties. Finally made the "Long Trek Back." Snowed about noon but 'twas nice walking thru the nice green pines. Read my prayer going up the trail, the one little prayer the church adds at the end of their letters to be read by them in church and servicemen everywhere the same day.

Waited on the road outside Peïra Cava for transportation to Turini. And while waiting lo and behold came B Company (2nd Platoon) and Crockett leading a mule, indeed a sight that greeted my eyes with joy—ha! Old Buster ending up being a mule herder, and he gave off with that sheepish grin and we talked fast for he was moving down to our old "home." We mentioned action, letters, home, etc., all in about 5 min, then he went over the hill and I piled in a truck with my boys along with Lt. Gosselin, C.O. of the 3rd Platoon C Company, and we all headed for Turini. Arrived a few minutes later and found we had "nice" dugouts to live in. Found Scotty and he had me fixed up with a bed. I'm with 3rd Platoon, HQ squad, and also in this dugout is company HQ, Capt. Hess, etc. Got situated about 2, ate a C ration and then viewed the place. Pretty close to Jerry forts and lots of artillery here I understand. Had supper of C rations about 6 and then batted breeze with Scotty in our "hole." He lets me in on the latest happenings and so on. Hazelton is now attached to C Company, the boy from Providence, Rhode Island. The fireman now makes 4 aid men to a company.

> A – Brown, Ladd, Flarity, and Kerr
> B – Schneider, Goldstein, Simon, Lehman
> C – Scotty, Mude, Hazelton, and myself

Rest of men in Aid Station I guess. Read some of the latest news in *Stars & Stripes* 25, the latest one. Have homemade board double-deck affairs to sleep on.

Mother to Richard

Dear Richard,

We were so happy to hear from all four of you kids Friday and Saturday. Your regular mail letters to Daddy and me and to Eleanor, both written November 7, were the ones we got. In this case V-mail was faster, for Daddy got the one about the allotment, written also November 7, four or five days earlier. We see you are a Pfc. again. Did you have to take one of those jobs you didn't want, to get a rating? Buster told his folks he was where his Dad was in 1917, so we know that means France. We have watched the papers but have seen no word of the Second Army in action. Maybe it is getting set to appear suddenly as the Ninth did.

Jonas and Mildred finally rented a nice apartment over at Miami Beach and moved into it last week. They share the apartment with a Lieutenant Arko and his wife, Jean. They sent advertising pictures of the place, even showing the floor plans. There is a private beach and sundeck just outside the back door. Jonas does not have to work on Sundays, so he said he could lie on the sand in the sun all day if he chose. Jonas said he was in an advanced class with two lieutenant commanders and the rest mostly full lieutenants. He was sixth in the class on the navigation exam.

I'll go on about the children's letters. Lucy said they had 200 charts sent into Hydro to be rushed immediately.[52] She was afraid they might not get much time off so she went sightseeing, through the Capitol Building, etc., and out to Arlington Cemetery and the Tomb of the Unknown Soldier. She had been roller skating again. David said they had never had regular huts but were getting them built now. He didn't have much to write about. Has never seen any of the Washington County boys yet.

I hear that Elmo Colglazier's got a letter from Jack's nurse. He wasn't able to write because his vision was impaired. She said he had had two or three operations and would have more, but would have to wear a plate in his head. I'm so sorry for the family. Marie has been so nearly blind for years that it's just a shame it had to be Jack's eyes. Last time I sent you Dale Rigdon's address and now Charlene has heard that he has been sent back to a hospital in England. Virginia got to see Ernie Pyle at convocation when Indiana University gave him the degree of Dr. of Humane Letters. He was very shy and wouldn't say a word. His old pals told about his former escapades. The funny thing was that Indiana University didn't give him a degree then; it's doubtful if he appreciates this one so much now.

---

52   Hydro: The Hydrographic Office was part of the Department of the Navy. Staff prepared and published maps, charts, and nautical books required in navigation. –Ed.

Jimmy Huffman and Martha came in Friday afternoon. He was supposed to get 100 hours in a bigger airship at Fort Wayne, after which he expects to fly transport planes.

Love,

Mother

The aid station at Peïra Cava. Courtesy of Norman Eliasson

November 27, 1944

Unit History

Pvt. Willard Arthurs, lightly wounded in action, transferred to unknown hospital.[53] Shell fragment wounds suffered in right leg at 1145 hours in vicinity of Turini.

---

53   "Lightly wounded" meant that the wounds were not considered life threatening. "Seriously wounded" meant that the wounds were considered life threatening. A "wound" was generally caused by enemy action. An "injury" was caused by an accident such as a fall or the premature explosion of a weapon. "Morning Reports: Commonly Used Abbreviations," *80th Division Digital Archives Project*, http://www.80thdivision.com/WebArchives/abbreviations.htm (March 20, 2014).

Richard's Journal

Slept very little, up at 5:45 and smoked out by the fire. What a transition, from summer to winter, from innersprings to boards, from sun to shadows, from low to high, from few Jerries to lots of Jerries. All just in a few miles from Moulinet to Turini. Had cup coffee and hamburger sandwich for breakfast, got light about 7:00, already had dungeon doors open to let out smoke. Read the paper a while and then Scotty and I walked up the mountain to visit our positions. Saw Hazelton at 1st Platoon Company and then went to HQ and fixed up Carlisle's boils, saw Mert Finger and started back down at about 11:15. A few rounds of artillery buzzed pretty close on way down. Had a very nice walk. Frozen all around this morn. But sun is out, excellent views and nice soft looking green pines with gray moss dripping from each and every branch. Had chow of two steak sandwiches and coffee. Hurriedly ate and went over to anti-tank company and got in ambulance to go back to Peïra Cava to hunt for lost barracks bag (with clean clothes, shoepacs and whatnot).[54]

Went to aid station with Cyphert and Martinez, saw all the boys. They are set up in a nice house in Peïra Cava with running water and all. Also have another aid station near A Company, some place I'm not familiar with. Went down to French barracks to look for barracks bag, but to no avail. Also lost gas mask with my towels included. Had chow at aid station about 5, Spam, corn, gravy, bread, butter, jam, peanut butter, sweet potatoes, peaches and whatnot. I haven't eaten a meal like that—well, I can't remember. Sowell and Steinman are the chief cooks and bottle washers. Cyphert and Boehringer rushed me back to front after chow. Arrived at A.T. Command Post at dark and that's where I'm at now spending the night. Can't get the 200 yards

---

54 Shoepacs were special boots with a 12-inch upper, a steel shank, and a rubber bottom. Unfortunately, these boots were not sufficient for the cold European winter. The rubber retained perspiration and many men suffered from trenchfoot and lost toes or feet as a result. If they could wash and dry their feet and socks daily, the risk of trenchfoot was less. Battle conditions often made this daily washing impossible. "WWII Shoepacs," *Olive-Drab.com*, http://olive-drab.com/od_soldiers_clothing_combat_ww2_shoepacs.php (Jan. 1, 2014).

to the dugout because of booby traps, guns, and whatnot. So, I'm here writing this about 7 bells, getting ready to hit the sack to see if I can get a little shut-eye. Luckily a guy has gone on pass to Nice and I can use his sack. Lt. Battenfeld says I can go on pass Wednesday, good deal, to Nice for 48 hours, have to round up some clean clothes. Letter from Mother, V-mail written the 12th, had finally heard from me after a month.

November 28, 1944

Up at 7:00 after a very unrestful night. Rolled all over the place, floor felt as if it were all sharp cornered rails. 2nd night I haven't slept. Guess I got too used to those innersprings of Hotel de Paris, Moulinet—ha! Spent the entire morning doing nothing whatsoever, but did manage to shave a while before dinner. Warm today. Did my laundry this afternoon and got it all dried. Have now given up hope of finding my long lost equipment. Sgt. Ross came back after a search of no avail. So far have lost my much-needed shoepacs, pair ODs[55], pair long underwear, mittens, cover, barracks bag, 2 towels, and gas mask—ha! Had big chow this evening, meat loaf, green beans, coffee, bread, bread pudding, and plenty of all. After chow stood outside as long as possible before we closed the iron doors of our dungeon. Then lit a candle and cleaned out my musette bag and repacked. Lay in awhile and read the life of Charles Dickens in prep for reading David Copperfield, one of the books I found in Moulinet—the only one entirely in English. Got sleepy and blew out candle about 9:30.

November 29, 1944

Up at 7:00 after little sleep, too hard, have to remedy that. Hope to sleep better tonight, expect to have a big day tomorrow. 'Tis Thanksgiving (the real one) and I'm going to Nice on 24-hour pass. Had chow and went to Peïra Cava and at last found my equipment that only yesterday I'd given up for lost. I feel much better now. Talked to Lt. Battenfeld in aid station and he says passes have been cut down

---

55   OD: Olive Drab, the color used for uniforms, paint of vehicles, and other Army equipment. In this case, it refers to clothing. —Ed.

to 24 so now can go since I've found my clothes. Talked to "Crazy" (and I'm serious) Sgt. Haggerty. He gave me a drink of alcoholic spirits he brews himself, tasted rather horrible. Also acquired 2 new flashlight batteries. Returned to dugout, had chow, shaved, washed, and made a complete change of clothing, first time since leaving Marseille. I indeed feel cleaner, got things ready for the take off in the morn. Warm sun this afternoon. Got *Stars & Stripes* of the 26th and 27th and read news, the best of all Indiana 14, Purdue 6—ha ha! Messed around tonight sorting things around and talking to Scotty about conditions in general.

November 30, 1944

Thanksgiving Day! And what a day—WOW! Got up at 7:00, rushed around getting my clothes ready, eats, etc., to go on 24-hour pass to Nice. Finally got ready at 8:45 and then huge bags of mail came and I received 3 from Julia, 2 from Mother, and one from the DeJeans. So I was much pleased with the day so far, lots of news in the letters that was indeed welcome, also Mother enclosed a book of airmail stamps. After reading the mail I went down to the A.T. Platoon HQ at Turini to get transportation to aid station at Peïra Cava to get pass only to learn that passes had been cancelled since we are to move tomorrow. So back to dugout and after a little messing around I decided, with the aid of Scotty, to go to aid station and probably go to Nice anyway. So drove Capt. Hess's peep into station and secured pass to Nice from Sgt. Haggerty and proceeded to hitchhike to Nice. Yes, back at the old game again and I did okay. Nice is 36 km from Peïra Cava and I started at 10:15 and got to Nice at 11:30, not bad.

Got rides with the Japanese boys from the 36th Division (Jap-American Division) that's relieving us tomorrow. Well, then the ordeal began. I walked to the seashore (with aid of maps), around a monument to World War I, then down Quai des États-Unis along the seashore, indeed a beautiful scene but much of the building on the right ruined by the Nazis. Concrete pillboxes, trenches, dragon's teeth,[56] and barbed wire on the right next to the seashore. These fortifications extended the entire length of the waterfront, however the town in general is not shot up badly. Workmen are already removing the dragon's teeth with blast hammers and filling up the trenches with cinders. Walked on down to the public park (Jardin Albert), a once beautiful palmed park now a sort of mess). North to Rue Massena then crossed Boulevard Victor-Hugo, passed Continental Hotel, up to railway station, east to Avenue de la Victoire, the main N and S avenue of town. All kinds of shops already displayed with X-mas assortments. How can one think about Christmas with the hot sun beating down? Then I went over to the Continental Hotel, taken over by GIs of the 7th Army to stay (front line troops only). Eats, beds, and all for only 25 francs, 2 days, okay. I cleaned up a bit, got the latest *Stars & Stripes* and then went down to the Red Cross in hopes of obtaining a snack that I could call Thanksgiving dinner. But they were evidently out of food, so my Thanksgiving dinner consisted of one large and one small chocolate (tropical) ration bar—they have a sickening taste.[57] The Red Cross is in the Cassina on corner of Promenade des Anglais and Rue du Congress, overlooking the sea. By this time 'twas about 1:30 so I decided I'd better think about hitching back since we are leaving tomorrow, so went to Adriatic Hotel (68th HQ) but found no transportation, so started walking back the way I came. Indeed I'd done enough walking by this time and 'twas hot but nothing else to do. So I think I must have walked half way back to Peïra Cava. Finally outside of Nice got a ride with the Japs to L'Escarène. Walked long way up mountain and finally got picked up by chaplain at Lucéram.

---

56   Dragon's teeth: pyramid-shaped concrete pylons laid in rows by the Germans to deter tanks and mechanized vehicles. —Ed.
57   A regular chocolate bar would melt in a soldier's pocket in the South Pacific or in summer temperatures in Europe. The army commissioned Hershey to create a four-ounce chocolate bar that would be high in nutrition (600 calories) and would not melt. These objectives were met, but unfortunately the resulting product didn't taste very good. "Ration D Bars," *Hershey Community Archives,* http://www.hersheyarchives.org/essay/details.aspx?EssayId=26 (Jan. 1, 2014).

What a walk! Got to aid station at 5:00 and decided to stay all night since was getting dark and traps were out. Viewed a beautiful sunset over snowcapped mountains (the view from Peïra Cava is terrific). So I took a hot bath, was it nice, oh baby. Then had a fairly decent supper cooked up by Sowell, Steinmann, and Sellen. I guess I can substitute it for a Thanksgiving dinner, had hamburger, dried sweet potatoes, pears, bread and butter, and sliced peaches. Not bad, after a heck of a day's walking. Messed around awhile and all medics took off but a few to enjoy their last night in Peïra Cava.

About 11 Sowell and some of the boys came in and naturally he was tight, so I, being kinda hungry, suggested he make some biscuits. So I fixed up a hot fire and he began, indeed a funny show. But he got a few made and they were good. We ate them with apricot jam and butter and cheese. Then he went to bed and left me, Cyphert, and Martinez in the kitchen. So, I decided to make some biscuits, and so I did, and they turned out okay. About the time the biscuits were done, Sgt. Haggerty came in with Steinmann, tight as a loon—ha. All the biscuits, although slightly tough, were immediately devoured. Am quite proud of them nevertheless. By this time 'twas 2:30 and so I decided to clean the joint up, washed a few dishes. Sgt. Haggerty began singing (not a bad voice—but he's crazy otherwise—and how) and soon all went to bed and left me alone. Swept the floor, banked fire, spread a shelter half on tile floor and lay down about 3:30 and said my prayers.[58] What a Thanksgiving Day—oh!

---

58   A shelter half was a pup tent with two half pieces that hooked together with a row of buttons at the top and a watertight closure. The shelter half was about 7 feet long and 5 feet wide and with stakes and poles weighed five pounds. "Tent: Shelter Half (Pup Tent)," *Olive-Drab.com*, http://olive-drab.com/od_soldiers_gear_shelter_half.php (Jan. 1, 2014).

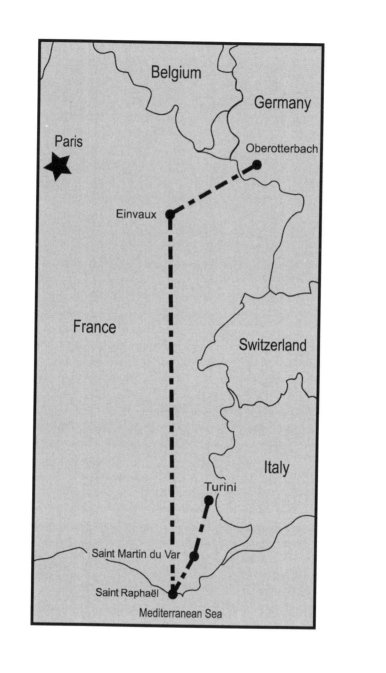

CHAPTER FIVE
DECEMBER 1944

December 1, 1944

Unit History

C Company—240 enlisted men and 6 officers left Turini, France, at 1330 hours on mounted road march to St. Martin-du-Var, France. Distance traveled—31 miles. Arrived 1530 hours. Medical Detachment left Peïra Cava at 1200 hours, arrived Saint-Raphaël, France for entrainment to destination unknown at 2300 hours.

Richard's Journal

Up at 6:00, feeling fit as a fiddle! Built up fire, woke up Sowell, and we began to fix breakfast. Made oatmeal (put fig bars in mine), cut bacon with pocketknife, mixed up dried eggs, and Sowell baked biscuits. I ate and said "bon jour" and Sellen took me to front at Turini at 8:00. Got to dugout in time to pack equipment and take off to Peïra Cava, only to have to go back to get bedroll. Ate C rations for dinner and took off for old factory again. Ride with HQ half-track. Some ride down the mountain. Arrived at old factory about 3 bells and fixed up things as we had 'em a couple weeks ago. B Company and Crockey pulled in about 4:00 and I went over immediately to see him and we talked about the latest happenings, etc. Glad to see him again, indeed glad to see him well. Went over after chow to see him again but had gone someplace so I hit the sack in the dirt, about 9:30 (did watch a movie awhile). Still feel bad from Thanksgiving—no wonder?

Lucy to Richard

Dear Richard,

For about six months, so it seems, I've been meaning to write you and as usual I end up writing the folks about every three weeks and neglecting everyone else. Even Mother and Daddy are disgusted with me. Really I don't know what's wrong with me except that there's so much confusion around the hall I can hardly concentrate on writing. Anyway here I is! I confess I was very sorry to hear you were seasick. I know you'll pardon me when I say I had to laugh picturing your big hulk leaning over the side and your face pea-green. "4 eye" must have been a beautiful sight. What I wouldn't have given to be there with a paintbrush and paper!

Just last night I went over to eat supper with one of the WAVES at Suitland Manor and coming back I saw the first ice of the winter on the puddles left by the morning's downpour. Gee, it seemed good to feel ice crack under my feet. It made me remember going down to the creek and testing ice to see if it was hard enough to stand on or to run the sled across. Those were the days! I remember when Mother used to get furious with me for sliding on the school grounds with all the boys! I'd usually be the only girl, and once had the record for going the farthest—to the railroad track and over!! Whew!!

The work at Hydro has been speeding up so's to get our charts to the ships faster, and scuttlebutt was that we'd have our usual privilege of every other Saturday off taken away from us. Therefore, I decided to hurry and catch up on my sightseeing. I visited the Capitol, the Smithsonian Institute (at least part of it), and Arlington Cemetery, where I saw the Tomb of the Unknown Soldier. I visited the cemetery on Armistice Day and watched them change guards and that was impressive. I felt very un-GI-like as I watched, for I'd just avoided saluting about 20 times that day! Bob and I had been to Mount Vernon in August when he was here on leave. We took the boat ride out, and sat in the sun—I mean on the boat. It's beautiful out there. I was surprised to see how high up Mount Vernon seemed from the river, for I'd always had a lower scene in my mind. One of the most beautiful places, tho', is the Lincoln Memorial and the Reflecting Pool!

Tomorrow is Captain's inspection, so I must get my room ready. Guess I'll have to go to that stinky Navy dentist soon as I broke two pieces out of one of my good teeth. Thankfully not in front! This life's killing me, ha ha! Ahem! What's more, I was eating a cracker. Gee, these bakeries are lousy since the war!

Well, Mr. Private Berkey, write me the news and tell me your latest gossip. I must make the old brain work for at least two minutes to clean up the joint before I crawl into my icy bed.

Write!

Love,

Lucy

December 2, 1944

Unit History

240 enlisted men and 6 officers left St. Martin-du-Var, France, on mounted road march of 45 miles. Arrived at Saint-Raphaël, France, at 1400 hours awaiting entrainment. Left Saint-Raphaël at 2300 hours by rail transportation for destination unknown. First and second sections of Train I loaded weapons, vehicles, and personnel for movement (HQ and HQ Company, Company A, Company B, Personnel Section). Train II carried Company C, weapons and vehicles.

Richard's Journal

Up at 6:00, chow, went over to see Crockey. Took him some candles and we talked awhile, helped him carry his stuff to half-track in preparation to leave. We moved out at 9:00. Rode down to and past Nice, thru Cannes, and at about noon arrived at an area outside Fréjus, the place we are to get on a train to take off for a new front up north. Cannes is a very modernistic and beautiful town, much like Nice. All along the shore are demolished Nazi installations. They sure messed up the entire seashore of the Riviera. Stayed in area at Fréjus till after supper and then moved to train station about dark. Sat around fire all evening till 12 while half-tracks were being loaded. Finally they loaded us in boxcars, 13 in the one I'm in, half of HQ and half of machine gun squads, good deal. Finally crawled in sack at 1:00 but got out immediately upon hearing a loud shout for a medic. Ran up the way a piece and found Shelton of B Company lying on ground, tight and had fallen out of half-track, about a 10 ft. fall, came to and was okay. Lucky he was tight. He and 4 other B Company boys missed their train so have to ride with us, so they stuck 'em on the cold half-tracks. So, finally got back in sack and guess the train soon started rolling. By the way, lost 350 francs in crap game at Fréjus —ha!

December 3, 1944

Unit History

Wheeled vehicle convoy left St. Martin-du-Var, France.

Richard's Journal

Got up at 8:00 while train was entering Toulon. Got a glimpse of blue harbor and then stopped at a little station in north Toulon and stayed entire day, that is till about 5 bells. Wrote V-mail Christmas cards to Folks, Julia, Grandmother, Martha Jean, Betty, Rodman, the DeJeans, David, and have one left for someone. Cleaned up and had chow, just messed around rest of time. Moved out at about 5 and saw very little in way of scenery since darkness approached very quickly. How interesting, at last we have something to look forward to during the next 4 or 5 days in our 40 x 8 boxcar. Heard lots about the 40 hommes 8 chevaux boxcars during last war, same as this I guess.[59] Toulon, what little I saw didn't seem to be damaged too badly. Suppose the Jerries messed up the beach as they did at Nice and Cannes. 13 of us in this boxcar and we have just enough room, quite comfortable for a boxcar. Before going to bed we all got to singing, all kinds of songs, stopped at a town and sang "We're Coming Over" for a Frenchie who fought in last war and evidently wounded. We also sang some Christmas songs that were indeed very pretty. Finally hit sack about 8:00 in the best of spirits.

Mother to Richard

Dearest Boy,

The last word we have from you was written November 7 and we ought to be hearing again. Maybe there will be a letter tomorrow. Martha Branaman said Lee Edward wrote that he was in a combat area. He said he was in a jeep when a German fighter plane came down on fire and exploded within 150 yards of him. He and the boys with him crawled under the jeep. If he can write things like that, I should think you could tell a little more about what you're doing. No, I don't want you to tell what the censors forbid, of course.

There are a lot of anxious people now. I talked to several at church this morning and almost every family has someone to worry about. Mattie Martin said Russell had just crossed and they had not yet heard from him. Their Junior leaves Wednesday, they think, to fly a B-29 in the South Pacific. Willie Lester is at home and was at church with all his family. He is going overseas shortly. Rev. and Mrs. Roach are upset because their

---

59   As France only had narrow gauge railroads, boxcars were half the size of those in the United States. Each 40 x 8 boxcar could carry 40 men or eight horses with dimensions of 20 ½ feet long and 8 ½ feet wide. Many soldiers reported on the uncomfortable conditions of these old, unheated cars. Some men even built fires inside them trying to stay warm. "Forty and Eight Boxcar," *Skylighters.org*, http://www.skylighters.org/encyclopedia/fortyandeight.html (Jan. 1, 2014).

baby boy, Hugh, had to report to Great Lakes Saturday.[60] They had thought he would get to finish this year of school. Mr. and Mrs. Marvin Martin have heard that Marvin, Jr. has been wounded. So it goes. Do you remember Basil Martin, son of the contractor who built the Ward Thompson house? He is missing in action.

The sun was bright this afternoon, even if cold, and I thought we should have gone to the farm to get a Christmas tree but Eleanor didn't think so. It should be put up two weeks from today if we are to have it a week before Christmas. Last year we didn't though. I am really not much interested in Christmas with so many of you away. I hope some of your packages reach you in time. Our women's group is meeting Friday to pack boxes for servicemen in this country. If you haven't already sent the request again for food, please send one. I want to send you some cookies and candy.

Daddy said he didn't have you here this fall to take the leaves out of the eaves trough in the back of the house and it was frozen up and leaking over the edge. He also said to tell you he was still using the maps you brought him. He also has a very good National Geographic map of Germany and its approaches, in detail. He is following the progress of the different armies. This week's *Life* magazine has a fine relief map, showing the rivers, hills, etc., and the position of the armies.

The big news in athletics is that we beat Mitchell here Friday night, 32 to 25. It was the first time Mitchell had been beaten this year and they had been running up big scores against their opponents. Eleanor said it was an exciting game. She said a funny thing happened. The boys were scuffling for the ball in

---

60   A thousand miles from the nearest ocean, Great Lakes Naval Training Station is located in North Chicago, Illinois. This facility supplied around a million soldiers during World War II. "Great Lakes Naval Training Station," *Encyclopedia of Chicago*, http://www.encyclopedia.chicagohistory.org/pages/543.html (Jan. 27, 2014).

the corner and got tangled up with a spectator and dragged him down on the floor with them. He got up looking dazed and brushed off his coat. Army beat Navy 23 to 7 yesterday in football at Baltimore. We got a letter from David. He said it was terribly hot now. They have huts with screens at last and he does not have to sleep under a mosquito net. We hear that Fred Kuonen is in the Philippines now.

Love,

Mother

December 4, 1944

Richard's Journal

Up in morning at 8:00, had chow cooked up by one of the boys, and then we pulled into Lyon, rather dirty and musty looking. We moved on after a time and continued to be jolted hither and yon in our little siesta. Half the boys here are HQ squad and half machine gun squad, guess I'm the odd 13th one. One boy, Sgt. Bush of machine gun squad, is from Jeffersonville, lives on Graham St. Another guy is from Seymour (Kramer). Still bouncing around in our little train car, went to bed later tonight, about 9:30.

December 5, 1944

The farther north we go we see more and more of the spoils of war. Passed thru Dijon this noon and then all along the way we saw bomb craters, cities that were practically nil, etc. People in wooden shoes and some none at all. Rainy today and rather cool, in fact I've been cold all day. Didn't do a darn thing today. Can't write because the car shakes too much, so just looked out the door. Some of the boys play pinochle all day and blackjack and poker and whatnot. Cold, so went to bed about 8 tonight. Still bouncing toward Germany.

December 6, 1944

Unit History

240 enlisted men and 6 officers arrived at Einvaux, France, at 1700 hours, detrained at 1730 hours on mounted road march to Schwindratzheim, France, and arrived at 2330 hours. Wheeled vehicle convoy arrived at Schwindratzheim at 1900 hours.

Richard's Journal

Moved very little last night but more this morning and are supposedly near Épinal. This evening, after lunch, we stopped by a hospital train and talked to lots of the soldiers on the train, namely cadre men. As luck would have it we stopped by the kitchen car and received from a most gracious Greek mess Sgt. some ground coffee, fresh bread, and canned milk. Heard they were carrying some casualties from the 62nd. About 4-5 bells we stopped and prepared to get off train. Unloaded vehicles about 6 and at 7 started out for some town 90 miles away. We rode in the cold half-track till about 2 bells and finally ended up in a town, and found a barn loft and hay and to bed. This hay is heaven, good night.

Virginia to Richard

Dearest Richard,

Having decided that I have neglected writing to you for far too long a time, I promised myself to do so tonight. Did I tell you I am working? Your old job, practically, as far as I'm concerned. I'm working here in Morrison Hall waiting, serving, and cleaning up tables at noon, and usually at night. Fun in a way, and earns me some pin money, if you know what I mean.

Tonight we went to one of the Auditorium Series programs. It was really super. The von Trapp family singers. Austrian immigrant family of high birth—baron and baroness! They have 10 children, seven girls and three boys. Sing beautifully, play on antiquated instruments, dress in peasant old country costumes, and do everything family-style. The second half of the program was best, all centering around old Christmas customs—all candlelit and there was a tall, lighted tree in the background. They sang carols in the languages in which they were written. Only the seven girls and mother sang. Two boys are in the service, one little boy, and the papa doesn't warble! A Catholic priest is their conductor and manager. They are very much Catholic.

The folks tried to talk me out of nurses training again when I went home, but I stood up for my rights. Might go to Yale. How does that sound? They had me really worried until I had to give a demonstration in home nursing the other day and did a darned good job, if I do say so. I like it a lot. Am so anxious to graduate, and get started. Wish I were over there with you now. Okay, I know you don't like to hear me blab about this, so I'll shut up. Ha!

Hoping you get this letter by Christmas. I wish you a very Merry Christmas, though frankly, I don't guess it will be for any of us. At home at Thanksgiving, we all said it hardly seems right to go ahead: even though we shall go through the motions the old spirit won't be there without you all. I wonder who will get our tree? Darn you anyhow, why didn't you teach me to drive? I feel positively brainless.

I think of you every day, and wonder how you are getting along. Well, I hope. Be good—take care of yourself. Praying that you will keep well and have at least a halfway pleasant Christmas.

Lots of love—your sis,

Virginia

December 7, 1944

Unit History

Unit reorganized and prepared for future operations. Platoons reconnoitered surrounding towns of Brumath, Geudertheim, Weyersheim, Hoenheim, Souffelweyersheim, and Reichstett. All reported roads only could be used by tanks and half-tracks. Bridges in good shape. All surrounding streams flooded, terrain flat, wet and boggy. Shoulders of roads clear of mines.

Richard's Journal

Three years of war. I wonder how much longer? For me this is really the beginning of war, oh my aching back. Up at 9 bells, boy was that hay warm. Rolled up bedroll and took back to half-track. Sat around till noon in track and then moved about a block to another hayloft where we are to stay till we move up. At last my meager knowledge of Deutsche comes in handy. This town of 1200, Schwindratzheim, is 42 km from the border, 12 km from Strasbourg, and therefore mostly German speaking French. We are billeted with a family who speak German, Herr Kreizer, wife and sister, and the Catholic priest next door. Goose and Ross sleep in the house and we sleep in the loft behind the padre's house in 2 rooms. They all seem very much Dutch. Everyone wears wooden shoes outside and neatly steps out of them coming to the door. I can converse with Herr Kreizer, an architect by trade, in America a bricklayer and carpenter I suppose, and I'm remembering much taught to me by Frau Ellis at IU. Those were the days, indeed. She told us how t'would be, and indeed she was quite *richtig*.[61] We all washed up in the neat kitchen and of course dirtied it up with our non-removable shoepacs. After chow of K rations we sat in kitchen till 9 bells and talked with the English-speaking padre and herr and frau and learned much from the padre about the Germans, etc. I also wrote a letter home and finished my Christmas cards in between times. The people here were not bothered much by the Germans. They fled the town and the main battle took place at now ruined Strasbourg. This is a great agricultural region and the people have plenty to eat. The padre was very interesting to talk to, and another man came in who spoke English and we had a

---

61   Richtig: correct. —Ed.

jolly time. About 9 we took off for bed after what I considered a most enjoyable evening. Flashes of artillery are visible as well as audible. 2 planes shot down by our ack-ack over town today.[62]

Richard to Folks

Dear Folks,

Finally getting around to writing again so will attempt to post you on the latest happenings. Saw Buster some time ago and we had a jolly get-together discussing the latest news received in our letters. Have not as yet received any *Leader* issues, so we must rely on letters alone.[63] Thanksgiving Day I received two letters from home from Mother, three from Julia, and one from the DeJeans. Quite a day I had with those letters and also a pass to Nice, and did I have a time! Ha! Hitchhiking included, back to my old tricks it seems, and was it hot! Could have gotten a nice sunburn if I'd have had my shirt off.

I notice the date today—3 years with the U.S. in the war—Wow! Too long.

Probably by the time you receive this 'twill be Christmas so wishing everyone a *Merry Christmas*! Will be thinking of you all, indeed where I'm now is nothing like last year at Cincinnati where I could hitchhike home. Ha!—Great life.

Guess if Lucy doesn't write I can never write her since I've lost her address. The other day I caught up with all my correspondence, except her.

I know where Lee Smith is but can't say I guess, haven't seen him though. I, too, agree with what you said he saw.

Would enjoy hearing the results of the local election, since after all I did have a voice (if only absentee). Buster also heard about Dale Rigdon. Would like to hear the latest about him. Guess I'll sign off on this page. Again Merry Christmas and

---

62 Ack-ack: nickname for anti-aircraft gun. —Ed.
63 *Leader:* Local Salem, Indiana, newspaper. —Ed.

Love,

Richard

Thanks loads for the stamps, Mother!

December 8, 1944

Unit History

One half-track was lost by Company C northeast of town of Niederschaeffolsheim. Track hit mine, blowing same up. Enemy fire exploded gas tank and vehicle was completely demolished. All personnel escaped without injury. Pfc. Franklin Bussert, injured, transferred to unknown hospital.

Richard's Journal

Up at 8 bells and fixed a little chow of 10 in 1. Drizzled rain and spit snow this morning. Very fine weather here, oh yeah, and mud knee deep. The old man says in this particular town it doesn't snow some years, not last, but without doubt this. Got a bedroll, naturally GI type and doesn't look too warm, probably be okay with blankets. After evening chow helped the old man carry water for cows. He has four large ones in the stable below where we sleep. Again this evening talked in the kitchen with the padre and had another most interesting time. They brought out the schnapps and we had a little shot. Boy was it strong! Today is a Catholic holy day. These people always bring out their schnapps on an important day!

December 9, 1944

Unit History

Pfc. William Staley, lightly injured in action as of 20 Nov 44 transferred hospital. S/Sgt. William Strowbridge, lightly wounded in action; Tec 5 Phillip Aragon, lightly injured in action. 1st Lt. John Battenfeld promoted to the grade of Captain, Medical Corps.

Richard's Journal

Up at 8:00 after a very warm night's sleep. Messed around this morn, cleaned up, shaved and did nothing in general, ate at mess hall for a change and naturally 'twas poor. We eat better when they let squads cook for themselves. Went up to aid station this afternoon for no reason at all, just messed around and learned more German. This evening wrote letters in the kitchen (warm) and of course had another interesting talk. Wrote Christmas greetings to Aunt Fannie, Belle, Minnie and Uncle Charlie, Martha Jean, Julia and family, and a letter to the DeJeans. Brought out my English Dictionary and the old padre really had himself a time going through that, asking questions, etc. Went up to an old guy's house for a while tonight, gave us wine.

Eleanor to Richard

Dear Richard,

Well, ye old holidays rolled around once more. When the folks get the tree, we'll get down the Christmas boxes and start throwing icicles around again. We have to be more careful though, because you can't buy them or lights for the tree either this year.

All the stores downtown have their Christmas displays out but Daddy. He says he's going to put one in his window though.

About four weeks ago I met a real cute boy at Corydon and I write to him now. Big thrill!

We got a crate of oranges from Jonas and Mildred from Miami. It also had a grapefruit and a coconut. Mother ground up the coconut to use because we can't buy it here. I eat oranges all the time. I'll grow to be an orange.

Merry Christmas and all my Love,

Eleanor

December 10, 1944

Richard's Journal

My German seems to be improving a wee bit and am having much fun. Today is Sunday and much the same as any other day. Messed around this morning but this afternoon at 2 went to the town Protestant church, a very nice one indeed. Had a very young chaplain and he had a Christmas service and the confession. Some of the boys got some Christmas boxes and we have been having good eats. After church, stopped at B Company and saw Buster and talked a while. He was frying potatoes, exchanged news for a moment, and I took off. Talked with the old padre a while tonight and then stayed up till 2 talking with the guards, namely old Niles. What a guy—ha. Kinda sick to my stomach tonight.

December 11, 1944

Up at 8:00 feeling like heck, washed my head, combed my hair, and didn't feel like eating anything so cleaned place up a bit and back to bed about 10:30 a.m. I found I'd taken aspirins instead of sodium bicarbs last night for my upset stomach, so kinda got an overdose of aspirin and also dysentery. Before going to bed this morn, I was blessed with a Christmas package from the DeJeans, indeed an unexpected event. Also got a *Yank* magazine and the first *Leader* (Oct 5) issue. They serve as goodly little morale builders. The DeJeans box contained a can of turkey that I shall save for Christmas or New Year's dinner, a 1 lb. fruitcake "we boys" ate this evening, a jar of spread, a large bar of fudge, and a bottle of olives that was broken—too bad for I really like olives. How thoughtful of the DeJinxes. I will write soon and thank them. Got up at about 4:30, after having a visit from Scotty, he took temp (100.2) and a couple bismuth pills and a visit from Biener and Bopp bringing me a shirt and taking a PX order for a can of peanuts and bottle of American beer and a cigar. After getting up I made a cup of hot tea and ate a few crackers, etc. About dark we got the PX stuff and I drank the beer, which was plenty good, gave the cigar to Fyda, and packed the peanuts in my musette bag. Talked to the padre about an hour. Showed him a *Coronet* magazine, which he seemingly enjoyed, and then hit the sack about 9:00. Terribly rainy weather and very unpleasant, feel much better this evening.

Claude Bush to Richard

Dear Richard,

Well I hope this finds you safe and well. We are all right. A big snow on the ground. We have just killed hogs and wish you were here to help us eat the sausage and backbones. Dee is coming home for Christmas. Did you get sick going over? Is there any pretty girls over there? If there is anything you want me to tell your girl back here, just let me know and I will see that she gets the word. Now listen Richard, I know you have a war to win, but if you can get off a few days I would like for you to come back and help me haul manure and some baled straw. Answer this, you big boy, or it will be too bad for you. Wish you could visit with us while Dee is home. Where are you?

Claude and Eska

Dad to Richard

Dear Son,

We sent Eleanor to the post office late Saturday night and got your letter saying you're struggling with verbs and idioms. Oui-oui. Glad to get it. That is the second letter. This last letter came by airmail. Expect we will get the others later. Mail is sure slow. We got a box of oranges from Jonas and Mildred just after Thanksgiving. Heard from David and Lucy last week. They are okay. Jonas will be there until about January sometime from what we can gather. He hasn't had any more attacks of malaria. Of course he may be there longer, we hope. Said he didn't have to go to school on Sunday this time.

From the way mail is I thought I better send this Christmas greeting and perhaps you would get it at least near the time.

We want you to know that we will be thinking of you that day. May you enjoy it as best as you can under the circumstances. We expect Virginia home from IU about the 21st. There will only be four of us this year. Good luck.

Your Dad,

James G. Berkey

December 12, 1944

Richard's Journal

Up at 8:30 and feel fairly well today. Drank some hot tea and ate very little. About noon wrote a letter home, received a letter from Dee Bush in Yuma, Arizona, Christmas card from Jean and Ida Berkey, a letter from Julia, home for Thanksgiving vacation, and a long newsy 12-page letter from Aunt Minnie. After writing, went around to see some guys that were a little sick, GIs etc. Washed and shaved, went up to see Scotty a while, and helped with another sick guy. Wrote a letter to Julia and to DeJeans tonight before hitting sack. Wrote in kitchen and talked to the people a while and learned a little more Deutsche. Anti-aircraft opened up, and me without my steel helmet—ha! Hid in old man's wine cellar and didn't swipe one single apple. Rainy and cold.

Richard to Folks

Dear Folks,

At last I've received a *Leader* and enjoyed the "latest" news (the issue was October 5—ha!). Also received a *Yank* and a Christmas box, the first from the DeJeans, indeed not expected, but nevertheless very inviting, since 'twas all stuff to eat.

I read that Eleanor is now school treasurer. If you keep it up, Eleanor, you'll have all the schools' money—ha! Today I got some mail and received a Christmas card from Ida and Jean, a V-mail from Dee—now in Arizona—a nice long letter from

Aunt Minnie with plenty of news, and am still looking forward to a letter from home. It has been quite some time since I've received one.

Finally saw Buster a couple days ago and as usual he was having a big time. He'd received a letter from home saying his folks, wife, Frankie, and all had moved to Louisville. Am well and fine, having a great time and enjoying myself as much as possible.

Love,

Richard

December 13, 1944

Richard's Journal

Up at 7 bells and supposed to move so ate and got things in order and in vehicle but sat around all day waiting to move and find myself again really hittin' the hay! I've a place dug out in the very top of this hay loft and am not using my bedroll, think I'll be warm enough. Have been standing around all day doing absolutely nothing. Still have dysentery. Ate chow at mess hall at 11:00, and of course no good, so ate C ration, hot tea and potatoes fried by Frau Kreizer for supper, very good potatoes and tea. Received a Christmas card from Jo, Billy, and Tommy. Sat around fire this evening and drank hot tea, talked to Padre a moment and gave Herr Kreizer some cigarettes.

December 14, 1944

Unit History

237 enlisted men and 6 officers left Schwindratzheim at 1040 hours on mounted march of 32 miles. Arrived at Oberbetschdorf, France, at 1250 hours. Company billeted in town awaiting orders. Cleared towns of Oberseebach and Aschbach, France.

Richard's Journal

Up at 8:00 and after groaning around for a couple hours, I finally got breakfast eaten, a C ration of hash and a couple cups of tea. At last we move. Took off at 11 and ended up in the middle of the afternoon at a town, Oberbetschdorf or something like that. Supposedly 10-12 km from border of Deutschland. The Germans left only yesterday and seemed to have taken most of the able men with them or ahead of them. We are staying in the home of what seems a very well-to-do farmer, who by the way has two very nice looking daughters. I'm in the basement to sleep this evening, but a very nice one and quite warm. Have bed rolled out and am ready to hit the concrete. The other guys are playing cards upstairs in the living room and all of course trying to make a hit with the gals (who are married). Cold today.

Mother to Richard

Dear Richard,

I have been writing notes to people on Christmas cards, and sort of neglecting my own children. I am not sure what day I wrote you last. Anyway, we are still alive and shivering, as it has been quite cold here. It has not been zero weather at all, but it is hard to keep the house warm. The coal pile is low and Daddy doesn't want Indiana coal. He has ordered Kentucky coal and may have to take egg coal.

Grandmother has not come up. Every week I think she will be ready to come, but she dreads to leave home.

Daddy has ordered a small turkey for Christmas. I don't know of any guests unless Virginia invites a "little" boy she wrote about. She has been robbing the cradle again. She will be home about next Thursday night. Mr. Bush brought us in some country sausage, so we're having good breakfasts. Dee is expected home next week. He will miss you.

Several of the wounded boys are getting to come home. Jack Colglazier is in a New York hospital and still can't see much.

Dale Rigdon had a broken leg after all, and will come home when able. Marvin Martin, Jr. gets to come home. John Robinson has been wounded—is in a cast from the waist down—and little Ervin Purlee has an arm injury. There are many others, so of course we are anxious about you and Buster.

We got your November 25 airmail letter last Saturday. You said you wrote another one a day or two before, but it has never come.

Do you live in tents? Do you have enough warm socks?

Lots of Love,

Mother

December 15, 1944

Unit History

237 enlisted men and 6 officers departed Niederbetschdorf, France, at 1530 hours on mounted march of 9.3 miles to Oberseebach, France, and arrived at 1630 hours.[64] Company billeted in town.

Richard's Journal

Up at 8:00 this morning after a good night's sleep on the nice warm concrete. Pretty cold this morning. Got around to eating a K ration and a couple cups of tea. Went up the street to see a guy that was sick and then messed around and had dinner about 1:00, then got Christmas packages from Virginia, Ida Berkey, and the church. Ida's had a box of cookies and a couple candy bars and other assorted candy. The one from the church had cookies, candy, and a card from Glen Cauble Davis. Virginia's had a biography of G.W. Carver, a bottle of malt tablets, an IU X-mas card and note (written Homecoming Day), a can of solidified Brilliantine,[65] 3 bars soap, a couple

---

64　Oberbetschdorf and Niederbetschdorf are part of the same community. —Ed.

65　Solidified Brilliantine: hair grooming product. —Ed.

snapshots of herself, 3 issues of Indiana University *Daily Student*,[66] and IU Bookstore playing cards. Indeed a swell Christmas box—thanks, Jidge! Lots of other guys got boxes and so we had a jolly old time and eats aplenty. About the middle of the afternoon (about the time we began enjoying the gifts—eats) the good lookin' gals brought out the wine—well!

Then we had to move up, moved to town of Oberseebach about 5 miles from Wissembourg where the boys are having some trouble with the Jerries. We parked in a barn and took over the house where we sleep tonight. Looks as if tomorrow may be *it*. Plenty of artillery bouncing around here, shakes everything. Tonight the boys are washing their feet and drying sox on stove, and since ol' Hoosier Sgt. Billhymer got a Testament from his wife, he reads it aloud for a while. Indeed a very happy bunch of guys always singing, into combat with Christmas carols on my lips, sleeping on kitchen floor tonight. Talked to Niles and Northcutt till about 11 bells.

Virginia to Richard

Dearest Richard,

Got your letter two days ago and just now have time to answer it. It was so good to hear from you. I had seen Julia the day before and she said she'd almost given up hearing from you— was a bit disgusted I think because she hadn't heard from you. However, the folks hadn't heard anything—during the same period of two or more weeks—so I figured you couldn't write then.

Thanksgiving didn't mean much this year—Christmas won't either. I haven't been able to get hepped up about shopping at all. Everything is so expensive, and nothing is worth it. Oh, of course, you know the Berkeys—always knock ourselves out trying to make things traditional—but frankly, I don't want to until you are all home again. Then we'll paint the town and

---

66   *Daily Student*: Indiana University student newspaper. —Ed.

everything in it barn-paint red. Have a hilarious time! I do hope what I sent you was okay—for Christmas, I mean. I never know what you'll like.

Am dating a sweet little sailor from out at Crane. Only been in eight months, is about 18, and very nice. No drink, no swear. Met him at the U.S.O. last Saturday night, spent the whole evening with him, and practically all of Sunday. We went to the Episcopalian church (my first experience) and kneeled and got up continuously during the service. Certainly have to get used to it before you can get much out of it. Very nice, though. Then we ate dinner in the Grill, and went to a movie.

More ASTP guys rolled in here last Saturday—now have about 550 men, in Navy and Army, here in school. Lots of medical students. Must stop now, since I can't think of anything else. Will make you some cookies over vacation! How does that sound? Hope you got the Christmas packages in time for the 25th.

Oodles of love. Be good to your patients and take care of yourself. Tell Buster hello for me.

Virginia

December 16, 1944

Richard's Journal

Up at 7 bells, packed up things and put in half-track. Messed around eating breakfast and Scotty came over about 10 and we went to aid station where I received a very nice combat jacket—boy, it's okay. Renewed my pill supply and got a couple candles and a large Red Cross flag. Washed up and shaved before dark. The old man around here seems to have a sort of cool atmosphere towards us staying in his house and barn. The barn here is a brand new one. Wonder how he rates it? When no one else for miles does. Had chow at kitchen in town of Oberseebach and sat round in kitchen tonight talking, etc. The artillery is really givin' 'em heck tonight. Talked till about 12 bells with ol' Niles and finally got around to crawling in the sack. Sun was rather warm this evening but cold tonight, heavy frost.

December 17, 1944

Unit History

At 1530 received orders from Commanding General, 14th Armored Division, to relieve 62nd Armored Infantry Battalion. At 1645 Battalion crossed Initial Point to begin relief of 62nd. At 2005 Company B and Company C moved up to line to relieve 62nd. Company left Oberseebach, France at 1615 on march of 7 miles. Crossed German border at 2330. Arrived at Rechtenbach, Germany, at 2345.

Richard's Journal

Up at 7, rolled up bedroll and put in half-track and acquired my mess kit and took off for chow at kitchen. Had coffee, bread, butter, and dried eggs. Went to church at 11:00 in town Protestant church and had a very nice service by the young chaplain. The artillery gave him quite an opposition. A very clear day today and the airplanes have really been buzzing. After chow saw one of our B-17s shot down, indeed a sight that makes one's blood boil! All kinds of fighters have been chasing around and once it seemed as if everyone this side of the ocean opened up on what was evidently a German fighter. Changed sox and powdered feet and dried. Very warm this afternoon. Sun comes up in southeast and sets in northwest, making a very small arc.

December 18, 1944

Unit History

At 0545 Patrol #1 reporting they drew several rounds burp gun fire. No activity noticed in village, but several lights appeared to be moving around on high ground north of village. Saw caliber .30 tracer fire going northward. Artillery falling all along high ground west of

Oberotterbach. Patrol #2 in at 0545 reporting being fired on by small arms. Flares on high ground above town.

Attack launched at 0745. Ten-minute preparation fired by 500th Field Artillery on Oberotterbach and streamline running through town. Company B on the right, Company C on the left astride the road. Two platoons Company B, 25th Tank Battalion, deployed on high ground overlooking town for close support of infantry. No resistance encountered until forward elements reached position about 300 yards south of bridge over the Otterbach River. At this time heavy mortar and some artillery fire was concentrated. The assault elements continued attack with Company B circling the town on east, reaching the cemetery. Communicate with Company C only occasionally. Tanks stopped by roadblock in southern edge of town holding up operations for an hour and a half. Tanks continued to move through village but were stopped by blown bridge in center of town. Dozer unable to find material to make fill. Smoke fired by artillery on possible enemy observation posts from high ground. Smoke drifted to north edge of town. Enemy launched counter-attack under cover of this smoke. Tanks and infantry forced to withdraw to high ground overlooking town from south. Two platoons, Company B, unable to withdraw due to automatic weapons and sniper fire.

At 1430 reorganization commenced and completed 1800. Numerous enemy snipers made evacuation extremely difficult. Heavy Machine Gun Platoon placed on right flank to strengthen defensive fires. Frequent artillery and mortar fire fell throughout sector during operation.

Evacuation of the town was very costly. Casualties were so heavy that the Battalion Aid Station was split and operated in two separate towns. Under direct enemy observation and amid intense mortar and small arms fire, medics gave first aid and evacuated many casualties during the most intense fighting. Forty-eight casualties were treated in a twelve-hour period at the Battalion Aid Station. Many wounded were left in buildings completely isolated by enemy fire and had to be rescued by night patrols many hours later.[67] Pfc. Richard Berkey, slightly wounded in action, transferred to 117th Evacuation Hospital. Captain Derl Hess, non-battle casualty, transferred to Battalion Aid Station. 1st Lt. James Devine assumes command of Company. Lightly wounded in action: Pvt. Seymour Bierman, Pvt. Robert Farris, S/Sgt. Paul Hoffpauir, T/Sgt. John Garwood, S/Sgt. John Fitch, S/Sgt. James Lollias, Pfc. Baker Grooms, Pfc. Billy Cook, Pfc. Robert Bunnell, Sgt. Edgar Van Voorhis Close, Pfc. Bernard Schnaus, Pfc. Arthur Irwin, S/Sgt. Lawrence Marro, Cpl. Charles Bobnock, Pfc. Andrew Saus, Pfc. John Burdine, Pfc. Richard Burke,[68] Pvt. Francis Dooley, Pfc. Charles Sheppard, Pvt. Glenneth Smith. Seriously wounded in action: 1st Lt. Paul Dixon, 2nd Lt. Frank Tangney, Pfc. Robert LaPoint, Pvt. Marvin Bernstein, Pfc. Kenneth Jennings. Pfc. Herman Karnes, killed in action, vicinity of Oberotterbach.

---

67   The troops met little resistance in the first hour of this battle. But, upon entering Oberotterbach, enemy fire from mortars, artillery, machine guns, and rifles became intense. The tanks and infantry became separated when the Otterbach River Bridge was blown. Wounded and dead lay among the "dragon teeth" of the Siegfried Line. The firing was so intense, medics could not get to the wounded. The enemy had a perfect line of sight from their protected pill-boxes and trenches. The 68th AIB was ordered to fall back 800 feet and the battle continued for five days and nights. Captain Joseph Carter, *The History of the 14th Armored Division,* (Atlanta: Albert Love Enterprises, 1947), Chapter V p. 1, Chapter VII p. 17.

68   This is a significant coincidence. Richard J. Berkey, the subject of this book, and Richard J. Burke, of Company B, were both wounded at Oberotter-bach on December 18, 1944. They had met each other previously on November 9, 1944, as they were both friends of Buster Crockett. —Ed.

CHAPTER SIX

WOUNDED AND WORRIED

December 19, 1944

Unit History

Right flank extended making front 3,000 yards wide. Troops dug in further and held high ground south of Oberotterbach. Heavy enemy artillery and mortar fire throughout day in our sector. 48th Tank Battalion fired on known pillboxes; effect unknown. Ceased firing with tanks at 1430 to allow artillery forward observer to adjust 8" howitzers. Visibility decreased making observed fire impossible. Harassing missions to be fired throughout night. C Troop 94th Reconnaissance and 3rd Platoon, Company C, 125th Engineers attached with 500th Armored Field Artillery in support. Recon Patrols #3 and #4 out, consisting of one officer and 3 enlisted men each.

Capt. Derl Hess transferred from sick at Battalion Aid Station to 84th Medical Battalion. Released from assignment and principal duty as Armored Infantry Unit Commander and assigned to Headquarters 68th AIB, 1st Lt. William Broadwater joined from A Company and appointed Armored Infantry Unit Commander. Sgt. James Gavin, Jr., lightly wounded in action. 3 men missing in action.

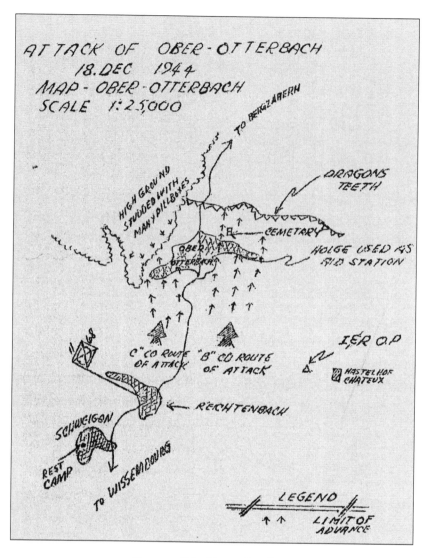

ATTACK OF OBER-OTTERBACH
18. DEC 1944
MAP - OBER-OTTERBACH
SCALE 1:25,000

Courtesy of the National Archives

December 20, 1944

Unit History

Patrol #3 in at 0030 reporting being halted by a German. They hit the ground and were fired upon with rifles. Enemy attempting to cut off patrol, so they withdrew. A large fire, which was so intense that it lit up one side of the town of Oberotterbach, was observed. After patrol withdrew, machine gun fire was observed striking the position they had been in. At 0030 Patrol #4 reported observing fire and hearing a tank motor in the same direction. They also observed what appeared to be tracks of horse-drawn caissons. Troops remained at dug-in positions on high ground south of town. Artillery active, firing on enemy positions and pillboxes. Pfc. John Kleban, lightly wounded in action. Pfc. Paul Driscoll, killed in action, vicinity of Oberotterbach, Germany, as of 18 Dec 1944.

December 21, 1944

Unit History

Recon Patrol that went out 2130 20 Dec 44 returned at 0100 21 Dec 44. They reported receiving tracer fire. They reached the stream and received two more rounds tracer from left front and two rounds mortar. They were in creek bed 20 minutes and received burp gun and machine gun fire. Stream is approximately 7 feet deep at that point with water 10 inches deep. Small arms fire went directly over their heads while in stream. They observed big glow over the ridge on left front. At 0600 Company C withdrew under cover of darkness to Line 1 where new positions were dug. Two platoons of 48th Tank Battalion moved into firing position accompanied by two 105 mm howitzer Sherman tanks. Company C, prior to withdrawing, set up emplacements with helmets mounted on stakes and "C" ration cans, simulating telescopes. At 1615 one German soldier walked into our lines and surrendered. At 1630 enemy artillery expended on dummy emplacements. Pvt. Alvin Northcutt, lightly wounded in action. Pfc. Ernest Ruggieri, seriously wounded in action as of 18 Dec 1944.

December 22, 1944

Unit History

Two platoons of 48th Tank Battalion moved into firing position to fire on visible enemy pillboxes and any possible enemy positions.

Tank fire had no apparent effect on fortifications. At 1630 Company B returned to forward dug-in positions. Pfc. Buster Stoots and T/Sgt. Leslie Younts, lightly injured in action. Missing in Action, vicinity of Oberotterbach, Germany, as of 18 Dec 1944: Pfc. Salvatore Bova, Pfc. Larry Gioia, Pfc. Lawrence Jensen, Pfc. Milton Kelly, Pfc. J.P. Fleniken, Pfc. Sidney Lieppe, Pfc. Minor McLain, Pfc. David Middleton, Pfc. Dean Peterson, S/Sgt. Laurence Poole, Pfc. Grover Shepherd, Jr., S/Sgt. William Stoyanoff, Pvt. Claud Wood.

December 23, 1944

Unit History

Company C holding positions at Line 1. Two platoons of 48th Tank Battalion moved into firing positions. Effect unknown; visibility very poor. Artillery supporting our troops, active on enemy fortifications throughout the day. At 1630 Company C returned to forward dug-in positions. At 1800 relief began; verbal march order issued. B and C Companies relieved by platoons from exterior flank. Companies to reorganize in Schweigen to proceed to Merkwiller. Complete relief to be effected by 2400. 180 enlisted men and 4 officers left Rechtenbach, Germany, at 2120 hours on mounted march of 16 miles and arrived at Dieffenbach-lès-Wœrth, France, at 2300 hours. Company billeted in town awaiting orders. Lightly wounded in action: Pfc. Thomas Boyd (18 Dec 1944), Pfc. Thomas Birckhead (22 Dec 1944), Pfc. Alphonse Savage (22 Dec 1944), Pvt. Thomas Garner (20 Dec 1944), and Pfc. George Ross (19 Dec 1944).

December 24-28, 1944

Unit History

Unit reorganizing at Merkwiller and Dieffenbach-lès-Wœrth. Training schedule being carried out. On 28 Dec 44, officers and key non-commissioned officers attended Counter Sabotage Demonstration held by VI Corps. On 28 Dec 44 unit plus attachments began mounted road march to Schœnbourg, Lohr, and Ottwiller. Training schedule being carried out. The commanding general, 14th Armored Division, decorated two officers and five enlisted men with Bronze Stars.

December 25, 1944 Christmas Day

Mother to Richard

Dear Richard,

We have been very anxious about you since the war news has been so bad. We watch the mail and newspapers for any possible information and were so happy to get your Christmas card (V-mail) and your letter this morning. The trouble is that the mail is so slow. Your letter that we got today was written December 7 and so much has happened since then. Julia told Virginia she got a letter the other day that must have been written a little later, for you told her about having a weekend with a French family. That must have been very interesting. How did you happen to be asked, and how did you understand each other? Was the food good? The French are said to be excellent cooks. Also I have read that the fruits and vegetables grown in the soil of Southern France have the finest flavor in the world.

From what we have heard from Carroll Moore's folks, Buster's, Lee Edward's, etc., we think you must be going along the Rhône Valley with the 7th Army. That is bad enough but at least you're not with the First—unless you have all gone to the rescue.

When we thought about your being in such danger, we hardly felt like celebrating Christmas but we knew you would want things to go on as usual here at home. Daddy and we five womenfolk managed to have a very, very nice day, with lots of presents, a beautiful tree (brought in by Mr. Weeks), and a turkey dinner. Grandmother came Friday morning and Lucy was here just two days. Both had such a good time.

We got the grandest big new photos of Jonas and Mildred. Boy, they are glamorous! Look like movie stars. I am so proud of them.

Lots of Love,

Mother

Virginia to Richard

Dearest Richard,

What a day—everything has been so perfect—that is excepting the absence of our "men" and Mildred. My gosh, but I wish you were here to eat the candy and nuts—I'm sure to regain all I've lost since I saw you. About 10 pounds, though you wouldn't think I looked it. I don't. Ha!

After the usual debating of us in our "old" age, we agreed to hang up stockings in traditional manner and did so—cutting up like nuts—yes, nuts, and more nuts—nuts galore. This morning, we managed to restrain ourselves from the mad scramble until after a bite or two of breakfast. The gifts were all lovely. One of the most beautiful Christmases ever. We always say we won't have much and end up by making each more plentiful than the last. It's worth it though. We thought of you all—Aunt Fannie says this is the first year one of you boys didn't come after the candy at Aunt Minnie's. Ellie and I got it.

Tonight, your high school class is having its reunion. I don't know where. I got here Friday but have been so swamped with Santa doings, I haven't even seen the kids. I doubt if many will be there. I gave Davis your address and he said he'd write you today or soon anyhow.

At our dinner we used the bright Fiestaware set of china and the delicate goblets, etc., very colorful and Christmasy with oranges, apples, nuts, and tangerines for a centerpiece on a huge red platter. David sent money for a family gift "for the outward appearance" and a beautiful mirror was selected. It now resides on the wall above the piano. Guess how I got home? By freight! On the caboose from Orleans to Salem—left Bloomington at 9:35 on the bus, rode to Orleans, got a freight (can carry persons between Borden and Orleans—new one on you boys) and rode in the caboose with the brakeman to Salem—only lady on the train—quite dusty, but fun—got home at 2:00 p.m. Best timing yet! Everyone in town is cackling about it.

Oh yes, dear Santa knew how badly I was needing bedroom slippers so he gave me three pairs! Ha! Will write you more tomorrow! Am making cookies for you sometime this week.

Lots of Love,

Virginia

Dad to Richard

Dear Richard,

Will add a note. Got your letter of Dec. 7 just this morning. Came just at right time. Lucy got home Sunday morning at 2:00 a.m. and had to leave at 6:45 from Mitchell. All had a good time. Had to have Weeks bring the tree from farm. It was 12 feet high but Virginia and Eleanor got it up. Looks good. Write and tell us where you have been.

Good luck,

Dad

Lucy to Richard

Dear Richard,

Your letter made today just right—we were lucky to get it on Christmas! Richard, I can't understand why you haven't gotten a letter I wrote you ages ago, but anyway Mother sent you my address and I'll write again! Today has been rainy but inside everything is cozy and Christmasy—and we did have such nice things this time. Wish you could see our tree— it's beautiful—

touches the ceiling as usual! I do hate to go back this evening, but I so enjoyed being home for Christmas! Wish we could have had you three boys, but maybe next year, I hope. That turkey dinner was something—I feel like running around the house two or three times!

Love,

Lucy

Eleanor to Richard

Dear Richard,

Guess I'll take time out from stuffing myself with the nuts, etc., to write you. This has been a wonderful Christmas. The tree is gorgeous and even stands straight, which is a miracle. Virginia and I put it up. To begin with it was 12 feet tall, and so, fools that we were, we cut a foot out of the top and nailed the base on. Well naturally for a 9-foot ceiling, an 11-foot tree is a trifle tall so we pulled off the base. You should've seen us! Then I proceeded to saw one foot off the bottom, which made 10 feet. Well, we were freezing to death and disgusted, so we struggled with it into the house where it practically ruined the ceiling. Virginia cut some more out of the top, we turned the tree and she stuck in a false top with Scotch tape. It doesn't sound very nice but it really is. I got scads of beautiful things. Mother even made me a darling pair of pajamas right under my nose and I didn't even know it.

Loads of Love,

Eleanor

January 2, 1945

Mother to Richard

Dearest Boy,

We are having a very cold spell now—0° in some places last night but 8° on our back porch—and we think of you so often and hope you're not suffering too much from the cold. You said last fall that you might sometime have to wear all your clothes at once—and maybe that sometime is now. The war news sounds so bad all the time that we cannot help but be very anxious though we know that worrying does no good.

Did you ever get any of your packages that have been on the way so long? I have waited and waited for a letter with another request for food in it, so I could send some things, but none has come. You know we can send only 8 ounces without a request. Virginia made you some cookies and could send only enough for a smell. Eleanor has been making different kinds of quick hot breads for home ec and all have been so good. Tonight she made cheese biscuits and we said we wished we could feed the surplus to you!

Dee is at home now but we haven't seen him. His dad said he meant to come to our house. Paul Davis finally went into the Army Air Corps. Was supposed to leave Friday. I think I told you Willie Lester has gone overseas. Jack Hollister got to come home for Christmas. He came alone from Texas, where he is in the hospital now. He can't see much but went back for an operation. Dale Rigdon is getting to start for the U.S. right away, maybe yesterday.

This afternoon I took the Christmas tree out and cleaned up the mess. Grandmother helped me take off icicles and then we burned piles of pine. We keep a fireplace fire going all the time during this cold weather.

Yesterday we got a letter and a telegram from Jonas. He and Mildred have had to move out of the nice apartment and go to the Beacon Hotel. His orders have not yet come. He said his grades were okay but the only thing he knew was that he had been recommended for a ship in a cold climate because of his malaria. That is the very thing he does not want.

We have not heard from David the past week. Lucy wrote that she got back all right after her leave, but the train was late; however, she was on night shift and did not have to work until 4 o'clock that afternoon. She thought she had such a good time at home that she was glad she came, even though she did get almost smashed by the crowds at times.

I'm so sleepy sitting here by the warm fire that I'm going to have to close. Grandmother has already gone to bed and Eleanor is going.

Lots of Love,

Mother

CHAPTER SEVEN

RELIEF

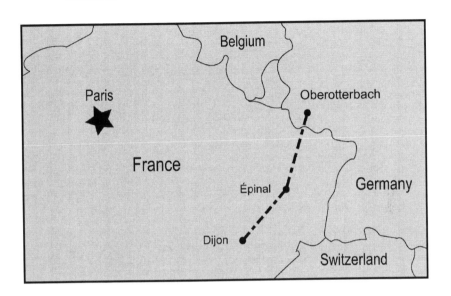

January 3, 1945

Richard to Folks

Dear Folks,

Finally around to dropping a line. Got hit in the upper right arm with a piece of shrapnel some time ago and I'm still in the hospital. Arm still sore but otherwise am okay as usual. The wound is nothing serious, so I see no need of worrying.

Haven't heard from home or anyone else for quite some time now. Hope everyone is okay.

Has been ages since I've seen Buster, but heard he's still around from recent reports. Since his folks have moved I guess you don't get the latest news from his mother. Had turkey for Christmas and also New Year's dinner. Will write more later.

Love,

Richard

January 5, 1945

Rodman to Richard

Hello Richard,

So glad to hear from you, old man. I have shifted to various places since I last wrote to you, but your mail caught up with me—a little late but I don't mind. I left Louisiana when I returned from my long-awaited leave. From Livingston I spent a spell in two camps in Texas. You hear a lot about that place but believe me that's the best place I have hit since I've been traveling in this Army. Why, if I had another week I would've been married by now. I suppose it was fortunate that I moved for that reason only. But really, Richard, I was near Austin, which is the seat of the University of Texas. I had the queen of the campus and I really had things boiling! She was a great kid! Maybe I'll dig my foxhole a foot deeper now that I met up with her!

So you finally are getting out of Kentuck? Come to think of it old Kentuck was pretty damned nice wasn't it? And how are things with you? I hope you get along well and who knows, I may be with you before long. You may be sure that it won't be long until I go somewhere!

I've been quite busy during all this moving and I'm pretty well through now. I was the unfortunate one to draw the job of company packing officer and if you took part in any packing you must know what a job it was. I'm having one heck of a time in New York whenever I can get there. I think I visited every bar and have seen every band and current show on Broadway. I have been here before so getting around the place wasn't so new. Had a darned good time New Year's Eve with some friends in Wilmington, Delaware. There is definitely an advantage to coming back to a place that you know. I have been hearing big Huffman is on his way over, too—also Bill Lester. DeJean is wearing bars of a First Lieutenant now. Davis finally got caught and is at Camp Atterbury the last I heard. I sort of hate to be leaving after all the fun I've been having the past few months but I guess I better help get it over with.

Played a little basketball this afternoon—my first in almost a year—sure had a lot of fun. Well, old man, keep in touch and who knows this is a pretty small world, we may meet in God knows where before this thing is over.

Hoping you had a nice Christmas and New Year; sorry you couldn't have one like I did. Best of luck and let me hear from you!

So long,

Rodman

January 6, 1945

Richard to Folks

Dear Folks,

Don't know much to write about but thought I'd better anyway since I presume you are probably somewhat worried about me since hearing that I got hit. However, I assure you I'm convalescing as well as is expected. My arm is still sore, especially the muscle. I still eat with my left hand, since I find it difficult to not only reach my face but also to extend my arm completely and straighten the joint. The wound is completely healed and I no longer have a bandage on it. Expect the soreness to go away, before long I'll be okay.

The wonders of the drug penicillin are surely brought out in these hospitals over here. Even with my small wound I received a great number of shots. It is given in the same manner as a hypo with the needle, etc. Seems to play havoc with a fever, as well as an infection.

I read in the paper that there was snow over the nation, so I guess you got some at home, too. Haven't received any mail for a very long time. I've used all the airmail stamps you sent, Mother, but since I'm in the hospital here I can go to the post office and get envelopes and all. Got a dozen a while ago so that will last a while.

I will attempt to keep you informed more regularly concerning my well-being. Hope everyone is well.

Love,

Richard

January 7, 1945

Mother to Richard

Dearest Richard,

Just last night we got the telegram telling us you were wounded almost three weeks ago. Daddy and I were listening to the president on the radio a little after 10 o'clock and a boy came from the telegraph office with the message. It made us pretty shaky but we are so thankful it did not say you were missing or a prisoner. We are hoping that we will receive a letter from you right away and feel that we will if your wound is not in a place that prevents your writing. We have not had any message from you that was written later than December 7. Of course there has been such a volume of Christmas mail and then such a lot of confusion and hard fighting that it must have been well nigh impossible to write home at all. Poor boy! No doubt you have been in a regular inferno. I hope you have been able to help save some lives. Do tell just as much as you can.

I know it is selfish but I cannot help but hope that you will not be sent back to work for a while. If your wound is "slight," as the telegram said, you may already be back, but I do so hope and pray that your life may be spared. A slight wound could well be a means of saving your life for future service.

Have you heard anything about Buster lately? We worry about him, too. Ida got a letter from Junior last week. He said he thought he might see you as you were probably at the front. Bertha Judy got a letter from Paul that was written December 22. The soldiers were making Christmas happy for the children of a French town who have not had good Christmases lately. I realize now that the same day you were wounded was the one on which the news came that Dale Huckleberry was really killed. Today they had a memorial for him at the Baptist church. Mrs. May Green stopped in afterward. She said they had a high school alumni class meeting at Huckleberrys before they heard Dale was missing and Gladys read several of Dale's cheerful letters. Once he said, "You ought to see Lee Edward driving a jeep. He certainly can sling the mud."

There have been new casualties reported almost every day. James Grimes who married Maxine Spurgeon is reported seriously wounded and the boy who brought our message said they had had to deliver three "killed in action" telegrams the past week. One was a Charles boy and two were from Hardinsburg. However, he said there were sometimes mistakes. One boy was reported killed December 7 and his folks got a letter from him written December 8. Another boy reported killed walked into his folks' home for a furlough. The dog tags of a buddy had been switched with his. The National Guard boys who have been gone so long are in the Philippines now and several have been injured. Pauline Colglazier who married Mancil Smith did not even hear from the War Department but Mancil wrote her that he had broken ribs, an injured back, and sprained neck.

We are all fine. Grandmother and I are sewing and knitting. Eleanor stayed all night with Jeanie Jarrett and they overslept and missed Sunday school. Daddy is busy again helping people with income tax reports as he always does in January. He hardly ever gets to meals on time. I called Virginia today and told her about you.

We heard that Dee left the very night he ate supper with us. Frank Norris told Daddy that Mr. Bush said his heater wasn't working and he wanted to borrow the Norris car to take Dee to Scottsburg at midnight. Lee Henry still won't write to his folks more than twice a year! When we talked about being uneasy about you, Dee said it would take a pretty good one to get you!

Daddy says to try and write us the details of your accident—just where and what the wound is and how it happened. And do take care of yourself. Mr. Roach spoke of their telling Hugh not to be afraid of those things that can only kill the body but of those things that can destroy the soul also. I agree that that is more important but we want to keep you as long as we can.

Lots and lots of Love,

Mother

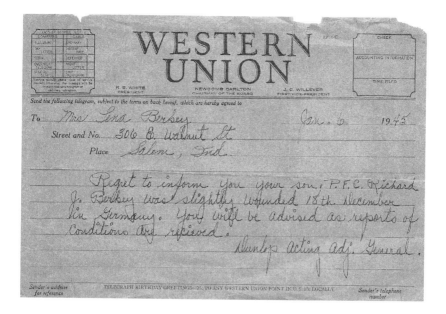

KAREN BERKEY HUNTSBERGER

Virginia to Richard

Dearest Richard,

Mother called me at noon today, and told me about the telegram saying you've been slightly wounded. I do hope it is only slightly and that you are getting along all right. I hope they send you home, too, but knowing the Army and the situation over there, I suppose that would be hoping for too much. Also, I hope you are getting your mail okay. This is the second time I have written you since our Christmas letter to you. Charlene says her husband hasn't got mail for months—he's in England in a hospital.

Not much out of the ordinary goes on here. Per usual, I had a silly mess of mix-ups at enrollment. My last semester I would have to act like a first-semester freshie. To begin with, it was so icy I fell all over myself on the campus building staircases and outdoor inclines. Some fellow saw me sit down beautifully just yesterday. Ha! We enrolled on New Year's Day and had to make it up by going to Monday classes yesterday. Joy! Of course, the Administration Office learned yesterday that I lacked three hours of enough 200 courses to graduate, so I had to change my schedule for the second time since regular enrollment. I'm taking zoology. I remember you once said that everyone should take it—ahem, yes, just taking big brother's wise advice! I like it so far. It will come in handy with my nursing later on, too.

I haven't seen Julia to tell her about you yet, but will tomorrow. Be good and do everything you're told—and take care of yourself. I told Daddy that you and I were going to start our hospital sometime. Do you have a nurse? Lucky girl. Wish I were there to take care of you and the others. I'll be in it next fall, though, and Daddy doesn't seem to mind now. The papers talk as if they will draft nurses soon anyway. Don't crown me for this Richard, but I hope you go to chaplain service whenever you can. There's an awful lot to this religion business. It makes life worth living.

Lots and lots of love to a swell brother,

Virginia

January 8, 1945

Captain Battenfeld to Richard

Dear Berkey,

Received your letter this morning and was very pleased to hear from you and to find out that you are getting along well. I extend my own and the rest of the detachment's wishes for a complete and speedy recovery.

I wish I could bring you up to date on the Battalion since you've been gone, but of course for security reasons most of the details must await your return. About that, the division has made arrangements to get its men back to it as soon as they are released from the hospital. I have requested Battalion to make sure that you return to us. I have no worries on that score since we have been getting many returns in the last week.

We have not done very much in the last few weeks, but have covered one hell of a lot of ground doing it. Fortunately, the detachment has not had very much work to do—of the type done at Oberotterbach.

I might add that we have had many questions from C Company men asking for you. With your letter at hand, we can assure them concerning your present state of health and whereabouts.

I hope this letter gets to you before you leave the hospital where you are at present.

Best of luck and see you soon I hope,

Capt. J.L. Battenfeld[69]

---

69   Captain Battenfeld was the doctor in charge of the Battalion Aid Station for the 68th Armored Infantry Division. —Ed.

Virginia to Richard

Dearest Richard,

I started to write December instead of January. Can't seem to get caught up with old man time. And how. Lessons galore. I go to the library every night and study! Believe it or not! Have to make some decent grades this last semester plus pass that English Comprehensive three-hour exam over all the lit I've had.

We had a beautiful 6-inch snow here last night and you know how happy that made me. Guess where you are, that blizzard I hear about doesn't sound too good—though better than mud, I should think. Have you seen the mountains? I bet they're beautiful.

I saw Julia yesterday on the way to class and I told her about you—it was awful to have to tell her there, but I managed it. It was really a shock since she had just gotten a letter from you that morning. It was written December 8. Took a month to get here. They don't have a telephone in their house now, so I couldn't get to her before.

Dee was home Christmas. I didn't see him, but he was planning to visit the folks before he left, his dad told Daddy.

Well, I must close this and get on the books for a while before bed. Be good and take care of yourself.

Lots and lots of Love,

Virginia

Jonas to Richard

Dear Richard,

Mother wrote she got a telegram a couple of days ago saying you had a little trouble with the Jerries. I hope it isn't bad. Malaria isn't exactly fun but I guess I'd take a few more attacks of it in place of being shot up.

I wrote a Christmas card to you but you'll never get it since it was never mailed. I didn't have your address at the time and didn't get it until a few days ago.

Too bad I didn't get back to the States a week sooner so I could've seen you before you left. Did you get seasick on the way over? I hope you didn't because it's not pleasant especially when you have it all the time out at sea like I do.

I finished school here in Miami two weeks ago and have been waiting for orders since. I was recommended by the board for duty in a cold climate because of malaria (which is all I've been able to find out), so I don't have any idea where I'll go. Probably get the run to Murmansk or some such duty, but I hope not. Take care.

Your brother,

Jonas

January 9, 1945

Richard to Eleanor

Dear Eleanor,

And how are you doing young lady? Enjoying snow? I read in the *Stars & Stripes* that you've been having plenty there lately, so you should be enjoying much sliding. And how is the school vacation? Or by now I should say how's geometry, Mrs. Bush, and English, and so on? Athletics too—playing basketball these days?

Thought you might be interested, as well as Mother and Dad, in some French money so I'm enclosing some for observation and souvenirs. The new little square pieces, 2, 5, and 10 francs, are our own issued invasion money and the other piece, 10 francs, is issued by France. The value of the franc is based roughly on 50 francs to the American dollar, so the 10-franc pieces are worth 20 cents, the 5F 10 cents, and the 2F 4 cents. See? There are also French coins of small values and I also have some German pieces that aren't suitable to send. These happen to be the only different types I have at present—maybe I'll send some different ones later.

Still in the hospital but I'm getting okay. Hope you all at home are okay. Haven't heard for a very long time and am eagerly expecting to get mail soon. Wrote sister Virginia a line a while ago. I received a very swell box from her for Christmas. Hope to hear from you sometime.

Love,

Richard

January 11, 1945
Richard's Journal

At last! After 3 weeks and 4 odd days, I again make an attempt to record the rough and rugged life of R.J. Berkey. This is the longest period of time I've missed writing in these four diary years, my mistake 5 years. Well, anyway since I last wrote, the peaceful sunny Sunday afternoon of Dec. 17, 1944, quite a few things have happened, indeed quite a few. Guess I might as well record a few things, but I know I shan't ever forget, especially that morning of the 18th. We moved up from Oberseebach during the night to another town, supposedly Wissembourg, and proceeded to carry out an attack at the town, Oberotterbach, Germany. As we moved through a vineyard we got a nice welcome of mortars and 88s, indeed my so-called "Baptism of Fire." As I lay on the ground waiting for one to drop on me and write *finis*, I was hit (8:30 a.m.) in the upper right arm by shrapnel. Boy! Was I prayin', sweatin', cursin', and whatnot—and what a sensation, sting as they say. Moved my fingers and was much relieved to see 'em move, then cautiously looked at my arm and about then heard a guy call in great pain, so I say to hell with my arm and take off. Crawled through to Pop Karnes and found in bad shape. Helped Sgt. Close who had a neck wound. LaPoint was all shot up. Dragged LaPoint to ditch and went back after Pop. With aid of Jennings who was half out of his mind, we finally got Pop to ditch. What agony! Makes me sick to think of it. Why I wasn't killed during that hour or so I do not know. Pop died in an hour or so with concussion and I'm satisfied I did my best under such conditions. I hope the other guys think so. The least I could do was say a little prayer for him. I hope it helped. It was terrible—enough of that. My arm started bothering me in the middle of the afternoon so I turned in to the aid station. Hazelton took my place and I really felt cowardly "chicken" or whatever one might say.

January 12, 1945
Mother to Richard

Dear Richard,

I have written you since we heard last Saturday night that you were injured, but I will try V-mail this time. Maybe this will get to you quicker than the other letter. We're still anxiously awaiting the mail each morning and evening, as we have had no word from you yet. We imagine all kinds of things about your condition and of course none of them are right.

We are all fine. The weather is wretched with lots of snow, sleet, and slush, but we are all pretty free from colds. Daddy is very busy, as usual in January, helping people with reports. Eleanor has a part in the annual school play, so she's going to be busy, too! Uncle Russell came out today and brought a lot of things to eat—apples, duchess potatoes, sausage and spareribs. They had killed a young beef so he brought a lot of that. Come home and help us eat! We hope you can come soon if your injury requires rest. I'm so afraid you are back in combat, or will be soon.

Did you ever get any of the packages we sent? David wrote that he got 10 boxes for Christmas. Probably most of it was spoiled in that climate. Jonas is still awaiting orders. We got a letter from him today, and one from Virginia. Virginia said she had written you twice this week. Let us know all you can. If you can't write, have someone else write for you.

With love and best wishes,

Mother

Indiana University Alumni Magazine, January 1945.
Courtesy of the Indiana University Alumni Magazine

Richard to Folks

Dear Folks,

Am still in hospital and am much better indeed! Still haven't received any mail from home or anyplace else. I find it hard to write letters and thus neglect to write, nothing much ever happens here so nothing to write about.

I occupy the time by playing cards, reading, and doing nothing. The magazines are a couple months old and the card games become exceedingly boresome. Usually play rummy or solitaire with one or both of the boys on either side. One boy is from New York, the other from Texas. The one from New York (Glens Falls) is French and the one from Texas (El Paso) is either Mexican or Spanish. We have been together most all the time in this hospital and have quite a time together. We also have a game of darts, a game of ring toss, and we did have a game of Monopoly that has disappeared lately.

The magazines we get are *Saturday Evening Post, Colliers, Liberty,* and *Yank,* and we receive the *Stars & Stripes* every day. That's our newspaper, all written by GIs. Has a column called "Pup Tent Poets" which is to me very enjoyable. GIs write poems about everything known to man and they publish them in this paper. A short but very funny example I remember is entitled "Some Fish" and goes thusly:

My girl left me to marry another.

But what care I? I'll marry her mother!

(Apologies to the GI who wrote it!)

Last mail I received was your Christmas card, very nice indeed. Thanks for the poem enclosed, Mother. I enjoyed it muchly. Also at the same time received a V-mail from Imy Humphrey. I must write her, too, some of these days. A couple of months ago I received three Christmas boxes, one from the church, one from

Virginia, and one from Ida and Jean. Indeed, very thoughtful of them. Guess Junior is around over here someplace, too.

I see by the date that I've been in the Army a couple of years to the day. Sure doesn't seem that long and I'm glad it doesn't. Guess I'll sign off—hope to hear from you all soon.

Love,

Richard

Claude and Eska Bush to Richard

Dear Richard,

It is with deep regret that we learned you were wounded. Hope you are not bad hurt, and that you will soon be fully recovered. Now Richard, I want you to write us and tell us just how bad you are hurt and how it happened. Dee was home a week Christmas and we thought of you and wished you could have been with us. Well take good care of yourself. I hope you will soon recover and be well again. Maybe this war will be over and you will be back to help me fill my silo again next year. I hope so. Be sure to write and tell us your condition.

Claude and Eska Bush

January 17, 1945

Richard's Journal

Didn't get far with last attempt at journal writing. Even wrote some letters yesterday afternoon to Folks, Ida and Jean for thank you for Christmas box, and to Bush. Have been in quarantine last 5 days but out now and go to mess hall and latrine again. Continues to remain cold and snowy. Had my arm x-rayed yesterday morning for foreign body, still little sore and stiff. After wounded, went from Battalion Aid to 117th Evac Hospital and was operated on, stayed 3 days at Épinal, and then put on hospital train one afternoon and arrived next afternoon at 36th General Hospital, Dijon. Operated on again morning of 24th. Very sick rest of day. Woke up okay and had turkey for Christmas dinner. That's the life, meals in bed, especially Christmas! Ha! I didn't do anything Christmas Day except talk to LaCross and Bailey and did even play a few cards. Nothing much happened from then till New Year's. New Year's Eve bed at 9:00, and had turkey again for dinner (still remember New Year's Eve last year—Cincinnati, hitch-hiked home, etc. ha!). In a prefab ward now and just today got moved away from LaCross and Rivera, the Mexican. LaCross has become my "buddy" from Glens Falls, NY, and do we have some terrific card games. He has a pilonidal cyst and was operated on yesterday afternoon and came back "drunk" from Sodium Pentothal. He's okay!

Mother to Richard

Dearest Richard,

We were tickled to death to hear from you this morning and to know that your wound is not serious. We had been afraid of a head injury. You have probably suffered plenty of pain and will still have a lot of discomfort but we feel that you are a lucky boy and just can't thank God enough.

I have written to Helen Crockett to see if Buster had written her anything about you and had a letter from her Saturday. Buster couldn't tell but had tried to hint at it, on December 26. He had said, "Richard is all right but I don't think we are going to be together anymore. I can't go into detail but I've got my fingers crossed." Naturally we imagined everything from that. Today I got another card from Helen. Buster wrote on December 30 saying they told him you might be back with your unit in a few days. That's the trouble! You may get another dose of shrapnel! However, it is much better for you to be able to join your detachment than to be sent back to the States practically ruined.

It is odd about these telegrams. Sometimes "slightly" proves to be more serious than "seriously." James Grimes was reported seriously wounded but soon wrote his folks that he would be out in a little while and back at work. Marvin Martin was reported slightly wounded but he had a serious leg injury and will come home. Bud Rigdon is back in a U.S. hospital with his twice broken leg in a walking cast so that he can exercise the damaged muscles in his other leg.

This is a beautiful day, although patches of snow and ice still linger. Grandmother is asleep in the big chair with sunshine across her and a khaki sock she is knitting for you in her hand. I got the yarn and she started the socks a few days ago, although we said "Poor boy, maybe he doesn't have any feet to put them on." As soon as one pair is done we will send them. First I'm going to send you some ordinary athletic socks that I have had for you about a month. If you have plenty, you won't have to wash them out as often. I'm also sending a package of Dentyne chewing gum that Frank Neal gave Daddy for you, 20 small packages.

You don't know how many friends you have, or how many have called to ask about you. Maude Pitts says to tell you that she is so happy to know you are all right and that she still loves you the same way!

I think I told you Rodman came home for five days and came to see us on Saturday. His bunch had to clear out of camp to make room for another unit that was shoving off. He has gone back to the port of embarkation. Matthew Marks and Bob Zink have gone across—two young doctors to join you over there. Stella said Otto cried so hard Saturday night. He is 75 years old and knows it will be a long time before he sees Bob. Our own Daddy was so tired at noon today that he said he felt more like going to bed than to town. He thought it was the letdown of relief after being worried about you. He has also been extra busy on income tax reports and it let up after the 15th. He is

WAITING *for* PEACE   135

really unusually well this winter, I think, and carries in wood, carries out ashes, etc., quite industriously.[70]

Eleanor is being initiated into the Home Ec Club. Today she had to wear an apron to school and carry a dishtowel and a big potato!

I'll have to tell you a joke on me. My brother Russell had a heifer he called "Sister" and he changed its name to "Toots." He said nobody knew whether he was talking about a woman or a cow. I said it was rather hard on me when he said, "Sister drank a bucket of slop!"

If you have talked to Buster or heard from him by the time you get this, you will probably know that his brother Bob has successfully completed his 50 missions. He is supposed to get to come home now.

Do send us a request for food, so that we can send you more than 8 ounces. Have you never received any of the packages we sent—even the toilet articles?

Lots of Love,

Mother

P.S. The mail has been so tied up that Aunt Minnie and Aunt Fannie just got the Christmas letters yesterday that you wrote on December 9.

P.S. #2 Daddy says to ask you if the bone of your arm was injured. He said sometimes the flesh wound heals and the bone later causes infection. Were you working in the aid station when hit?

P.S. #3 Mr. Bush just brought us some fine steak.

---

70   Richard's mother comments on this because Richard's father had spent a year in bed in 1935-36. His recovery was exceptionally slow following surgery for a lung abscess. He had trouble walking for the rest of his life. He was 63 years old at the time this letter was written. —Ed.

January 19, 1945

Dee to Richard

Dear Berk,

Received your card. Thanks a lot. I was home for Christmas and New Year's. Had dinner with your folks one night. They were all okay. Heard you had a little tough break. Let me know how you are and how you feel. Will be over here about four months after I leave this place. Should be leaving here in about two or three more weeks.

Saw IU play Nebraska. IU won but still is no good. If we were there, we would be all Big Ten.

Write,

Bush

January 21, 1945

Richard to Folks

Dear Folks,

I seem to have lost all sense of time, since I've been in this hospital. Can't even remember the last time I wrote, but don't think it was too many days ago.

Still haven't had mail. I was just thinking that it was sometime around Thanksgiving that I last heard from home. Hope everyone is okay. Suppose you're having the regular run of colds. So am I, in fact I think I'm catching one now, even in this place. Also I presume you are having the usual trouble with the furnace. I read in the paper that the fuel situation is rather acute. Hope you have enough coal, and too, wood for the fireplace. Is Grandmother at home this winter? I was noticing the date and remembered this is sometime near her birthday isn't it? And Aunt Minnie's too, never could get 'em straight.

Have occupied the greater part of the day reading. Read a baseball book this morning about the famous pitcher Rube

Waddell and Connie Mack. Read the *New Yorker* magazine this afternoon and played a couple of games of cards with the boys on either side of me.

Arm is much better but yet rather stiff. Imagine I'll be okay before so very long. Hope to hear from you all soon.

Love,

Richard

Mother to Richard

Dear Richard,

I'll try another V-mail, as we are urged to use them. We have found that the ones from this section are photographed in Chicago and an airmail stamp is unnecessary.

We're fine, except that Grandmother is not very well. Tomorrow is her birthday but we celebrated this past Sunday. We had baked chicken with the trimmings and Eleanor baked an angel food for her birthday cake. We also got some flowers for her. She is 87. She wished you could be here to eat. Aunt Minnie will be 70 tomorrow. I made her a new green smock and Grandmother made the buttonholes.

We got a letter from Jonas this afternoon. He has no orders yet. The weather has been rainy down there the past week so they have done little but eat and sleep and go to a show now and then. He had heard from his former skipper. He is now an executive officer on a Patrol Craft and is at Portland, ready to go out again.

We feel that you are probably back at work again. Tell us how your arm is—whether it is still sore and how much of a scar you have. Had the piece of shrapnel gone on through or did it have to be picked out?

Love,

Mother

War Department to Mother

Dear Mrs. Berkey:

I am pleased to inform you that the latest report states that your son, Richard, was making normal improvement on 24 December. You will be notified immediately when additional information is received.

Sincerely yours,

J.A. Ulio, Maj. General, The Adjutant General

January 24, 1945

Virginia to Richard

Dearest Richard,

Mother's last letter brought me the news I've been craving to hear—that they heard from you and that you're comparatively all right. I feel much better now knowing that. I signed up today to give blood the 8th of February. I hear everyplace that they need more than they are getting, and I want to do my share, even more to help you—or anybody else's brother, for that matter.

I really mustn't write anymore now, since I have a paper for social philosophy on "The United States as a Society" due tomorrow afternoon. Doesn't that sound gruesome? It does to me.

I hope you got the cookies. Please write me and request some and I'll send a lot. Also anything else you want. Take care of yourself! I haven't heard any news about your old cronies or I'd tell you.

Lots of Love,

Virginia

Mother to Richard

Dear Richard,

Yesterday we thought we were getting a second letter from you since you were injured but it was an old letter dated December 12. We also got a letter from the War Department reporting that you were making normal improvement on December 24. That wasn't very recent either! They sent a blank on which we were to write a five-word message to you, to be sent as a radiogram. We wrote it and mailed it this morning. Let us know when you get it. It may be another month but they do well to accomplish all they do, when there are so many casualties.

Marvin Martin, Jr. finally wrote his folks that one of his legs is off 6 inches below the knee. He is coming home as soon as he is able.

Write us just as often as you can. We are always anxious. Are you back with your detachment?

Lots of Love,

Mother

January 25, 1945

Richard to Folks

Dear Folks,

I'm starting this letter without the slightest notion of what I'm going to say after this line. I feel that I should write you more often than usual to let you know of my well-being. Am in the hospital yet. Learned a couple of days ago that I still have the small piece of shrapnel in my arm. I thought it had been taken out but X-rays proved different. I can feel it in the muscle. It's peculiar indeed because it's on the opposite side of my arm from the original penetration. I don't know yet if it will be removed, it seems probable that it should since 'tis rather sore, or rather causes soreness.

I haven't heard a word about Buster from any source for a number of weeks now. And too, I'm still looking forward to receiving some mail, from anyone, suppose they are keeping it all at the detachment till I return.

I finished reading *Low Man on the Totem Pole* this evening. All I can say is that H. Allen Smith must have a unique imagination or else he's slightly buggy. What do you think, Dad, you read it?

Love,

Richard

January 27, 1945

Rodman to Richard

Dear Richard,

How's my boy by this time? Here's hoping you are getting along better. I heard good news about you saying that you were writing with your injured arm. I hope that is true. Perhaps you would like to hear more about things at home. I've lost track of most of the gang but perhaps you hear from a great number of them through other sources. Eddie Alberding is taking pictures or working in an Air Corps photo lab. He's still studying German, hoping to find a woman of his type, and his latest mathematical achievement is the calculating of the conjugate foci of his camera lens at a variable or something like that! Hmm, maybe we wasted our time at Indiana University! Incidentally, I was there on my last leave. The old place is getting pretty war struck! Those beautiful women going out with those puny kids! Drop me a line when you can!

Rodman

January 30, 1945
Richard to Folks

Dear Folks,

Finally got some mail yesterday, one from Mother, Virginia, and a church letter. By the way, could you please inform them of my correct address? Thanks. Mother's letter was of December 15 and the one that contained stamps. Thanks loads for them! Thanks also for Lucy's address. Maybe I can drop her a line now after about six months.

It was interesting to learn about the guys being wounded and how. Was glad to learn that Bud Rigdon wasn't too badly hit. Buster was always talking about him and made me feel as if I knew him, too, although I've never met him. I'll tell Buster about him when I see him again, although he probably now gets news before I do.

I assure you Mother that I have plenty of warm socks and for that matter everything else, so don't worry about that. Besides the comforts of home etc., I guess I miss ice cream the most.

I'm supposed to have another operation tomorrow to remove the foreign body in my arm, so guess I'll be here a while longer—I hope.

Saw the picture show *Rhapsody in Blue* a few days ago, 'twas very fine. I got so interested I strained my neck attempting to gather it in its entirety.

Love,

Richard

January 31, 1945

Mother to Richard

Dear Richard,

So far, the last letter we've had from you was the one written January 6, the second one you wrote in the hospital. You had not then had any mail from home for a long time. I hope you have by this time.

Daddy was just reading in the *Times* a list of divisions now on the Western Front and the 14th Armored was among them. Of course we already knew it was there. Today we got a letter from Jonas. After waiting five weeks for his orders, he was finally sent to the Naval Hospital in Key West for a checkup in regard to his malaria. The letter was written Sunday and he and Mildred were going Monday or Tuesday. It was to be only a four-hour ride. He said Mildred had always wanted to go to Key West but he was afraid it would be so crowded it would be hard to find a room. He said he had no idea how long they would keep him—maybe days, maybe weeks.

We had a very sad thing happen this afternoon. The Church of Christ burned down. We are having quite a cold spell and the thermometer was only about 10 above zero all day. This was prayer meeting night and somebody built a hot fire in the practically new furnace.[71] The trouble seemed to be in the flue. We could see the big blaze and see the small tower burning. We heard that they thought the furnace was saved but everything else seemed to be a total loss.

We also got a letter from David today, written January 17. He was okay but seemed bored with his surroundings, as usual. He is lucky to be out of a combat zone, and I hope he will not be moved. He sent a negative of himself and we had a bunch of prints made for him. He looks quite natural but a little older. His hairline seems to have receded more.

---

71   Most all furnaces were fueled with coal at this time. —Ed.

Lucy still remains silent. She has written only once since she was here Christmas. I wrote her a very urgent letter Sunday so maybe she will write.

We saw the Crockett car down by the house Sunday but didn't get to talk to any of them. I see by the paper that Bob has now been decorated *six* times for bombing missions. That must be the way they encourage those fellows to keep on at such dangerous work—lots of decorations.

Dale Rigdon is still in a Pennsylvania hospital. His mother and Charlene went to visit him and then he came here last weekend to see their little girl. Charlene says he has to have another operation. His heel lacks about three quarters of an inch of touching the floor. The muscle has grown to the bone.

In the last issue of *Life* there is a fine write-up and a set of pictures on George Lott, casualty. It shows every step from the time the boy was badly wounded in both arms until he was brought back to this country. It made us almost able to see what had happened to you. Lott was a medical unit member. They had their Battalion Aid Station in the cellar of the village house, with straw on the floor. He left shelter to answer the cries of two wounded men.

I am sending you an article that came out in the *Star* about our Indiana boys. Of course, other articles give credit to other divisions as well, especially the 28th, the 101st Airborne, etc.

I sent the first pair of socks Grandmother knit for you, and she has the other pair almost done.

Lots of Love,

Mother

CHAPTER EIGHT
FEBRUARY 1945

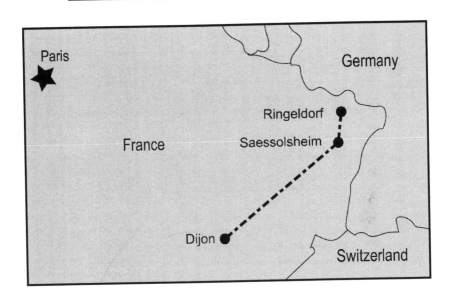

February 1, 1945

Junior to Richard

Hiya Berk,

Heard you got hit. I hope it isn't bad. My mother told me about it. I understand you are a fightin' medic. Your Medical Corps deserves all the praise it can get. Everyone agrees there is no braver or better man than a combat medic. I've been pretty lucky so far. We've been strafed, bombed, and shelled, but I've not seen much action and no front line as yet, even though it was close at times. When did you get hit?

It looks as if we might get home this year if the Reds keep rollin'. I forget what the States look like, though it's been only a year ago when I was home. I think I would like to go huntin' or fishin' again. You know there isn't any place like the States.

WAITING *for* PEACE   145

I haven't seen much of the big cities, but I don't think they could compare to little old Salem. I had a chance to see Reims though. It wasn't too impressive. I was at Nancy, France, for quite some time and thought it stunk. I visited Verdun on a pass. It was an interesting place, but after a couple of hours I was ready to hitchhike back.

Say, I have a picture of you and Lucy in my billfold. How does Lucy like the WAVES? She sure looks snappy in her uniform, doesn't she? David's in the Pacific now, isn't he? And where's Jonas? We are scattered all over the world, aren't we?

I've been intending to drop you a line since I first heard you were over here, but was short of time. It keeps us jumping these days. Write when you can and if there is anything you want or need let me know.

Your cousin,

Maurice

February 5, 1945

Richard to Dad

Dear Dad,

I see it is now February and remember that you have a birthday about the 18th, so here's wishing you Happy Birthday, although this will reach you somewhat late. And I see, too, that David has one about Thursday. I received a letter from him the first of the month and now have his address so I must write him. I also received 15 more letters along with his. Even one from Lucy and two from you, five or six from Mother, one from Aunt Fannie, and the remaining from the three or four girlfriends I manage to communicate with—ha! I almost forgot Virginia. Got three from her and one of them was one of those "very, very serious" types that had no end of laughs. Guess I shouldn't make fun of the *dear child's* "serious convictions" but I'm sure in no position to receive such absurd diddle daddle—ha! That surely must be the job of a devoted father, your job, pity you. I see that your own children are your most troublesome clients.

All the letters I received were so old that I find I'm about 2 to 3 months behind time with news at home. However, one of Mother's letters was of December 15. Guess my mail is slightly mixed up. I noticed some of the forwarding addresses were the same as the one Dale Rigdon had, as Mother enclosed in one of her letters.

A doctor removed the piece of shrapnel from my arm last Wednesday and this is the first letter I've written since then. The piece was small, approximately 1/2 inch long, and was removed by a "local" much to my satisfaction. I have now acquired two nice-looking little scars in remembrance of my grand entrée into the Fatherland.[72]

Once again, I've found that all the time spent at the institution of higher learning was not in vain. I've found considerable use of my limited vocabulary of Deutsch. My French was practically nil, but have learned a few words and phrases, enough to get along anyway.

Had a couple of fried eggs this morning for breakfast, first since I left home. Boy, were they good! Also had toast, Cream of Wheat, and raisins. Chow is okay here. I've really been eating oatmeal again, surprises me. Guess it must be the change after eating so many K rations. In fact there's been a radical change. I, believe it or not, now eat slower than brother Jonas, if that's possible.

Haven't seen or heard from Buster for a couple months now, just hope he's okay. Hoping you're all okay.

Love,

Richard

---

72   The initial surgeries (December 18 and 24, 1944) removed several pieces of shrapnel. When Richard developed an infection and did not improve, the doctors realized there had to be more shrapnel inside. This third surgery (January 31, 1945) revealed that the shrapnel took a piece of his new combat jacket inside his arm. The fabric had caused the infection in his arm. The third surgery removed the fabric and another smaller piece of shrapnel. —Ed.

February 6, 1945

Mother to Richard

Dear Richard,

Saturday we got your letter, written January 16. So sorry you have never received the many letters we have written. Yesterday we got another War Department report saying you were making normal improvement on January 22. This is the first time they have given your hospital address. I'll use it, though you may be moved before this gets there. Guess you know Buster was wounded January 18. If you find out anything about him you can tell us, please do. They are as anxious as we were. They were at home last week because June was leaving Saturday to go into the Army or Navy.[73] Helen brought Frankie in so Grandmother could see him. He is a dandy with a sweet one-sided grin. He is so well and fat. Lucy is coming home next weekend from Saturday until Monday evening. Virginia is coming then, too. We've had two more letters from David. He is okay.

Jonas is not sick but has been sent to the Naval Hospital in Key West, Florida, for a checkup on his malaria. Mildred is still with him and will get a job if he has to stay awhile. We still want you to tell us how your injury happened.

Yours always,

Mother

---

73   June was Buster's brother. —Ed.

Unit History

Headquarters 36th General Hospital APO 380 7 Feb 1945

GENERAL ORDER NUMBER 12
AWARD OF THE PURPLE HEART

Under the provision of Army Regulations 600-45, as amended, the Purple Heart is awarded to the following for wounds received in action against the enemy:

Berkey, Richard J. Pfc., 35694330, MD, 68th AIB, Germany, 18 Dec 44. Entered service from Salem, Indiana.

Sunday, February 11, 1945

Mother to Richard

Dear Richard,

I guess it's time to write again with the hope that your mail will finally get through to you. We have read that quantities of mail were lost when the Germans broke through and captured so much stuff. Maybe some of your letters and packages were in that mess. We have not heard from you this past week. The last we got from you was written January 16 and the government report said you were still improving on January 22.

Lucy came home this weekend. She came Friday morning and Daddy sent Ivan Roberts to get her in a taxi because the roads were still icy. He charged $5 plus tax, which Daddy said was much cheaper than having a possible wreck or ruining a precious tire.[74] The weather then turned warmer and most beauti-

---

74   Tires were the first rationed items as 90% of the world's natural rubber became unavailable to the U.S. when Japan moved to conquer SE Asia. Tire rationing began December 27, 1941 and ended December 31, 1945. Civilians were allowed to keep five tires per automobile. "Take a Closer Look at Ration Books," *The National WWII Museum*, http://www.nationalww2museum.org/learn/education/for-students/ww2-history/take-a-closer-look/ration-books.html (Jan. 24, 2014).

ful. We took her back to Mitchell this afternoon and, though the wind was still sharp, it seemed like spring. A few robins are already back. I hope you are having some nice days in France.

Lucy was the same little old complainer, sweet as ever but worrying about her eyes and teeth and constipation—and about being an old maid! She's going to have a rest for her eyes. She applied for a transfer to some other kind of work. The big boss told her she was valuable to the department because she did excellent work and was cooperative so they are allowing her to work in the basement a while, in the finishing and distribution department. They stack, fold, etc., and do not do anything that requires much eyesight or brains. After a month she is supposed to go back to her regular job again and see how her eyes get along.

We got a letter from David again yesterday. He was 20 on Thursday. He writes pretty regularly but doesn't have much to write about either. We also heard again from Jonas. He checked into the Key West Naval Hospital a week ago Saturday and had to stay there all the time the first week. He had no idea what they would do to him or how long he would have to stay, but said if it seemed it was going to be quite a while, Mildred would get a job. He said the town was jammed. The first night they slept in a rat-hole of a place, which used to be a good hotel. They told him General Grant once slept there when he was president! Dee Bush was still at Lincoln, Nebraska, the last we heard.

I want to remind you again about the requests. We have such a time wanting to send you things and can barely send 8 ounces at a time. Put a request for something in every letter. Lucy has been waiting a long time to send you some stuff. We think about you all the time and look for a letter constantly. We are so afraid you are back with the fellows in combat.

Lots of Love,

Mother

David to Richard

Dear Richard,

You should give me a good kick in the pants for not writing to you a heck of a lot sooner but I figure you have plenty to think about besides me.

As you can see by the address, I am now aboard ship but only arrived yesterday afternoon. I was the only one to come on this ship but one other sailor who I went to radio school at Chicago with is also going on a PGM (Patrol Motor Gunboat) today so we'll very likely get to see each other now and then. There were six of us who had the least time up at NAB 158 and two of us had to be on a PGM so we drew cards and I drew a 2 and here I am.[75]

The duty here as a radioman is not very bad at all. Up at NAB 158 we had a three-section watch but here we don't really have a watch except when at sea and so I get almost every night in except every three or four days I have to stand a four-hour watch.

I received a Christmas card from you and enjoyed it very much. I'm sorry I didn't send you one, but I wrote you a letter some time before Christmas. I doubt if you ever got it for that was around the time you were in a little action and your mail situation is somewhat disrupted as I gather from the news at home. Christmas out here sure was different from last one but about all I did was drink a little beer and had a headache the next day. I don't drink it as a rule but it's the only thing we could get cold up here so it's always a relief from the heat. We get Cokes also but not very often. Mother said you got a Christmas package from DeJean so you'll probably get your others about next Christmas. I think I got all the Christmas packages that were coming, so I consider myself lucky. Most of the candy

---

75   Naval Advance Base 158 was located at Torokina, Bougainville Island, in the Solomon Islands. —Ed.

was spoiled but on the whole they were in pretty good shape. Just getting something from home made me feel better anyway.

Maybe next time I'll have more to tell you but can't recall much at the time of importance. Get that arm well quick but don't get in too much action for I don't want anything to happen to you.

Your brudder,

David

February 12, 1945

Richard to Folks

Dear Folks,

Boy am I in a rare mood this eve. Just finished writing dear sis Virginia a letter and probably flattered her out of this world or else made an enemy for the rest of my born days—ha. Called her butterball, chatterbox, ol' fatty, and all. She'd probably ring my neck if she could get a hold of me. I told her that her letters are so newsy, probably because she's so nosy, which ain't far from the truth. I guess all this unexpected eruption of energy is due to my convalescence, no doubt. I'll probably be leaving here in a few days, back to duty. My arm's pretty good now, just as usual.

Today I got in a little physical therapy sorting mail over at the post office. The prime result, I got a letter from little Eleanor and Dad (Christmas card and letter combined). That's the latest mail I've received as yet.

Got my Purple Heart Saturday. It's a very nice medal, will send it some of these days. It's for wounds received in action against the enemy in Germany (you probably know that by now though). Will write more before I leave here.

Love,

Richard

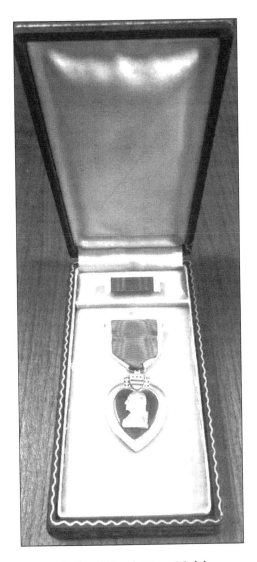

Richard's Purple Heart Medal
Courtesy of Eric Berkey

February 13, 1945

Richard's Journal

Well, here it is Feb. 13, 1945—a little reminiscing of the past month or so. Was operated upon again 31 January and Captain

Crook removed a piece of shrapnel about ½ inch long from my arm. It had a piece of my combat jacket neatly wrapped around it and was causing infection. 1st of February I got 16 letters and really enjoyed 'em although they were a couple months old. Got 2 from Dad, 3 from Virginia, 6 from Julia, 4 from Mother, and one from Aunt Fannie. Groundhog Day was quite sunny, although much snow on the ground. The old groundhog sure saw his shadow. When the sun comes out everything around here seems more cheerful, but sunny days are so few. Got the Purple Heart Medal Feb. 9, the day after Dad's birthday. Wrote him a letter, having received one a couple days before from him. The medal is very nice looking, took it over this evening to the Red Cross to have them send it home. Yesterday, the 12th (Lincoln's Birthday), I received 3 Christmas cards from Dad and letter, too, from Imy and Geneva Head, and a letter from Eleanor. Also wrote 7 letters last night to Martha Jean, Imy, Julia, Virginia, Folks, and a V-mail and regular letter to Mrs. Owens, who mother said she hoped I'd write to so they could get some overseas mail. Also, yesterday the doc took a look at me and pronounced me almost ready for duty—ha! And also yesterday I sorted mail at the post office, first work for ages. I got a cablegram from Mother and Dad. It said, "All fine–Happy you are better–Mother Daddy." Evidently they have heard from me by now as well as the War Dept. Also worked in post office this morn and a little this aft.

Richard to Folks

Dear Folks,

Received your cablegram today and was glad to learn you are all fine and also that you have heard from me, and the War Department, too, I presume. I assume by the message you sent that you've received a letter from me informing you of my well-being. Assuring you that I'm very well and will probably be leaving the hospital shortly. I gave my Purple Heart to the Red Cross to send you. Indeed, a nice-looking item. I've just returned from a movie and enjoyed it very much. It was crazy and comical like I enjoy. Thanks for the cablegram.

Love,

Richard

February 14, 1945

Richard to Folks

Dear Folks,

A few days ago I was over in the Red Cross and was looking through the registry of patients who had visited there. Ran across Lt. Richard (Buck) Land's name and a Salem, Indiana, following. So I remember he was wounded last summer in Italy. I also ran across a book, *History of Indiana*, and read some things about Salem and Washington County I had never had the pleasure of knowing before. One story said John Hay despised the very name of Indiana and claimed some eastern state as his home (I believe Vermont).[76] He called Indiana the "Wild West"—ha! Maybe it was then. Worked in the post office today sorting mail but never ran across any of my own. Expect to leave here soon.

Love,

Richard

February 15, 1945

Mother to Richard

Dear Richard,

Yesterday Daddy got your letter of February 5 in which you told of having the piece of shrapnel taken out. Was it the only

---

76   Born in Salem, Indiana (Richard's hometown), John Hay was personal secretary to President Lincoln. He also was secretary of state under Presidents McKinley and Roosevelt. "Birthplace: John Milton Hay," *John Hay Center, Stevens Memorial Museum,* http://www.johnhaycenter.org/index.asp?mod=2 (Jan. 24, 2014).

one that did the damage, or had another one been taken out earlier? If there are no more fragments, surely the arm will improve rapidly now. It must've been worse than you told us, or you would not have remained in the hospital so long. We're just thankful that you've been warm and dry and safe. As far as we know, Crocketts have not yet heard what Buster's wound is. Glad you got some letters, even if old.

We are all okay. Lucy and Virginia were both at home last weekend. Jonas is still tied up at the Key West Naval Hospital, being examined for malaria. We hear from David often. Eleanor is flitting around at her various high school duties and social functions. She was too old to care about Valentine's Day yesterday but the neighborhood kids passed around a lot of them. Dale Rigdon has a 21-day furlough. He and Charlene and their little girl are at Warsaw this week. Bob Crockett is at home. The weather here is beautiful today being warm but windy like March.

Love,

Mother

Richard to Eleanor

Dear Eleanor,

Will make a feeble attempt to answer your letter. And thanks so much for writing. I enjoyed your little pictures and your keen way of expressing our street number—ha!

I see that yesterday was Valentine's Day. So let this be mine to you, and will you be my Valentine? A Red Cross gal gave me a large heart-shaped cookie today and 'twas a nice surprise and tasted good, too. It was left over from a Valentine party they had last night. I just got back from the picture show, *Carolina Blues* with Kay Kyser, pretty good. Saw a real good one the other day, *Animal Kingdom*. I shall attempt to write you a regular letter later. These V-mails usually don't seem much like letters.

Love

Richard

February 16, 1945

Mother to Richard

Dear Richard,

I just wrote you last night but have more news. Today we got another letter from you, older than the one we got yesterday. It was written January 25. Glad you got that piece of shrapnel out! Tonight Daddy said he talked to Bob Crockett as he went to town. He found out that Mrs. Crockett and Helen and the baby are here. They have heard from Buster and have found out that his injury is to his eye. He says he will be able to see. The other piece of news is that David is being moved. He wrote February 9 and gave an address on a ship, PGM-5, but said that was not permanent and we should not use it to write to him. He stopped at an island and he and Frank Arthur, one of his buddies from school in Chicago, were waiting for orders. He thought they would probably be stationed on a ship but wasn't sure. I hope he is not going to the danger zone. I learned today that a new double capsule has been invented for giving penicillin by mouth. The inner, oily capsule is not dissolved by the stomach juices. We are all fine here.

Love,

Mother

Richard to Folks

Dear Folks,

Received Mother's V-mail of February 5, 1945 this afternoon. This is the first news from home since I've received your letter of December 14.

I had not known Buster was wounded, since it was a month after I was, and I haven't received any news from the outfit. He's not in this hospital, I checked the roster. I hope he's not bad, but guess you don't know or you would have mentioned it. I have been worried about him all the time I've been here, but have been consoled knowing that he sure knows how to take care of himself, but one never knows here.

I was wounded in an attack by a shell fragment. I was an aid man, and carried only medical supplies. It's real exciting being a medic, sometimes a little too much, but I enjoy nonetheless.

Love,

Richard

Richard to Folks

Dear Folks,

I will write to you tonight since there are some more things I want to say. Received a V-mail from the Bushes dated December 11 and have already answered it. Also Mother, I wrote Mrs. Owens both a V-mail and regular letter as you suggested.

I'll probably be leaving here soon, so by the time you receive this you should no longer use the hospital address.

I have managed to catch up with all my correspondence, since I've been here, as well as get a nice rest the past few weeks. I've been sorting mail at the post office for the last few days. It sure occupies the time, and I managed to find a few of my letters amid the mess. I have received none of your packages as yet, maybe in time for next year—ha!

Love,

Richard

Mother to Richard

Dear Richard,

Yes, this is the 20th and Daddy brought me a box of chocolates in a sack for Valentine's Day as boxed chocolates are now hard to get. He had a very nice birthday Sunday—a Swiss steak, birthday cake, etc.

Helen came up Saturday to get your address for Buster and read us one of his letters. He said a rock flew up and hit him just above the eye. The eyeball was still sore after the bandage was taken off, but he had been to church and to a show. Said he was glad to be warm and dry (in Hospital 35) but was anxious to get back with his outfit as he kept thinking of them in the mud. This is the nice thing he said about you:

"Whatever happened to Richard? I know he is all right, as I talked to the doctor and he said it wasn't serious. He did a great piece of work and the boys are all proud of him. He wouldn't leave until everybody was taken care of. When they tried to make him leave he said now is the time they need me and I'm staying! I would certainly like to talk with him about that day. Tell his folks I said 'Hello' and that I commend him for his work."

Wasn't that nice of Buster? That's the first thing we've heard about you on the day you were wounded, though we were sure you were doing your best always. We are proud of you!

Love,

Mother

February 22, 1945

Unit History

Unit outposting Ringeldorf and remaining in defensive positions. Sector generally quiet throughout day, except for occasional 50 mm mortar harassing fire landing in Uberach. Assault gun fired on estimated 75 mm towed anti-tank gun and observed a direct hit. Artillery fired on enemy working party, dispersing enemy. Pfc. Richard Berkey, joined company from Headquarters 3rd Reinforcement Battalion.

February 23, 1945

Unit History

Continued improvement of defensive positions. Sector generally quiet throughout the day. Maintained contact with 19th AIB on left and 3rd Battalion 502nd PI (Parachute Infantry) on right. Prisoners of War taken this afternoon are from the 2nd Company of the Grenadier Regiment 935 of the 245th Infantry Division. They have 130 men in Bitschhoffen with command post in the schoolhouse. There are 3 platoons of 4 squads each, one machine gun per squad, 2-3 Panzerfausts per squad.[77] They occupy positions along sunken road west of town, change reliefs between 2000 and 2030, and remain in foxholes 24 hours a day. They have no kitchen and have to forage for themselves, living off rabbits, chickens, and anything they can find to eat. At 2300 reconnaissance reports that Lt. Hood and one rifleman stepped on Schu-mines and are unable to walk.[78]

---

77 Panzerfaust: German anti-tank weapon. —Ed.

78 Schu-mines could not be found by a metal detector. Made of wood with dimensions of 6 by 6 inches, the mine was activated with a hinged lid. When stepped on, the lid pressed down on a striker setting off 200 grams of TNT. This mine was built to maim, not kill. "German Weapons: Landmines," *Blanco County WWII Museum*, http://ww2blancomuseum.com/german_weapons/german_weapons_-_landmines (May 31, 2014).

February 24, 1945

Unit History

Sector generally quiet except for occasional artillery fire throughout the day. One enemy high-velocity self-propelled gun was seen by our observation plane. Direct hit was made on it by our artillery. At 1500 civilian in Uberach reported tanks and horse-drawn vehicles going from Mietesheim to Bitschhoffen. Took prisoner at 2200 hours who states they are making a patrol in force in the vicinity of Neuburg with mission of taking prisoners.

Dee to Richard's Folks

Dear Folks,

I think, if my memory serves me correctly, I'm supposed to find out if the "big one" is still kicking on the other side.

I can tell you this. I received a letter from him dated January 16 in which he stated his condition. He said that it was only a piece of shrapnel in the upper part of his right arm. He also said that it still hurt him at times but thought that in the end it would turn out to be as good as new.

I am glad that he told you practically the same thing or else I would've been forced not to tell. Being in the Army I understand perfectly how the family worries back home. I'm sure that is all that is wrong because I know he would've told me.

I am here in the sunny south and liking it very well. The Robbins boy from home is here also so we enjoy a gab session now and then. Sure wish I could be back in dear old Indiana.

As ever,

Dee

Dee to Richard

Dear Berk,

Well how is the wound by now? I am way down here in the sunny south. Instead of using pursuit planes for gunnery practice we use mosquitoes. Boy those babies can really peel off and fly formation. Will be here until May 14 doing nothing but flying and more flying. After that I don't have to tell you where I'm heading. I see you ground stools are never going to get it done so I guess I will have to come over and get it over after all. Hope this finds you in good enough condition to answer.

So long,

Bush

Richard to Folks

Dear Folks,

Finally got out of the hospital and back to the outfit. Received a letter yesterday from Mother, and too, the box of chewing gum—thanks lots! The letter was of the 11th, so guess mail is quite a bit faster here of late. This is the first letter I've written in about 10 days.

Mother, you are always asking for me to request something. What, I don't know? The time I did ask for some stuff I learned later I probably wouldn't need, and have never received anyway. Now, I don't need any toilet articles or stuff like that since we get it okay. Since you want to send me something so badly I'll ask, but seems as if it's a lot of trouble for you to fix it up. If you don't wrap it well, it's not worth sending. Would like some of your cookies, Mother, and too, candy and also peanuts or something of that nature and good candy bars. Thanks. Am okay and arm is well.

Love,

Richard

February 25, 1945

Unit History

Occasional mortar and artillery fire fell in our sector throughout the day. At 1047 hours Battalion Observation Post reported seeing what appeared to be leaflets falling just north of Uberach. At 1340 hours, 68th AIB Command Post reported that men were observed entering a dugout, one at a time at irregular intervals. One carried a machine gun. Our artillery fired on them. Effect not determined, but aid men observed going to dugout and evacuating 2 enemy.

Mother to Richard

Dear Richard,

Yesterday we got a V-mail from you written February 13. Mrs. Owens also got hers and was much pleased. Glad you got your cablegram and hope you have mail that is more recent by this time. Guess you are out of the hospital now.

This is a beautiful spring-like Sunday. I saw Logan and Mattie at church. They asked if you were in the 7th Army and I said I thought so. Russell wrote that he was reading the 7th Army news and saw something about "Richard Berkey's buddy." Wonder what it was. Russell is in Belgium. Frank C. is home for a week and was at church with Helen. I saw Dale Rigdon without crutch or cane. He only limps a little. Grandmother feels better than she has all winter and went with me today. Haven't seen anything of the Crocketts this weekend. Will be proud to receive your Purple Heart.

Love,

Mother

February 26, 1945

Unit History

68th remained in defensive positions. Sector generally quiet with increasing sporadic artillery and mortar fire during the latter part of the day. Made contact with 19th AIB on left and 1st Battalion, 142nd on right. 1st Lt. Woodrow Miller joined company and appointed principal duty as Armored Infantry Unit Commander.

Rodman to Richard

Dear Richard,

Well, how is everything with you, old man? Are you recovered, recovering, or still having difficulties? I haven't heard about you from any source recently so I'm hoping things are going much better for you. It feels as though spring is just around the corner here; things are getting green and the trees are beginning to bud. It's still very damp though and it feels pretty chilly. I suppose I'm not used to such a damp place. Personally I'll take Texas for more reasons than one. I received a letter from a very beautiful girl from there just yesterday who said it was so warm that she was sitting outdoors in her shorts writing it! Sounds good, doesn't it—especially the shorts!! I visited London last week and loved it. It's really an old historic place; hope I can spend more time there sometime. One never knows when he will run into someone he knows in this Theatre. Maybe I'll see you some day; can't never tell! I've already met a few of my old buddies! Write when you can and I'll write later.

So long,

Rodman

February 27, 1945

Unit History

Sector generally quiet, except for occasional heavy mortar fire falling in vicinity of Uberach. Relief of 68th AIB by 62nd AIB began 2100, troops en route to Saessolsheim and Ingenheim.

February 28, 1945

Unit History

Plan for defense of Saessolsheim: Outposts manned 24 hours per day. Two-man roving patrols operate from 1830 until 0630. Patrols to keep all civilians off the streets, enforce blackout regulations, and guard against acts of sabotage. In case of alert all company commanders will immediately report to Battalion Command Post for instructions. In case of infiltration by enemy at night all troops will fight for their own houses and courtyards, firing on anyone in street. All personal weapons and an ample supply of ammunition will be kept in billets. Maximum use will be made of vehicular automatic weapons. In case of enemy air activity all vehicles and troops will seek cover and concealment and not fire on planes unless they display hostile action, and then only on order from a commissioned officer. J.E. Foppiano, Captain, Infantry. Company left Ringeldorf, France, at 2330 hours 27 Feb 45 and arrived at Saessolsheim, France, at 0130 hours 28 Feb 45. Distance marched 18 miles. Company billeted in town. Performed maintenance of vehicles and weapons and outposted the town.

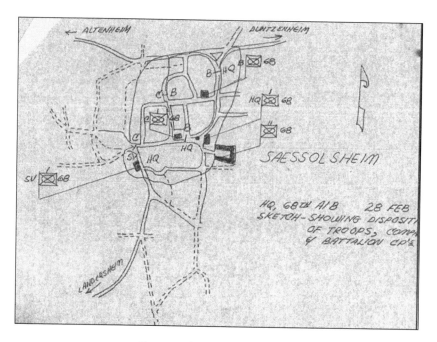

Courtesy of the National Archives

KAREN BERKEY HUNTSBERGER

CHAPTER NINE
MARCH 1945

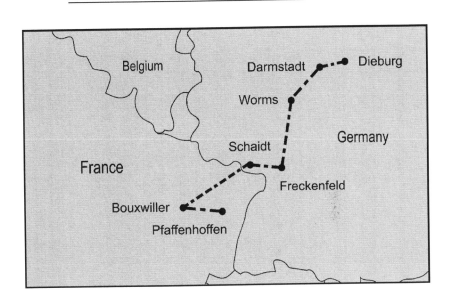

March 2, 1945

Unit History

2nd Lt. Harold Hanhardt joined company from Headquarters 3rd Reinforcement Battalion and appointed principal duty as Company C Armored Infantry Unit Commander.

Dad to Richard

Dear Son,

Last Monday we received your two letters of February 16. Hope you get okay before you go back. Guess you have heard from Buster by this time. Bob Crockett is home but will leave Monday. He took supper with us last Tuesday and I enjoyed talking with him. He made thirty-five missions over Germany and none of the crew was wounded. Mother talked to Buster's wife yesterday. Frank Richard has three teeth now. Some boy. Let us know if you hear from Buster.

Jonas is still in hospital in Key West. David is now on the USS PGM-5 and has been since February 10. Said he liked the boys on ship. Got a letter from Lucy this morning. Said she got your letter at Christmastime. Frank C. Neal was home for a week and was at Lions Club last night. Afterwards he and his father came up to the house and talked. He left this morning for Purdue. Says he will get about another year of training in the V-12.

It has been pretty bad this winter for outside work, snow and sleet and in last week snow and rain. The Ohio River is out of its banks. It commenced to rain last night and has rained all day and still at it. Water all around the cheese factory and over Highway 60 in places. Don't think we can get down to the farm. Eleanor is in high school play. Guess you will read it in paper. Hope you are getting the paper.

If you want anything send a request in each letter and we will get it to you. You have to make a request each time we send anything, so each time make a separate request. We have to show it and have it stamped at the post office. Write us and let us know what places you have seen. Good luck.

Your dad,

James G. Berkey

Buster Crockett in France, 1945.
Courtesy of Lynn Manship

March 3, 1945

Unit History

Pfc. Wiley Foster from missing in action, vicinity of Oberhoffen, France, as of 7 Feb 1945, to killed in action 7 Feb 1945.

March 4, 1945

Richard to Folks

Dear Folks,

Received Mother's V-mail of February 20 this evening and also received a letter from Virginia of the 22nd.

Most of the letter was concerning Buster. I received his address a couple of days ago and dropped him a line and will probably hear from him soon. What he said concerning me was the general idea, I guess, of what happened to me. Wednesday the 28th I received orders for the award of the Bronze Star Medal for what I did, most of which was my job anyway. Tomorrow I'm supposed to receive the medal from the General. I'll tell you about it.

More fun—helped a farmer with a cow that was having a calf this morning. You have been asking for me to write request letters, so finally someone mentioned something that may be useful to send. There happens to be a baking powder shortage or something of the sort around, so would appreciate a can or box of the stuff. You probably think I'm a cook instead of a medic, but the stuff sure comes in handy for biscuits and cakes and such. We get lots of chances to make stuff like that to help out with the none-too-tasty concentrated rations. Made a nice batch of fudge the other day and was going to make some this afternoon but couldn't get hold of any butter. Think I'll make it tomorrow anyway. Guess the box would be kind of empty with only baking powder so any eats would be swell for filling out the corners. Am well and fine—thanks.

Love,

Richard

*Pfc. Richard J. Berkey receives the Bronze Star from
Brigadier General Albert C. Smith. Photographer Tec 4 Sidney Blau,
163rd Signal Photo Company.
Courtesy of the National Archives*

WAITING *for* PEACE   171

Richard's Bronze Star Medal.
Courtesy of Eric Berkey

March 5, 1945

Dad to Richard

Dear Son,

This morning we got word that Dee was killed Saturday night about eight in flight at Alexandria, Louisiana. We understand that body was recovered and will be sent here. When he was home on leave last month we had him up for supper the night he left. Will write you more when we learn about the details.

Take care of yourself and write us. Virginia was home over the weekend. We took her to Paoli at 5:00 p.m. to get the bus back. On account of high water we couldn't get to Orleans. Good luck.

Your dad,

James G. Berkey

March 6, 1945

Unit History

Training Schedule: 0830-0900 Policing of area, 0900-1000 Dismounted Road March, 0900-1100 Radio School (3 men in each platoon will attend), 1000-1030 Map Reading, 1030-1130 Use of Compass at Night, 1030-1130 Gunnery & Crew Drill (AG Platoon, 81mm Mortar Platoon, Heavy Machine Gun Platoon), 1130-1200 Military Courtesy & Bearing (Stress Saluting), 1300-1400 Use of Binoculars, 1400-1500 Maintenance of Weapons & Vehicles, 1500-1600 Athletics. 255 enlisted men and 7 officers left Saessolsheim, France, at 1815 hours on mounted march of 15 miles and arrived at Pfaffenhoffen, France, at 2100 hours. Company setting up defensive positions around town.

March 7, 1945

Unit History

Patrol record: Patrol heard small amount of movement and talking in sand pit. Found unoccupied foxhole along east side of trail at crucifix. Foxhole approximately 4 feet deep and 3 feet in diameter. Could hear vehicles moving in Bitschhoffen. Vehicles would stop moving when "artificial moonlight" was turned on. Patrol returned at 2250.

March 9, 1945

Mother to Richard

Dear Richard,

Daddy and I have just come from Dee's funeral, so I want to tell you about it. It was this afternoon at our church. I told you, I am sure, that the Church of Christ burned, and the congregation is meeting in the library basement. The house was full and the Legion members did not even get in. The young Church of Christ preacher was the speaker and he was very good. Five people did the singing. Of course the casket could not be open. They just had a photograph. Stanley Robinson escorted the body home, and came in with Mr. and Mrs. Bush. They are just completely heartbroken. Mrs. Bush had a cold anyway and this sorrow nearly killed her. They thought for a while she couldn't even come to the funeral.

We went to the cemetery. Dee's grave is the second one to be dug on the right-hand side of the road as you go in the first entrance. It is back of the cottage, which is almost directly west of the Catholic church. We sent flowers for ourselves and a separate spray for you. Betty Nelle and Martha were collecting for flowers for your high school class, so we contributed a little to that fund, too. We have not yet been out to the house, but we will go later. There has been such a mob out there.

If you ever get back, you will have to be more of a son to the Bush folks than ever. They certainly need you. We are so sorry for them. I saw that Jane was at the funeral. Dee went to see the Coffmans the night he ate supper here. We heard afterward that he left on the late train from Scottsburg that night.

Did Daddy and I tell you we had a letter from Dee written February 24? He called you "the big one." He had promised to write when he heard from you. At the time he was here, we were wondering just how badly you were wounded. He told us in the letter that the Robbins boy was down there at Alexandria, Louisiana.

This is a beautiful bright day, but windy. We have a row of yellow crocus blooms. Also, we have a bouquet of pussy willows.

We got a letter from you today. We are glad you are out of the hospital but are afraid for you to be in combat again. We also heard from Jonas. He will be at the hospital another two weeks and then go back to Miami. They have promised him shore duty for six months, which we think is wonderful. He says the PGM David is on is a Patrol Motor Gunboat, which patrols the islands where there are still Japs and helps maintain a blockade. He said he is probably based on an island 100 miles south of Bougainville. We are thrilled to hear that part of the First Army has crossed the Rhine.

Love,

Mother

March 10, 1945

Unit History

Company in defensive position, vicinity of Pfaffenhoffen, France. Receiving few rounds of artillery, sending out occasional patrols. Enemy action—light. Weather cloudy, intermittent showers. Morale of troops high.

March 11, 1945

Unit History

1st Lt. William Broadwater promoted to Captain, principal duty Armored Infantry Unit Commander.

Mother to Richard

Dear Richard,

Eugene Rodman's mother stopped this afternoon to leave some of your property, the brown student lamp and *Heath's German Dictionary*. I didn't know they had them. She said Rodman was in England. They've been staying with the Everett Graves this winter but are going back to the farm right away. We had a light milktoast Sunday night supper, as Daddy was "off his feed" and the rest were not hungry. We are listening to the radio and the war news sounds hopeful at least. This commentator predicts the complete breakdown of Germany in April. He says Jap shipping is about ruined, to the Dutch East Indies and around the China Sea, but warns that the Jap Army is still intact and will have to be met on the mainland.

Have you ever heard from Buster? Ida says Junior had written you, but got no reply. He has been around Luxembourg. The First, Third, and Ninth are in the news a lot now. We hope the Seventh is chiefly holding territory. Plenty of mountainous country ahead, it seems.

Love,

Mother

March 14, 1945

Unit History

Cpl. Garold Betters, killed in action, vicinity of LaWalck, France.

March 15, 1945

Unit History

Medical Detachment—1 officer and 9 enlisted men became medical component of Task Force Blue leaving 3 officers and 13 enlisted men as medical component of Task Force 68th Armored Infantry Battalion. 9 enlisted men attached to companies as aid men. Vehicles left Ettendorf at 1430 hours and arrived at Pfaffenhoffen, France, at 1500 hours. 5 officers and 245 enlisted men left Pfaffenhoffen at 1700 hours on mounted march of 9 miles and arrived at Bouxwiller, France, at 1745 hours. Company billeted in town, reorganizing and awaiting orders. S/Sgt. Ralph Huff, killed in action, vicinity of Pfaffenhoffen as of 14 March 1945. Pfc. George Young, lightly wounded in action.

Rodman to Richard, writing from France

Dear Richard,

How's everything with you by now, old man? I still haven't heard of your condition from any source. I'm hoping for the best for you. I did receive two copies of the *Leader* quite recently and in one of them I read an article about Frank Crockett who I think is in your outfit. I take it from that that you are somewhere in Southern France. I have read quite a few articles about your outfit and it seems to be pretty hot. I still say we may meet over here sometime.

As for me, I don't think too much of this #$%^&* place!! We have a better setup here than we had in England but I miss going out to the towns and places for general sightseeing. We lived in a lousy place in England but the towns around were very nice. Of course I spent a good time in London, which is almost like civilization again.

And I managed to stay single during all my tours of the world and over here I feel pretty safe. While in England I met up with some big English lady wrestler who just about killed me. It's good that I left there!

Did I tell you I had a five-day leave at the port? That was some time ago but I had a real nice time. I saw some of the old gang. Julia has lots of new records I had to hear. Very good ones they were, too! It looks like a big dance coming once we hit the U.S.A. again. She is also planning a trip to San Francisco this summer. Doesn't sound bad, does it? That gripes me to no end. Here I am touring the world under the worst conditions and I haven't even seen the West Coast yet.

Well, I'm about dead with a cold so I'll close for now and write more later. Here's wishing you all the luck in the world and I hope to hear from you!

Yours,

Rodman

March 17, 1945

Unit History

Pfc. Joseph Zabadah and Tec 5 Robert Wood, lightly wounded in action as of 15 March 45.

March 18, 1945

Unit History

Beginning at 0337, 68th and attachments (25th Tank Battalion on right and 3rd DIA on right)[79] launched attack on axis Surbourg, Rittershoffen, Niederrœdern, Oberlauterbach, Salmbach. Proceeded along route meeting no enemy resistance until held up by blown out bridge. Captured Salmbach and completed mopping up of town at 1905. Outposting town with tanks and infantry, preparing to probe as directed. Night patrols reconnoitering roads and bridges. One prisoner turned himself in to the battalion surgeon. 240 enlisted men and 5 officers left Bouxwiller at 0350 hours on mounted march to Salmbach, France, and arrived at 2000 hours.

Mother to Richard

Dear Richard,

We got your letter of March 4th last Thursday. You seemed to be quiet then, but we have been reading of the advance of the Seventh. Hope you got your Bronze Star before moving. We are proud of you. Today we have been reading about the collapse of the bridge over which the First, etc., were passing into Germany. The news said it was almost repaired already.

This afternoon we visited the Claude Bush family a little while. Glad to see the old farm where you have so often been. It's greening up and looks pretty. It has been almost hot today. The Bushes are still very sad. Mrs. Bush says she is so weak because she can hardly eat. She has had lots of letters and messages, some

---

79   3rd DIA: 3rd Algerian Infantry Division, a French unit. —Ed.

from people she does not know. We saw a picture of Dee's girl, Marilyn Thompson, of Cedar Rapids, Iowa, to whom he was engaged. She has written to them several times. Dee wrote home and to his girl on the Saturday he was killed. He told the girl he somehow felt he shouldn't go up that day, but had to. Since Dee's death they have learned that Marilyn's father wrote to a prominent Salem man to ask about Dee because he "was paying attention to his girl." The man said he wrote back nothing but praise. Your packages are coming—cookies and candy in one and baking powder, etc. in the other. Please read the newspaper around the baking powder. The obituary of Dee is enclosed.

Love,

Mother

March 19, 1945

Unit History

245 enlisted men and 5 officers arrived at Oberseebach, France, at 0130 hours. Company billeted in town. Sent 1st and 3rd platoons to Schleithal, France, to secure town. Remainder of company left Oberseebach at 0700 hours on mounted march of 8 miles and arrived at Schleithal at 0930 hours. Company advancing toward the Lauter River to make a crossing. 68th relieved of responsibility in Salmbach sector by 3rd DIA at 1510. Unit and attachments began mounted motor march from Salmbach at 1745. Closed in Schweighofen at 2135. Maintaining contact with 25th Tank Battalion and elements of 36th Infantry Division.

Virginia to Richard

Dearest Richard,

I'm afraid I've been neglecting you again, dopey, but here goes at last. Last week when I learned about Dee, I tried to write but couldn't. The only thing I *can* say is: I feel all the things you always want to say but can't. I guess there isn't any answer to death. I've always believed in immortality, still do, and I don't think I'll be afraid when my time comes along even though I don't anticipate it for about 50 years. But then you know more of its meaning than I.

It looks as though in a couple of weeks I'll be saying goodbye to the man in my life who means the most to me, outside of you boys. Phil wrote today, he's still in Washington and may see Lucy. He is going to try to make it here before going out as a brand new ensign on a cruiser or battleship. No he isn't a new one, the one I've known for two years, met him up here. Not too serious, but we agree with you along those lines.

How do you like the new stationery? Crane's, best there is. They make the government currency, you know.

Well, dopey, I just had my locks whacked off, now they are beautifully short and unruly. The kids teased me and called me "Maria" as in Maria from Hemingway's *For Whom the Bell Tolls*, you know. Or do you? They made a movie of it.

Last week, the Mortar Board sponsored a Red Cross drive and it was a whopping success! Approximately $2,500 was raised in one night. President Wells "sold" his car and a gas coupon for the Junior Prom, Dean Katy "sold" a chocolate cake of her own concoction, Mr. McClintock "sold" a shoeshine (his red beard is shaved off as a result of Dewey losing), and Pronco "sold" his singing table waiter performance for one evening, etc. It was fun and worthwhile. Also at the theater, they have been driving for money, and getting it. Two wounded boys from Indianapolis talked this weekend, very well, too. One had been in Burma, one over Berlin, and both have one leg in a cast.

Tonight it poured rain and I got caught in it and fairly drowned. I met Julia, or rather ran into her at the library and she told me about hearing from you, about being obstetrician to a cow—ha! Not bad! I guess, after such experience, I need never worry about being caught. Ha. I'll bring my pet poodles to you.

Spring is really here, the forsythia is in full bloom, the violets, the trees shading that tender new green of the buds. Is the scenery, any you've seen, beautiful, very different? Mr. Thompson tells about his three trips down and up the Rhine, of the Lorelei Rock, etc. Old windbag, but nice. He's written too many books.

Well darlin', must do a bit of bookworming before I get some shut-eye. I'm keeping up with the Seventh in the paper daily. The ring seems to be closing in and I know that as they push, you are back in there working yourself to pieces. Do be careful. I know you're all doing more than your share and I'm proud of you. But do be careful. You know, somebody's going to have to help me with those six kids I'm going to have. On second thought, three would be plenty. Ha.

Write when you can.

My Love,

Virginia

March 20, 1945

Unit History

Patrol #1 left Schweighofen at 0200 using route 500 yards south of main road in a northeasterly direction to Kapsweyer. At Kapsweyer, checked a few houses and no signs of enemy were found. Fresh tank tracks observed south of town. About No. 6 type wire cable was observed stretched between houses. Gun flashes were observed directly north of town. Position of guns believed to be from 3-5 km north of Kapsweyer. Fresh foxholes were observed. Patrol returned at 0320. Lightly wounded in action: S/Sgt. Leonard Sciullo, Sgt. George Morris, Pfc. Frank Christlieb, Pfc. Abraham Wisotski, Pfc. Frank Libecki, Pfc. Robert Turner, Pfc. John Carfagno, Tec 5 Elvin Mude.

Sgt. Harold D. Bush Killed In Plane Crash

Funeral Service Scheduled For Friday Afternoon. Body To Be Buried With Military Honors In Crown Hill.

Mr. and Mrs. Claude Bush, of Salem Rt. 4, received a message Sunday night from Colonel Quentin T. Quick, Air Corps Commanding Officer, that their son Sgt. Harold D. Bush, 23, radio operator, lost his life at approximately eight o'clock Saturday night in the crash of an airplane near Alexandria, La. Army Airfield, while on a routine flight. All eleven members of the Flying Fortress crew were killed.

Mr. and Mrs. Bush had been notified Sunday afternoon by Colonel Quick, that their son was reported missing in an aircraft flight from the station. "The aircraft departed from this station at 4:15 o'clock March 3, for a six-hour local flight. No report from the aircraft has been received since 7:45 p. m. Further details will be furnished as they become available from searching facilities, which are now being utilized to the greatest extent."

A message was received Wednesday morning stating the body escorted by Cpl. Stanley Robbins will arrive in Salem Wednesday night.

The funeral service will be held at 2:30 o'clock Friday afternoon at the First Christian church by the Rev. Richard Lee Curry, pastor of the Salem Church of Christ. The body will be interred with military honors in Crown Hill cemetery.

Sgt. Bush was graduated from Salem high school in 1940. He was a highly valued member of the S. H. S. basketball team.

Sgt. Bush entered service in July, 1942. During his period of service he had been stationed in Florida, West Virginia, North Carolina, Iowa, California, South Dakota, Arizona, Nebraska and Louisiana.

Surviving are the parents and an only sister Mrs. Arthur Lee Maudlin, who resides west of Salem.

Newspaper clip courtesy of the Salem Leader; Dee Bush courtesy of the Washington County Historical Society

182   KAREN BERKEY HUNTSBERGER

March 21, 1945

Unit History

20 March 45—245 enlisted men and 6 officers left Schleithal, France, at 0230 hours on mounted march of 3 miles to one mile north of Altenstadt, France. Company dismounted and marched on foot to Kapsweyer, Germany, and set up positions. Pfc. Hermerigildo Martinez lightly wounded in action.

March 22, 1945

Unit History

Company on outposting and patrolling duties. Pfc. George Benesh lightly wounded in action.

March 23, 1945

Unit History

Company left Kapsweyer, Germany, and moved on foot to Schaidt, Germany.

March 24, 1945

Unit History

Company left Schaidt, Germany, on mounted march at 1900 hours 23 March 45, distance 6 miles. Company closed in bivouac area at 0230 hours at one mile west of Hatzenbühl, Germany, awaiting orders. Left bivouac area at 1130 hours on mounted march of 10 miles, closed in bivouac area at 1430 hours approximately 1 mile south of Bellheim, Germany, awaiting orders. S/Sgt. James Kollias lightly wounded in action as of 23 March 45.

March 25, 1945

Unit History

230 enlisted men and 6 officers left 1 mile south of Bellheim, Germany, at 1730 hours 24 March 45 on mounted march of 8 miles to Freckenfeld, Germany. Company billeted in town awaiting orders. Pfc. Neil Rich lightly wounded in action as of 23 March 45.

Richard's Journal

Received mail and very sad news. Dad wrote me that Dee was killed in flight near Alexandria, Louisiana. It makes me feel so bad, all the suffering his folks must endure.

Mother to Richard

Dear Richard,

Again we are quite anxious. Our last word from you was written March 4. We have been eagerly listening to and reading news about the big offensive. Tonight we learned that the 7th Army is on the banks of the Rhine, just ready to follow the armies that have crossed. A great show, but dangerous! May you come through safely!

The Crocketts were out today. Said Buster did lose the sight of one eye. He is now in the Instrumaster Division doing mechanical drawing. Mattie thought his APO was 170, but will write me. We are fine. Beautiful weather continues and flowers are blooming. Easter Sunday preparations are underway. No letter from Lucy lately. Virginia's commencement is April 22. Jonas was still waiting around the hospital, the last we heard. David's PGM-5 has a new base. He went north and crossed the equator again. He must be in the southern part of the Philippines.

Harold and Mary Elizabeth Cook, Junior Paynter, and Roger Moss are recent ones at home. Brooks Baynes and Billy Seat are still missing in action. Max Collins was wounded in the side at Iwo Jima.

Love,

Mother

March 26, 1945

Unit History

Company left Freckenfeld, Germany, at 1830 hours 25 March 45 on mounted march of 5 miles to Rheinzabern, Germany. Company guarding ammo dump.

March 27, 1945

Unit History

Headquarters CC "R" 14th Armored Division,
A.P.O. 446 U.S. Army, March 27, 1945
Subject: Commendation
To: Officers and Men of 68th AIB, 62nd AIB, and
Company A, 48th Tank Battalion.

1. In the operation just past, this combat command played an important part in breaching the Siegfried Line and the closing of a pocket, which resulted in the destruction or capture of all the enemy forces in the Palatinate.

2. The line through which you passed was part of the greatest system of fortifications in the history of warfare. That part of the line which you overcame was one of the strongest links in this entire system. The enemy who were driven before you

made a strong and determined defense until their will to fight was broken by the force of your attack.

3. The officers and men of the 68th AIB, 62nd AIB, and Company A, 48th Tank Battalion, showed dogged determination and great courage in the face of intense artillery, rocket, and mortar fire over a period of days and an aggressive attitude, which carried them to their successive objectives through a hail of small arms and supporting antitank fire.

4. I give my thanks and my congratulations to you who succeeded so brilliantly in the difficult task presented you. Your successful assault upon this fortified area with minimum losses is an achievement which burns bright in the action which swept the enemy to the Rhine.

D.H. Hudelson

Colonel, Infantry, Commanding

Richard's Journal

Am at aid station now. My dental bridge fell out and Capt. Miller just put it back in.[80] Went through a pillbox, indeed quite a thing, never saw anything like it.[81] Am going back up to ammo dump with C Company tonight.[82] Has been so much news and so little and late mail I hardly know which end is up. I haven't written in here since Feb. 13. I need to record it now so I won't forget. Discharged from hospital Feb. 22. Back to outfit after messing around a couple of days at outfit at Ringelsdorf, France. Sure glad to be back. Boys have really been through plenty (hear lots about Hatten and Rittershoffen). Buster was hit in neck and eye at Rittershoffen. Received a letter from him saying he was reclassified, etc. Sure glad to hear that. On Feb. 26,

---

80 Miller was the Medical Battalion dentist. —Ed.
81 Pillboxes were made of concrete and dug into the ground. They were often circular or hexagonal in shape, resembling the containers in which pills were once sold. Pillboxes had openings through which weapons could be fired. —Ed.
82 Ammunition dump: military storage area for explosives and ammunition. —Ed.

went back on line with 3rd Platoon C Company. Ross is Lieutenant now. Strowbridge, Deck, and Billhymer made Lieutenant and have 2nd Platoon. March 1—Received orders that had won a Bronze Star citation for Oberotterbach, Germany, back in December. March 5—received the Bronze Star from Brig. Gen. Smith, CO of 14th Armored in the afternoon. Scotty received a Silver Star and Mude a Bronze, too.[83] Had the whole 68th AIB out in a wheat field outside Saessolsheim, France. Cold blue Monday and a French farmer was plowing with oxen in a field ahead of us. Had to borrow all the clothes I wore since all mine were dirty. March 6-7 we moved to Pfaffenhofen and La Walck. 36th shoved off thru us to open drive of 7th on Siegfried Line about the 16th-17th. Ross left outfit to go to colored infantry outfit, good boy. March 18-24—cracked Siegfried Line and moved back in Germany. Am in Freckenfeld now, the town taken by ½ of 3rd Platoon C Co. with Medic Richard Berkey attached. Also took Schaidt, the town, back on the 23rd. The 23rd was the most fun had since I've been over here.

Unit History

Headquarters 14th Armored Division, AP0 446, U.S. Army

General Order Number 23, 26 Feb 1945

AWARD OF THE BRONZE STAR MEDAL

By direction of the President, under the provisions of Army Regulations 600-45, 22 September 1943, as amended, the

---

83   Tec 3 Glenn Scott received the Silver Star for bringing casualties from exposed positions under fire to a cellar in a house. He treated them there and left the ones who could not be moved. The next afternoon, evacuation of these men was attempted, but the aid men were fired upon. Scotty, under cover of darkness, set out with a patrol of four men to retrieve the casualties. Along the way, the patrol encountered some of the walking wounded making their way back to the aid station. Arriving at the cellar, they found the wounded had been removed by the enemy and only the dead remained, identified from dog tags. Hazelton, Ken, *Unit History, 68th Armored Infantry Battalion Medical Detachment, from Port of Embarkation to V-E Day*, Booklet (1945).

Bronze Star Medal is awarded by the Division Commander to the following named individual:

RICHARD J. BERKEY, 35 694 300, Private First Class, Medical Detachment, Armored Infantry Battalion, 14th Armored Division. For heroic achievement near Oberotterbach, Germany, on 18 December 1944. Early in the attack against the town, Private Berkey was hit by a shell fragment that lodged itself in his right arm. Despite his painful injury he continually circulated among the wounded of his platoon administering first aid. Before going to the rear to have his own wounds attended to, he made a search of his platoon's area to ascertain that all casualties had been evacuated. Private Berkey's courage and commendable devotion to duty were an encouragement and a memorable example to his platoon. Entered military service from Salem, Indiana.

Richard to Folks

Dear Folks,

Has been quite some time since I've written, but finally got around to it. Got back in Germany again it seems and at least this time I didn't get hit. However, 'twas quite tiresome and I'm completely worn out, generally speaking. My bridge fell out the other day and I had it put in by Capt. Miller this evening. Have received some mail recently, but was not so new.

Just finished cooking up three pigeons and they sure smell good. Was going to make biscuits but couldn't find any baking powder. Think I'll go eat. Am well and fine.

Love,

Richard

March 29, 1945

Virginia to Richard

Dearest Richard,

Even though I have not been writing often, I want you to know that I think of you often and pray that all is well with you.

News about the 7th Army these past few weeks has been spectacular. Today it tells about Mannheim and about a prisoner of war hospital the Seventh found in terrific condition. I wondered if maybe you were around.

Three weeks from Sunday on April 22, I graduate. The folks will come, maybe our neighbors, the Cooks, too. This Monday evening, the dorm gave *me* a banquet—I'm their only senior! Gave me a beautiful plastic and mirrored compact. Was I surprised! They told crazy stories on me and gushed about, too. Ha.

I haven't yet decided what I'm going to do this summer. Probably help houseclean first, maybe paint or sew a little. Have even been contemplating getting a job at DuPont for the money.

Doc Paynter is home, also J.W. Colglazier, Jim Huffman is on New Guinea, Rodman is in England, V.A. Smith was telling me yesterday.

I've been taking shots for next year, three typhoid so far. The last made me sick, my arm swelled and was so sore I couldn't touch or move it. I thought about you and knew you must have been that way two months instead of two days.

Well, dopey, guess I'll say bye for now, have got to get ready for the last meeting of the English club. Ugh.

Lots of Love,

Virginia

March 30, 1945

Unit History

Training Schedule: 0830-0900 Policing of Area, 0900-1000 Dismounted Cross Country Road March, 1000-1100 Basic Instruction on Mines & Booby Traps (Use War Dept. Pamphlet 21-23 "Don't Get Killed by Mines & Booby Traps"), 1100-1130 Military Courtesy, 1300-1400 Security, 1400-1500 Maintenance of Weapons & Vehicles, 1500-1600 Weapons Inspection (all individual weapons will be inspected).

March 31, 1945

Unit History

6 officers and 232 enlisted men left Freckenfeld, Germany, at 1830 hours en route to destination unknown.

Richard's Journal

We moved out and up the Rhine through Bergzabern and Worms crossing the Rhine River in that vicinity on March 31 about 2:30 in the morning. There was moonlight and it was very beautiful on a pontoon bridge, but nevertheless just another river. Afterwards we went up the autobahn to Darmstadt and to Dieburg and spent the day there, moving out again that night. Easter but didn't go to church. Thus we started our big drive thru Germany, town after town after town. Some we fought for, some we passed thru like a whirlwind, always stopping, most of the time, at night in a town and had us some nice ham and eggs—what a life. During the day eat K rations and at night the Jerries' food.

CHAPTER TEN
THE FINAL PUSH

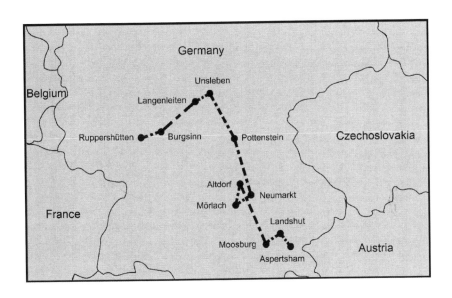

April 1, 1945

Unit History

C Company—232 enlisted men and 6 officers arrived at Dieburg, Germany, at 0600 hours from mounted march of 114 miles. Roads good, weather clear, and morale high. Company billeted in town awaiting orders, outposting assembly area and performing maintenance and resupply of vehicles. Battalion remained on alert status.

April 2, 1945

Unit History

Battalion and attachments (B-68, C-68, HQ Co-68, 1-A-636 TD (tank destroyer), 1-C-94, 1-C-125, Medical Detachment, Combat

Trains)[84] crossed initial point at Dieburg, via route Babenhausen, Schaafheim, Großostheim, Großwallstadt, stream crossing over Main River, Wintersbach, Heimbuchenthal, Weibersbrunn (passed through elements of 3rd Infantry Division) attacking within their zone, Rothenbuch, Partenstein, Burgsinn, Schönderling with objective Ostheim. 500th Armored Field Artillery in direct support. Company dismounted at 1700, began attack on Partenstein with B-68 on left and C-68 on right, tanks supporting. Attack moved from west to east along railroad. Company C was in town by 1955 hours.

April 3, 1945

Unit History

At 0900 B-68 and C-68 cleared Partenstein and outposted. 350 civilians held, requested military government personnel or CIC to take over prisoners. Left Partenstein on mounted march at 1030 hours bypassing blown bridge by crossing stream. At 1210 captured trainload of explosives, ammunition, and miscellaneous material. Captured Ruppertshütten without resistance at 1620. At 1900 moved into Rengersbrunn with tanks and dismounted infantry. C-68 held up by unknown source, unable to advance. Half-track knocked out at 1950. At 2000 medics report too many casualties, ambulances needed immediately. Rengersbrunn finally taken at 2020 with 4 personnel casualties, loss of tank and half-track. Total prisoners of war taken—33, plus 27 Russian forced laborers.

April 4, 1945

Unit History

At 0845 leading elements halted by roadblock. Moved up tank to blow it out. Dismounted infantry heading into town. Receiving enemy resistance from far end. Fellen cleared at 1000 hours. Timber

---

84   Combat Trains: attached support elements of a combat unit. The trains usually consisted of trucks with fuel and ammo, maintenance, the medical detachment and other headquarters elements. —Ed.

roadblock encountered at 1050 hours when leaving Fellen and small arms, machine gun, and burp gun fire came from left flank. At 1245 stiff enemy resistance encountered in Burgsinn by enemy occupying high ground east of town. Must resupply ammo and bring in tanks with infantry. Burgsinn cleared by 1520 hours. Captured trainload of medical supplies, ordnance, and signal equipment. 32 prisoners of war taken. Lightly wounded in action: Pfc. Monte Peterson, Pfc. Stanley Richardson, 2nd Lt. Harold Hanhardt, Pvt. Willard Arthurs.

April 5, 1945

Unit History

At 0330 column was held up by heavy fire on outskirts of Gräfendorf. Attack resumed at 0645. Gräfendorf cleared by 0910. Russian prisoners of war reported munitions factory at Wildflecken guarded by SS troops. Left Gräfendorf at 1230 hours on motor march to Waizenbach. Defense bypassed after heavy fire at Wartmannsroth. Dismounted troops entered Völkersleier at 1740, cleared by 1820. 38 prisoners of war taken today, 2 through medical channels. Billeted at Völkersleier. Lightly wounded in action: T/Sgt. William Strowbridge, Jr., Pfc. Claud Wilson, Pfc. Wallace Engle, Tec 5 Herbert Mullins, Pfc. Robert Colvin, Pfc. Leland Elmore. Sgt. Alex Robb, seriously wounded in action. Killed in action: Pfc. Waymon Temple and Pfc. Charles Wright as of 4 April 45.

April 6, 1945

Unit History

6 officers and 219 enlisted men left Völkersleier at 0930 hours, Schönderling taken at 1340. Proceeded past friendly infantry in Schondra. Passed through Geroda, Waldfenster, Burkardroth, Stangenroth, Gefäll and attacked Langenleiten. Langenleiten cleared at 1930 hours. Three half-tracks knocked out. 21 prisoners of war to cage, one through medical channels. 10 PWs handed over to military government in Völkersleier, knocked out three enemy trucks. Lightly

wounded in action: Pfc. Robert Brown, Pfc. Aaron McGlothlin, Pfc. Maryus Rowe, Pfc. Elmer Woods. Pfc. Larry Sanders seriously wounded in action.

April 7, 1945

Unit History

Jumped off at 0615. At 1000 hours attacked Sandberg with dismounted infantry under cover of smoke. One of our tanks hit three times. Sandberg cleared and outposted by 1100. Attacked Kilianshof at 1400, cleared by 1500. Twenty horse-drawn vehicles fired on by our artillery on road from Wegfurt to Schönau an der Brend. Approximately half destroyed, balance dispersed. At 1850 head of column at Weisbach (friendly troops already there). At 1945 leading elements at Simonshof sending in dismounted patrol. Entered Unsleben at 2120. Total prisoners taken—18. Pfc. Louis Barton, lightly injured in action. Pfc. Frank Fillippo, lightly wounded in action. 1st Lt. Woodrow Miller, Armored Infantry Unit Commander, lightly wounded in action as of 6 April 45. Pfc. Charles Nelson, killed in action as of 6 April 1945. Died of wounds as of 6 April 1945: Pfc. Larry Sanders, Pfc. Richard Dunn, Tec 5 Alvin Spoerl.

April 8, 1945

Unit History

Occupied Unsleben at 0122 hours. Discovered in former Jewish Tabernacle in Unsleben great amount of electrical equipment, calipers, grindstones, pumice, etc., that had been partially looted by civilians. Freight cars contain medical equipment. Mellrichstadt cleared at 1610, bridges blown. 99 prisoners of war taken, 30 evacuated through 1st Battalion, 15th Regiment.

Richard to Folks

Dear Folks,

It has been quite some time since I last wrote. Have a few minutes now so will let you know I'm okay. Seems as if I've only written a couple of letters in the last month or so. I imagine not only you, but all my other correspondents are wondering what's happened to me. Pardon the bullet hole through this stationery, 'tis a Jerry infliction. The bullet went right smack through all my stationery, envelopes and all. Don't get the wrong idea, I wasn't even close to this at the time.

I've learned about Dee from Dad's V-mail and Mother's letters of yesterday and today. I really don't know what to write to the Bushes. Thanks for telling me all about the funeral and everything, Mother. I'm sure glad he finally got home for Christmas. I know it meant so much to his folks. Last time I saw him I guess was when he last took me back to Darnell two years ago. I didn't know Dee was engaged.

Received a fruitcake from Lucy today and was sure good. Also received two pairs of socks from her some time ago. And well and okey-dokey—

Love,

Richard

Sunday night!
Apr 8 1945

Dear Folks,

It has been quite some time since I last wrote. Have a few minutes now so will let you know I'm O.K. Seems as if I'd only written a couple of letters in the last month or so. I imagine not only you, but all my other correspondents are wondering whats happened to me ———→ pardon this hole — tis a Jerry infliction — the bullet went right smack through all my stationery - envelopes & all! Don't get the wrong idea, I wasn't even close to this at the time.

The letter with the bullet hole

KAREN BERKEY HUNTSBERGER

Richard to Folks

Dear Folks,

Dad said something about writing requests on a separate sheet so would like some pancake flour. Some buckwheat stuff, Aunt Jemima or something like that. Also cookies or something of the sort, whatever is convenient. I hope these requests don't cause too much trouble—thanks!

I've never received the Christmas packages, only from DeJeans, Ida, Virginia, and the church back in December. Thanks again—

Love,

Richard

April 9, 1945

Unit History

Road reconnaissance made to northeast and northwest. Balance of unit and attachments except those guarding bridges and acting as left flank security for XV Corps remained in assembly area at Unsleben, carrying out maintenance of vehicles and weapons. 1st Platoon outposting town. 2nd Platoon outposting Mittelstreu, Germany. Weather fine and morale very high.

April 10, 1945

Unit History

Battalion remained in assembly area at Unsleben on alert status. 1st Sgt. Charles Harwood, lightly wounded in action. Pfc. Freeman Nicholas, killed in action as of 6 April 1945.

Virginia to Richard

Dearest Richard,

After about a month of silence where your letters were concerned had passed, I was getting worried, but today I learned that Julia heard from you Saturday so I feel better. I've been keeping up with you in a vague sort of way through the daily maps and news (I really do read them) and half learn what you couldn't say anyway. It looks to me as though covering so much territory so fast you wouldn't have time to even sleep, but I hope you are well. I read Tolstoy's *War and Peace* this weekend for class and contrasted as much as I know of this war with that. Doubtless and obviously (as you laugh over my usual stating of the obvious) there are many similarities with the human and mechanized sides as well as vast differences. The book contains the most vivid pictures of the horrible situation at that time from the medical viewpoint. Each time a death was described, it struck me that almost all could have been prevented with the knowledge of today, and it makes me proud to know that since you have to be in war, that you are in that part of it. Also, more and more I'm anticipating next fall and my introduction to it.

School looks the best to me it has for a long time. That is because I'm graduating, naturally. Today was my last Monday in classes here, a beautiful spring day, hot sun, the redbud trees still flowering. Spring has come so early that for a month, we have had fairly decent weather. Everything has been especially verdant and beautiful, the dogwood and forsythia, the magnolias, the budding leaflets, violets. I took my English Comprehensive and passed it. Ah, sigh of relief. Diploma paid for, finals, graduation the afternoon of the 22nd. Then goodbye IU for me. I am both sad and glad, as any senior is. Will send you a picture of me in my cap and gown.

Just read the news and it says the 7th Army is at Crailsheim. Well, dopey, I must get to work on that dear zoology. I've promised myself to have all my lessons this last week. Ha. Fine time to start studying. Be good and take care of yourself!

Lots of Love,

Virginia

P.S. We'll clean house when I go home, but if you'll write *me* and say, "How about some cookies?" I'd love to make you some!

April 11, 1945

Unit History

C Company—211 enlisted men and 4 officers left Unsleben at 1600 hours on mounted march of 24 miles and arrived at Gompertshausen, Germany, at 1900 hours. Passed through Heustreu, Hollstadt, Wülfershausen, Aubstadt, Bad Königshofen, Eyershausen, Trappstadt, Linden, and Schlechtsart. Company billeted in town outposting. Awaiting orders. 3 men joined company from 71st Reinforcement Battalion.

April 12, 1945

Unit History

Left Gompertshausen at 0615, cleared Rieth at 0700, Helligen at 0710, and Poppenhausen 0730. Four men with white flags came out of Dürrenried. Cleared Lechenroth at 0900, Oberelldorf at 0913, Unterelldorf at 0930, and Rothenberg at 0940. At 0950 head of column passed Report Line No. 4, Heilgersdorf, friendly troops in Memmelsdorf. Cleared Setzelsdorf at 1030, Memmelsdorf at 1040, Bodelstadt at 1150, Pülsdorf at 1207, Eggenbach at 1212, and Döringstadt at 1230. C-68 went into Dittersbrunn with a dismounted squad at 1640. Battalion closed 1855 in Unterneuses, Pferdsfeld, Dittersbrunn, Prächting, command post in Pferdsfeld. Prisoners of war taken—18.

April 13, 1945

Unit History

0800—road to Dittersbrunn impassable, other route passable but very bad. 1315—towns of Kümmel, Unterküps, Oberküps, Kleukheim, and Roschlaub all occupied by friendly troops. Two enemy medical officers, 10 enemy aid men, and 17 wounded enemy in civilian hospital in Kutzenberg. At 2040 69 Hungarian prisoners of war with six horses surrendered. One enemy anti-tank gun captured. At 2240 Scheßlitz almost cleared. Total prisoners of war—90.

Richard to Folks

Dear Folks,

Have a little time again to drop a line and will do so. I'm writing this in a German home. Fixed myself ham and eggs this morning for breakfast. And had the famous German black bread along with it, or I guess 'tis black bread, big round loaves hard on the outside and very soggy in the middle. It ain't so hot but I can eat it.

Baked some more biscuits the other day. Also made some drop raisin cookies and ended up making a chocolate cake, which wasn't too bad I didn't think. At least I didn't sleep any that night—ha! Baking powder still seems to be the hardest thing to get hold of. Had some pancakes the other morning, too—boy! They were really okay. Put a couple eggs in 'em and a can of milk. I'm beginning to think I'm learning more about cooking than anything else over here.

The other day I sent a Jerry flag. Maybe you'll get it in a month or so. It's a captured item. I know because I got it myself out of a town hall in one of these towns. Took down the flag and put up a white one—ha! More fun.

Had some Limburger cheese the other day, Dad, 'twas really good. It was Jerry stuff in a big number 10 can, part of their soldier rations I guess.

What gets me in these houses is the barn next door. You open a door thinking it's going into a bedroom and whatcha know you're in a stable with three or four cows. You walk out on the front porch and there lies a stinking pile of stuff they cleaned out of the stables. Some of these houses stink so bad I don't see how people can stand to live in them. The higher the pile, the higher the status—ha! Sometimes animals are even kept in the cellar below the house.

They also use the cows to plow with. Have seen only a few horses and relatively little modern farm machinery.

Saw a new scarecrow yesterday. White chicken feathers stuck in a potato and suspended from a stake by means of a string. Looked rather effective. Saw about a dozen of them in a garden.

Guess I can use more baking powder and pancake flour if you care to send it. Would also like any kind of eats. Have never received a box from home yet. Mind sending a book of airmail stamps? Thanks! Am well and fine.

Love,

Richard

April 14, 1945

Unit History

Scheßlitz taken at 0010. Captured 3 motorcycles, destroyed 2 track personnel carriers vicinity of Scheßlitz. Large crater, not repairable, caused delay. Two 500 pound bombs found under road. Forward elements now at Steinfeld—0900 hours. At 1250 caught enemy convoy of 12 vehicles leaving Drosendorf an der Aufseß. Captured 29 prisoners of war, 4 vehicles destroyed. At 1410 destroyed one more motorcycle, towed 75 mm gun, enemy kitchen trailer, and records of enemy battalion. Found abandoned small ammo dump. Head of column arrived Neuhaus at 1400. Aufseß cleared at 1435, Sachsendorf at 1505. Vehicles destroyed: 6 trucks, 4 personnel carriers, 4 towed 75 mm anti-tank guns, 3 motorcycles, 3 flak wagons, one light tank, 3 horse-drawn wagons. Captured 4 ambulances, 12 horses. 3 enemy killed. 156 prisoners of war evacuated to headquarters, 4 through medics. Total prisoners for today—253.

Buster to Richard

Hello Richard,

I received your most welcome letter today and it was post-marked March the 3rd. I sent you a letter in care of C Company and I hope you got it alright. I didn't know whether you were back with the outfit or not. I was in hopes you was lucky like I was and wouldn't have to go back up there. Yes, I was really lucky cause my eye isn't too bad. Anyway I'm off the front at the present and every day back here means that much closer to the END of this damn war. In a way, I feel rather guilty but I didn't ask to get hit. I often wonder how you were and if you were alright.

I get mail all the time from Helen and she tells me that Frank Richard has six teeth and the first of January he weighed 19 pounds. Sure will be glad when you and I can get back cause you and I have got lots to learn him before the women folks get too much hold on him. Wonder if he will ever be able to throw the shot put like you or run the half.

You probably want to know what I'm doing, well in fact, mostly nothing like always. I'm in Regimental Headquarters Company and fool around in the S-3 section and that is about all. Well Richard, that's about all I can think of at the present so I'll close by wishing you all the luck in the world.

Your best pal,

Crockett

April 15, 1945

Unit History

C Company left Aufseß at 0615 hours on mounted march of 25 miles. Forward elements at Albertshof at 0915. 121st Cavalry proceeding on our route—road very narrow, difficult to pass them. Column reached Gößweinstein at 1330, surrender party coming out from town. Town cleared 1350. At 1605 head of column vicinity of Weidenloh. One armored car knocked out by enemy bazooka. Moving forward with dismounted infantry supported by tanks and tank destroyers. Weidenloh cleared at 1840, 5 large fires observed vicinity of enemy barracks—appears to be fuel or ammo dumps. Kirchenbirkig cleared 1930. Regenthal cleared at 1945 hours. Entered Betzenstein at 2130, assembling there. Prisoners of war today—139, one enemy vehicle captured.

April 16, 1945

Unit History

C Company left Betzenstein at 0630 hours on mounted march of 8 miles and arrived at Pottenstein, Germany, at 0800 hours. C-68 plus one platoon A-48 moved out to assist 48th in attack of Pottenstein. Approximately 240 prisoners of war, 100 nurses, 10 ambulances, 3 motorcycles, and one anti tank gun turned over to C.O. 48th at Pottenstein. Received mortar and small arms fire from Plech at 0900. Prisoners of war report large prison camp at Langwasser, vicinity of Nürnberg. American ambulance captured from enemy at 1030. Cleared Riegelstein at 1130, between 1200 and 1345 cleared Eichenstruth, Gerhelm, Henneberg, Illafeld, and Bernhof. At 1520 captured enemy trailer with two bazookas, 100 cases bazooka ammo, 8 cases 20 mm ammo, 7 rounds 105 mm, miscellaneous electrical equipment, and record chest. Following towns cleared between 1345 and 1630: Spies, Plech, Hormersdorf, Reingrub, Menschof, Wallsdorf, Raitenberg, Kreppling, Steinensittenbach, Treuf, Schlossberg, Kreuzbühl, and Bondorf. Contacted elements 45th Infantry Division and provided left flank security along line Riegelstein-Steinensittenbach, Oberkrumbach. Outposted towns in which assembled. Prisoners of war today—563.

April 17, 1945

Unit History

C Company left Steinensittenbach at 1130 hours on mounted march of 38 miles. Reached Kirchensittenbach at 1430, Altensittenbach at 1500, Entenberg at 1530. Found large quantity medical supplies at Altensittenbach. Reached Altdorf at 1640, Rasch at 1645, halted in Hausheim with forward elements. Remainder of command in Grub. Road from Voggenhof to Hausheim barely passable. Civilian reports 24,000 enemy with 160 tanks in Neumarkt. Total prisoners for today—150.

Mother to Richard

Dear Richard,

All okay at this end of the line. A slightly chilly spell is on again, but all the trees and flowers are lovely. The campus should be beautiful when we get to Virginia's commencement Sunday.

We got the picture of you receiving your Bronze Star, and we thought it was excellent. The location of the camera, however, made you look like a little, short fellow, instead of your 6'2" self. We showed the picture to Crocketts when they were at home Sunday. They say Buster finally wrote that he got some mail from home—25 letters from Helen at one time. By the way, we never did get your Purple Heart. Maybe that Red Cross gal needs her memory revived.

What did you all think about the death of the President?[85] It was a shock but not so surprising. It seems that Truman is going to do all right. He has been a soldier and understands what you are enduring.

Love,

Mother

---

85   President Roosevelt's health had noticeably deteriorated in the months prior to his death on April 12, 1945. He had gone for a rest to the "Little White House" in Warm Springs, Georgia. He was having his portrait painted when he suffered a cerebral hemorrhage that killed him in minutes. —Ed.

April 18, 1945

Unit History

At 0630, 1-C-94, 1 platoon A-48, and C-68 launched attack on Berg. Hausheim-Berg bridge prepared for demolition, but taken intact. Cleared and outposted Berg at 0700. Hospital with 58 enemy personnel taken in town. At 0822, C-68 in Berg receiving small arms fire and 88mm fire from south, believed from Neumarkt. Forty 88 mm rounds fell from 1145 to 1200. Dillberg taken 1210, road from Dillberg to Gitz very poor. Recon elements receiving small arms fire from west edge of Pölling, Gitz taken, and our column moving on Pölling. At 1700 C-68 and one platoon A-48 joined B-68 continuing attack on Pölling, dismounted. Pölling cleared at 2020. 14 prisoners of war captured and approximately 65 enemy killed. Knocked out 3 enemy sedans, one motorcycle, one personnel carrier, one 88 gun. Captured approximately 25 tons ammo. At 2300 knocked out 2 enemy vehicles, 2 anti-tank guns and liberated 2 American PWs in Pölling. Lightly wounded in action: S/Sgt. Taylor Emens, Tec 4 Jesse Wollard.

April 19, 1945

Unit History

Nothing but civilians yet observed in Neumarkt at 0800. Liberated American prisoner of war reports five anti tank guns in west edge of town. Companies A, B, C signal at 0930 that they have made contact with the enemy in Neumarkt with direct anti tank fire coming from west edge of town. At 1525, all of Company C over canal. Two platoons C-68 in town, B-68 attacking from northwest, meeting fairly heavy small arms, automatic weapons and mortar resistance. At 1725 have made contact with friendly troops in factory, C-68 holds 10 houses. Approximately 38 prisoners captured today. Pfc. Russell

Thuermer, lightly wounded in action. Sgt. George Wheeler, seriously wounded in action as of 18 April 45.

April 20, 1945

Unit History

At 0400 troops withdrew from Neumarkt to permit air mission on town shortly after 0800. Forward elements remained in assembly at Pölling. At 1315 alerted for movement south to seize Danube River crossings. At 2020, C-68 and one platoon B-68 attacked dismounted from Pölling, attacking along railroad northwest with mission of clearing Heng and Köstlbach. Heng taken at 2300. Prisoners of war today—43. Lightly wounded in action: Pfc. John Meixsell, Pfc. Ross Parker. Pfc. Edwin Boehringer and Pfc. Robert Primm of Medical Detachment, missing in action vicinity of Plech, Germany, as of 16 April 45.

Richard to Folks

Dear Folks,

It's a problem to get down to this letter writing business. I'm sure out of the habit, as usual. About a week ago, I guess, I did finally get around to writing most everyone. I haven't heard from Buster for a long time. I think he is in some kind of service outfit now. I'm glad for that and hope he never gets in an outfit like this again. I've neglected writing my aunties and hope you pass these letters on to them, as I know you do.

I sent Mrs. Phillips some wildflowers that I picked and halfway pressed.[86] I know she'll enjoy them. She wrote a letter and asked for me to pick a leaf and send. I'm sorry to hear of the president's death. It seems to me to be quite a blow to us at this time. Am enjoying the springtime. There are so many different kinds of flowers and trees over here.

---

86   One of Richard's elementary school teachers. —Ed.

Hoping you are all well at home. Guess you'll all be going to the farm. Are you going to have a garden this year? I saw some people planting potatoes yesterday and was wishing that that was what I was doing. Am okay and feeling fine. Occasionally my arm bothers me, usually when I get rather exhausted, but otherwise am okey-dokey.

Love,

Richard

April 21, 1945

Unit History

Köstlbach taken at 0015 and outposted. Kemnath cleared at 1230. Prisoners of war taken—12. Pfc. Henry Sims, from missing in action to killed in action 20 Jan 1945, vicinity of Rittershoffen.

April 22, 1945

Unit History

At 0740 C-68 and B-68 moving steadily through woods, B attacking Rittershof and C attacking Tyrolsberg. At 1130 C-68 cleared Tyrolsberg. Rittershof cleared by 1255. At 1910 all drivers ordered that speed down mountain around curves will be 4 mph and column vehicles will be kept moving at all costs. Instructions of Engineer guides will be fully complied with. American prisoners of war escaping recently tell of enemy vehicles other than of medical type with Red Cross markings. Also many enemy soldiers carry civilian clothes if capture is imminent. Began motor march to Altenfelden assembly area at 2115. Company C left Pölling at 2130. Total prisoners of war today—34. Pfc. Clifford Elwood, seriously injured in action, transferred to unknown hospital.

April 23, 1945

Unit History

Battalion continued motor march from Pölling area to new assembly area at Penzenhofen, head of column arriving at 1205. Went through Buch, Grünsberg, and Altenthann. Roadblock en route at Grünsberg consisted of tank recovery unit which fell through bridge. Recovering same. At 1350 all troops closed Penzenhofen except portion of Service Company, Battalion Maintenance, A-48, 1-A-636, and Company C. Company C arrived Morlach at 1900 hours and billeted in town. One Platoon B-68 on each side autobahn patrolling in zone. 1355 hours—remainder battalion now in Penzenhofen to move to Allersberg without delay. Prisoners for today—6.

The medics at Morlach with Richard leaning against front of jeep. Courtesy of Norman Eliasson

April 24, 1945

Unit History

0155 hours—Road conditions have delayed departure of C-68 from Mörlach, engineer squad requested. Battalion began moving at 1100 hours, arriving at Zell at 1315. All leaves and passes cancelled. Closed Alfershausen 1505. Head of column held up by friendly column at 1735 at Thalmässing. Again held up by friendly column at 1805 at Kleinhöbing. Unit closed Großhöbing and Schutzendorf at 1855. Began movement to Esselberg and Morsbach at 2040. Arrived at 2215 for night. Prisoners of war—3.

April 25, 1945

Unit History

Remained in assembly area at Morsbach and Esselberg, performing maintenance of vehicles and weapons. Combed woods vicinity of battalion area for any enemy remaining there. Prisoners of war—6.

Mother to Richard

Dear Richard,

I've been flying around too fast for letter writing lately. House-cleaning, gardening, Virginia's commencement, study club guest meeting, washing and ironing, etc., have kept me on the run. We are fine, however. Daddy is going to Indianapolis tomorrow and Virginia, Eleanor, and I are going along.

We had a nice day at Bloomington Sunday. The weather was perfect and the commencement program enjoyable. The class numbered only 257 this year, so there was plenty of room. Virginia is all excited because her application to Yale School of Nursing next fall has been accepted. If she can take a 30-month course there, she will get an A.M. in nursing instead of an

R.N. Of course she expects to join the Cadet Nurse Corps.[87] It is now up to her whether she decides to go to Yale or IU at Indianapolis.

We are watching the news about the 7th Army with interest. Some have said it was a greater feat to take Nuremberg than to enter Berlin. We are scared though. The last you wrote that we know about was Julia's letter of April 10th. We saw her Sunday and brought her records home.

I hear that Dee's folks have bought the Highfill farm just east of town. Imy H. said when Dee was home he was wishing his folks would buy a home. He said, "If anything happens to me, I don't want people to say they used my insurance to buy a farm. They've got the money!"

Have I written you about David lately? He was finally allowed to tell us he is based in the Philippines. Jonas is still at Miami and while waiting, has a job with the Naval Court, which tries court-martial cases. He was 27 last Saturday.

Lucy is having to move from her hall into barracks. Suitland is a government dorm and they won't rent it to the Navy any longer, as so many civilian girls are working at the census building, and they need the rooms. She says she will go to Anacostia nearby, or to Barracks K, across town. It will be harder for her, to have to go to work by bus, and to have no room of her own. Did you ever get your baking powder? Or your cookies and candy? Billy Seat, who has been missing, is a German prisoner. James Grimes is missing now.

Love,

Mother

---

87   The Cadet Nurse Corps was formed to remedy the lack of trained nurses both in the U.S. and abroad during World War II. The training was free for women who qualified for the program. By 1945, Cadet Nurse Corps nurses were providing 80% of the nursing care in U.S. Hospitals. "Join the U.S. Cadet Nurse Corps," *The U.S. Cadet Nurse Corps*, http://uscadetnurse.org/sites/default/files/RecruitmentBrochure.pdf (Jan. 24, 2014).

David Berkey. Courtesy of Nina Seven

*On the PGM. Front row L-R: Deal, Merer; Back row
L-R: Gallagher, David Berkey. Courtesy of Nina Seven*

WAITING *for* PEACE 211

Richard to Folks

Dear Folks,

I received a letter from Mother written the 9th and stating that it had been quite a long while since you all heard from me. I guess the mail transportation is rather slow now or something so you'll probably not receive mail so regularly. I wish you all wouldn't be so worried when not hearing from me for so long, 'tis only the mail situation. I saw a letter yesterday I'd written a week ago, never been mailed, no way to mail it.

I thought I had a pass to Paris yesterday, but something happened! But I'm still looking forward to it this week or next. We're in the 3rd Army now and guess that's the mixup.

Am okay and well. Read a letter the other day that Buster wrote to another boy in the outfit. He seemed okay but wasn't sure how his eye was getting along. Will write often.

Love,

Richard

P.S. this is Jerry stationery—not bad!

April 26, 1945

Unit History

Departed for new assembly area at 1230. Arrived new assembly area northwest of Hirnstetten at 1345. At 2345, battalion was outposting Pettling and Demling (assembly area) and placing blocking force (B-68) on roads to north.

Richard to Dad

Dear Dad,

Has been quite some time since I've written you. Just yesterday I received your letter of the 17th January, rather old. Also received about 20 more old letters, one from November even.

Also finally got a box, the one that had the toilet articles in it. At this time it is muchly appreciated since I'm all out of all kinds of that stuff. Also received a box from the Neals, cookies and candy, and received a small box of cookies from Virginia. It was all broken open and the cookies tasted like gasoline. Also got the can of baking powder, thanks loads for that. A kid made some pancakes with some of it last night. We have been eating mostly off the fat of the land here lately. Ham and eggs and black bread, beats Army rations. We eat a lot of that type of rations that I brought home one time, the one in the little box. I think you remember.

I'm just now getting around to sending my subscription to *Yank*. It will be sent to you now so you can enjoy it. We get an issue of *Yank* over here and there's no use for a subscription since it's a couple months late on this subscription business. I'd like for you to do me a favor. Would you mind sending a dollar to the IU Alumni Association for my subscription? I've received two notices lately but have no way of sending even a dollar to them. I enjoy receiving that magazine. The other day I received the one with all us kids' pictures in it. Thanks lots for this favor. I'm enclosing 10 marks invasion currency, which is a buck to repay you—ha!

Am still sweating out a pass to Paris. Sure hope I can get to go. That's the only town over here I really want to see.

The mail lately is rather slow, so hope you won't be so worried about me when you don't hear for a while. Am fine and okay.

Love,

Richard

April 27, 1945

Unit History

At 0845 civilians report large number of storm troopers in civilian clothes in Demling. Request CIC to screen population. At 0920 civilian source, believed reliable, reports 300 SS troops passed south through Pettling at 1700 yesterday accompanied by 3 trucks, 4 large tanks, ten to twelve 77 PAK Guns, and three 37-40mm guns. Also reported that approximately 10 days ago one group of 2,000 and one group of 3,000 Allied prisoners of war passed south through this town. 3-D-94 made road reconnaissance locating favorable road to bridge site over Danube River at Ingolstadt, in prep for crossing. Outposted towns in which assembled. Prisoners of war today—53. Pfc. William Stuckert, from missing in action 12 Jan 45 to killed in action 12 Jan 45.

April 28, 1945

Unit History

Remained in assembly areas at Pettling, Demling, and Pleiling, performing maintenance of vehicles and weapons until 1215. Battalion order to capture Mainburg. Held up by machine gun and small arms fire at Lindkirchen at 1830. At 2045 towns of Buch, Meilenhofen, and Lindkirchen clear. C-68 plus one platoon B-47 continued attack after capture of Lindkirchen, clearing Gumpertshofen and Wambach approximately 2215. Contacted friendly elements in Mainburg and assembled there for the night. Prisoners of war today—91. Approximately 35 enemy killed, 1 wagon load of 105 mm ammo captured. Lightly wounded in action: Pfc. J.P. Edwards, S/Sgt. George Wilson. Seriously wounded in action: Pfc. James Simon, Sgt. Lawrence Vining. Killed in action: Sgt. George Ringeisen, 2nd Lt. Robert Billhymer. Pfc. Clifford Elwood died of wounds.

From back of photo: "Near Mainburg—passing prisoners of war.
This is where Ringeisen and Billhymer were killed."
Courtesy of Norman Eliasson

WAITING *for* PEACE   215

Mother to Richard

Dear Richard,

We just got your letter of April 13th yesterday, and your Purple Heart finally came then, too. We were very glad to get both. It is always a relief to hear from you, the way things are. I'll try this V-mail for speed, but will send the airmail stamps in another letter. I will also try sending more baking powder and the pancake flour today. Wish you could get your packages, but that's a minor thing. Your being safe is what counts. You are getting to be such a cook that I plan to retire and put you in the kitchen! We enjoy your description of German homes. I always thought they were cleaner than French ones. Will look forward to getting the flag *you* captured. The news that the Yanks and Russians have met is thrilling. Everybody is interested in the peace conference, now on.

We are fine, but have had a dreary, rainy week, and it has been chilly. Virginia and I had a nice trip to Indianapolis with Daddy, on Thursday. It was rainy, so we could not have made garden. Aunt Fannie has just set out 600 strawberry plants.

Love,

Mother

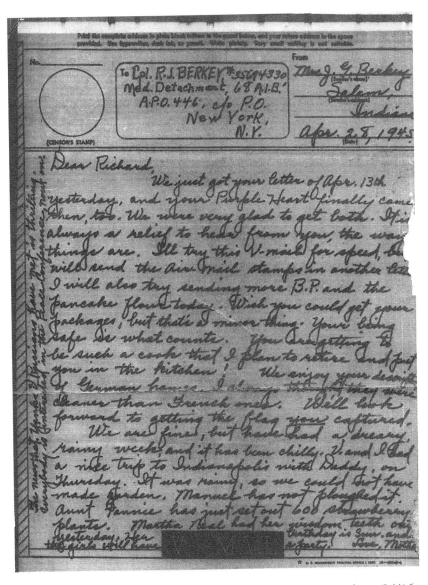

Mother's V-mail to Richard, April 28, 1945. Actual dimensions are 4 ¼ x 5 3/16 inches. The V-mail form she originally wrote it on was 7 x 9 1/8 inches.

April 29, 1945

Unit History

Moved out at 0600, Untergolzaberg cleared at 0810. Combat Command A states troops approaching Gendorf and Altötting should be warned that I.G. Farben Plant known as Montagewerke or Anorgana probably has a stock of poison gas capable of penetrating respirators. Cleared Obermünchen at 0900, Niedermünchen at 0927, Warzlberg at 0945. At 1110 captured hospital in Furth, two officers, 13 enlisted men on staff. Two officers, 96 enlisted men patients, 52 nurses, 12 teachers, 11 Italian laborers. Bridge in Moosburg blown at 1200 as lead vehicle entered—no casualties. At 1540 received small arms fire from Altdorf, attacking with tanks and one company infantry dismounted on axis of advance and one company infantry dismounted along railroad to right. At 1715 two Mark V tanks destroyed in Arth, enemy ammo dump in first house on right in Pfettrach. Altdorf cleared by 1935. At 2100 company pinned down at outskirts of Landshut (Company C) by heavy machine gun fire and direct fire. Total prisoners of war today—387. Approximately 140 enemy killed. Destroyed 11 vehicles, 3 tanks, 1 self-propelled gun, 1 towed gun, and 4 motorcycles. Captured 1 vehicle, 1 trailer-load bombs, and 1 ammo dump. Lightly wounded in action: Pfc. James Highfill, Pfc. William Usher, Pfc. Stanley Williams, S/Sgt. Louis Vega.

Near Furth on road to Altdorf and Landshut, April 29, 1945
Courtesy of Norman Eliasson

WAITING *for* PEACE

Virginia to Richard

Dearest Richard,

Well, old dear, it seems that a lot has happened since I last wrote you. The folks went to the farm this afternoon so I'm radioing and writing letters. It's been a sunny day, but it's still cold. Home a week, the college graduate is well rested and fattened up, though not too much. I'm much thinner than when I saw you last really.

I guess congratulations are in order for that medic corporal brother of mine who has the Bronze Star and Purple Heart. I feel so proud of you. I'm glad you sent the picture. It's so clear and looked awfully good to me. You're thinner, but doubtless you get around much better than when you were so heavy. We almost split laughing over that letter of yours we got yesterday, the one about the chocolate cake and German homes.

Wish you could have been there graduation day. The sun shone and the campus was perfect. Martha Neal came with the folks and Eleanor, all looking spiffy in new clothes. Daddy gave Mother a corsage of pink carnations, me one of pale yellow ones tinged with rust and blue ragged robins to go with my new gold suit. Eleanor looked darling. All the guys really stared until I popped laughing.

Julia and I got to march together, we were so glad. We were afraid we'd have to march with just anyone. However impressive the service was, we felt shaky and very much humble in the sight of those rows of gowned and beribboned profs. Goodness. During the service they paid tribute to the men and women who would be graduating if they had been able to. I was pleased with it all, their 125th anniversary, 257 graduates this spring. My A.B. in English looks good, but wait until I get that Masters of Nursing from Yale. Yes, I've been accepted and even though I haven't definitely decided, it seems likely that I should go there October 1. Daddy is reconciled and will help me get started before I get in the Corps. Guess I'll be seeing you in New Haven, Connecticut, in a few months.

Well, dopey, not much else to say now. I got lots of nice presents for graduation. Be good and take care of yourself. I'm expecting a present from you—your coming back and finishing school. I know now you'll make a wonderful doctor.

Lots of Love,

Virginia

Virginia's Graduation Day—L-R: Virginia, Mother, Dad, Eleanor
Photographer unknown

Rodman to Richard

Dear Richard,

Well, old man, what's cookin' with you? I haven't had any mail for so long, I've lost contact with everybody. These armies travel too fast for anything to catch up. I'm just assuming that you have recovered and that you are back with your outfit again. I hope I am right. It sort of looks like this thing is going to end some of these days and there again I hope I'm right.

I just had a suspicion that you were with the 7th Army from all indications but still in doubt. I can't seem to find out much about the 68th AIB. As for me, I'm with the 7th Army now and have been for some time. We've really traveled quite a distance with them. Right now I'm deep in the heart of the Alps and about to freeze to death! I suppose it's the snow on the peaks that makes me shiver.

What do you hear that's new from home? Still losing some of our buddies back in the States. Sorry to hear about Dee Bush.

Well, I'm sorry to say I have no more time at present. About the time I get settled to write, I'm interrupted. Hope to hear from you soon and hoping this finds you okay.

So long,

Rodman

April 30, 1945

Unit History

Following 15-minute artillery, mortar, and assault gun preparation at 0500, troops launched attack on Landshut. C-68 attacked along railroad to northeast while A-68 attacked along stream to northeast to clear houses north and west of railroad, succeeding in clearing that sector by 0700 without meeting enemy resistance. Combat Command R Rifle plus 1 platoon A-25 and B-62 , attached to 68th for operation, passed through Companies A and C, CCR Rifle on right of road and B-62 on left of road. Succeeded in reaching Isar River by 1030, thus accomplishing mission, despite burp gun fire and self-propelled gunfire from other side of river. B-62, CCR Rifle, and A-25 reorganized and upon contact elements of 99th Infantry Division withdrew, reverting to CCR control. A-68 and C-68 reorganized and returned to Altdorf, upon passage of 99th Infantry Division elements through our units to continue attack on Landshut. Units reassembled Altdorf, outposting town for night. Prisoners of war captured—181. Approximately 750 enemy patients under guard in hospital at Landshut. 48 enlisted men joined company from 17th Reinforcement Battalion.

Lucy to Richard

Dearest Richard,

I received a wonderful letter this afternoon, saw it in my mailbox as I was going thru the lobby on my way in from work. Boy, I was really excited because it was the first time I'd heard from this guy in ages—it made me feel 100% better. Best I've felt since they denied the surrender story Saturday night. Jeepers it was good to hear from that brother of mine! Thanks a million for the ritzy emblem, even if it is a Nazi one! Janet Knight, one of my best friends here, was having more fun with that badge, going around with it pinned over her rating and getting everyone in the place as curious as could be! They all thought she was crazy, and she is, that's why we all get along so well! Really, she's as fine a friend as I've met since I've been in the WAVES!

Guess I'm a bit late on congratulations, but well, raking in two medals at most is not bad duty to my way of thinking, kid! Mother must have thought she told me about the Purple Heart and Bronze Star; but she hadn't at all! Last week she wrote, "Did I remember to tell you we got a picture of Richard receiving his Bronze Star?" I almost fell over dead, rushed down to Janet to tell her there was a medal in my family and, well gee, I was some proud specimen! After all it's not every day a G.I. Joe gets such an honor bestowed upon him. Then, I received a church letter from home where it told of two medals, and so I found out about the Purple Heart that way! After that, well, bragging must be in my blood, for the more I rave the better I get, what an explosion! Anyway, without all the sugar stuff, it's that I'm trying to tell you I knew you had it in you all the time, and of course I'm darn proud such an honor came to you, though I must say I've always been proud of my brother, regardless of medals.

Well, Virginia graduated at last and I wasn't there to see it all. I had hoped to get to go home on leave, but can't get away 'till about May 26, when I expect to grab my seven days with two days travel time. I'm so glad for Virginia, for she's safely graduated, which is something in wartime, and has been made plenty happy because her application to Yale School of Nursing has been accepted for the fall term. However, Mother said Virginia wasn't sure yet whether she'd go to Indianapolis—to IU or Yale. I agree with you concerning Virginia's letters, Richard, but she's just going through a crazy stage when she gets these high-flown ideas and waxes too sentimental all over the place!! But, at heart she's as goodhearted a kid as you can find, and she does so much to make the folks happy. Gee, at Christmas time you should have seen her! I guess they told you how David sent her money to buy something for all of us, and something for the house. Poor old Virginia nearly went nuts trying to get suitable things and did a smack up fine job, in fact, she did a million things to make our holidays fun as much like always as possible. So, brother, guess that makes up for all her craziness in her letters, huh?! It probably bothers her as much as it does me to go home and find so many women, as if I hadn't seen enough of them since I've been in the WAVES. Yes, men are welcome creatures, especially nowadays, and especially some brothers I know! Here's hoping this mess will be over soon.

Oh, yes, I meant to explain about the surrender business! Saturday night I was sitting here in my room calmly reading a good book when the radio announcer seemed so excited I stopped my reading to listen more closely. He said Himmler had said Germany would surrender unconditionally to all three great powers, and the only thing they were waiting for now was for Eisenhower to make a final, definite statement, and for that to be confirmed by President Truman. Honestly, I was so excited I could hardly sit still enough to listen! I heard girls everywhere, in all the wings, yelling and telling their neighbors the wonderful news. Every few minutes, announcers of the Blue Network would interrupt programs to tell us a statement was expected momentarily.[88] This kept up for an hour, with announcers and commentators wondering why they hadn't seen any celebrating in the streets yet. Then, suddenly, it was stated that President Truman had cut short the bright hopes going around, by saying the former statement was only a rumor, and that there was no real basis for it. He said he had called an official in Europe, and that it was not true. This was really a sad place after that, long faces and plenty of the silence that gets you, the kind we felt around here just after we heard of President Roosevelt's death. However, things certainly can't last much longer, and the paper today feels that they are holding off VE Day till after Russia declares war on Japan. Sometimes I think these papers are crazy.[89] You could probably tell me things that would make all this seem like a big laugh! However, I thought you might like to know about how things seem to us over here.

News that you had finally received my packages was welcome indeed! Gee, I'm so glad you got them at last! Now I won't be afraid to send things. After you didn't receive those things from the folks, I felt sure my packages would be lost, too. I'm anxious to know how the fruitcake came through—was it awfully stale? I tried wrapping wax paper all around, but sometimes moisture gets in anyway. If there's anything special you want, please tell me, for I can get things here in Washington easier than the folks can at home. Would you like more socks, fruit, cake, dried apricots, pears, figs, dates? Or do you get those? Anyway I have the day off Wednesday and I'll see what I can muster up in town. *Be sure* though, to ask me to send something in every letter you write, so I can take the request letter with my package to the post office. That's the only way I can send you a package, so it seems. So, kid, say the woid and I'll send it!

---

88   The Blue Network was one of the original NBC (National Broadcasting Company) radio networks. —Ed.
89   Victory in Europe Day was commonly referred to as VE Day or V-E day. —Ed.

I must sign off, write to the folks, and do a washing and ironing. Write me when you can find time, ha! And take care of yourself. Here goes the screwball off again!

Loads of Love,

Lucy

May 1, 1945

Unit History

Company left Altdorf at 1100 hours on mounted march of 25 miles and arrived at Geislbach, Germany at 2130 hours. Billeted in town awaiting orders.

Near Moosburg, May 1, 1945. Courtesy of Norman Eliasson

Near Moosburg, May 1, 1945. Courtesy of Norman Eliasson

Karen Berkey Huntsberger

May 2, 1945

Unit History

Company left Geislbach at 1000 hours on mounted march of 19 miles and arrived at Aspertsham, Germany at 2130 hours.

May 3, 1945

Richard to Folks

Dear Folks,

Finally got round to writing again. I haven't heard from you for quite some time now. Must be the mail transportation here on the continent. I did receive a line from Sis Lucy the other day and was quite surprised.

We have been having most unusual weather here lately, snow flurries seem to be quite dominant. Very beautiful along with the apple blossoms, but I imagine due to the cold, they will be kaput, strawberries, too!

The news is very good and we here are sweating out the finis as I know you are also. Am okay and having a great (ha!) time. I don't think I weigh that 200 anymore. Down to about 185 which is about right. Hoping you are all well at home.

Love,

Richard

May 4, 1945

Richard to Folks

Dear Folks,

Received a box containing cookies and candy—boy! Thanks lots! Upon receiving the box I was in the act of making a cake and, well, the cookies kinda put kaput to the quality of the cake.

Also received Mothers V-mail of 17 April. Seems as if that type of mail isn't so fast as it was in the winter. Some airmails have been coming in about 12 days.

Some of the boys cooked up some chickens today and I tried to make some dumplings, but alas! They ended up in one big mess. Think I had a little too much milk in the dough and they didn't stick together.

Guess you got Virginia all graduated, etc.? I can see her at home now with all her big ideas concerning housecleaning, garden beautification, and possibly suntanning—ha! How's Eleanor and high school?

Would you mind sending me some pictures, small ones in preference? I've lost practically all, except of Lucy and Jonas. I lost the folder with Mother, Dad, David, and Eleanor's pictures that you all gave me a couple years ago Christmas. Thanks, I will enjoy them.

Have used most of the little can of baking powder and would like some more please. Also, vanilla extract flavoring if possible to send. Cookies, too. Received IU alumni magazine dated March and enjoyed it muchly. Hoping all are well at home. Assuring you I'm very well and fine.

Love,

Richard

May 6, 1945
Richard to Folks

Dear Folks,

Recently I've been writing quite a bit more than usual so you should be receiving more mail from me by the time you receive this one. Some of the boys picked up a radio yesterday and we have been enjoying some good American jive. Boy does it sound good! We also listen to an occasional newscast, if it's in English—ha! The news is plenty good and we are sweatin' the official notification of the end, which I hope is in not too many days, but one never knows how soon I guess.

Just finished listening to "Don't Fence Me In," a great time— boy, did that sound good![90]

Still sweatin' out a pass to Paris or someplace, oughta be getting it before long, I hope. Scribbled off a line to Buster a minute ago. Haven't heard from him for a couple of months. At least I figure he's okay in the rear echelon. Am okey-dokey.

Love,

Richard

90   The song "Don't Fence Me In" was written in 1934 by Cole Porter and Robert Fletcher. —Ed.

CHAPTER ELEVEN
IT'S OVER

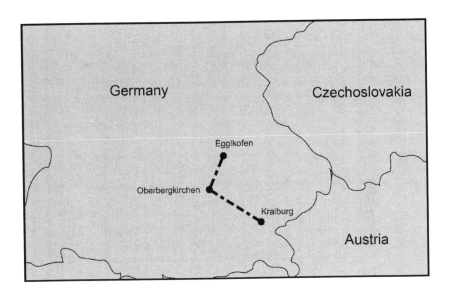

May 8, 1945 VE Day

Virginia to Richard

Dearest Richard,

On VE day, I think it most fitting to write you who have played one of the important parts in it. We got your letter of April 20th today and are so anxious to get another addressed on May 5 or 8 or later. Hope you can get some rest now. We are also hoping you'll get home for furlough, at least, but doubt if you will of course.

We got up before eight to hear President Truman's address officially declaring VE Day. All the generals spoke—we heard Patch! Salem businessmen took the day off, so Daddy went to town and shortly came home. We ironed, then went to the farm this afternoon.

This farming and gardening—my first experience for this season—wore me out. Certainly have gotten soft! The sun was hot but the wind cold and strong. We planted cucumbers, lima beans, and set out tomato plants, cut asparagus, gathered poke for a dish of "greens," and ate soda crackers. Daddy knocked himself out cutting down trees across the road from the garden, where he discovered a big bed of tiny asparagus plants coming on. Mr. Weeks has cleared out the road, but it is full of ruts and snags. Daddy hopes to fix it up so we can drive in. Daddy also sawed off the limbs of trees that always overhang and shade the garden. The place looks pretty good, but needs so much work. Daddy says one of these days he's going to put you boys to work on it. The orchard is a mess. I got overly ambitious and tried to dig new sassafras roots there where we got them last summer. Ha. You can laugh now! I forgot about the grub hoe and tried to use a light garden one. Ugh. Exertion and no result!

Mother saw Buster's baby last week—says he looks like both Buster and the Bush family. Be good and take care of yourself. Have a good time. Much celebration? Not over here. Some in New York and Detroit. Too much yet ahead.

Lots of Love,

Virginia

May 9, 1945

Unit History

S/Sgt. William Stoyanoff, from missing in action 18 Dec 44 to killed in action 18 Dec 44, vicinity of Oberotterbach, Germany.

Richard to Folks

Dear Folks,

Yesterday and today we have all been in quite a bit better mood than we have for quite some time. Yesterday I listened to speeches by Churchill, the King, and Mackenzie King of

Canada.[91] Also listened to the Salute and Tribute to the King from all the colonies, which was quite impressive. All this came over the British Broadcasting station, so therefore, we missed hearing the president. Nevertheless 'tis over over here and that's what counts and for which we are thankful.[92]

I've often thought of this day and naturally thought of celebration. But it seems as if the conquering feeling is elsewhere. It seems to me as if everyone has a feeling of relief, of course, and humbleness, or at least a sort of security and safeness.

I can imagine that you at home are rather excited about the war being over, but guess there is still that feeling of Japan yet that all the announcers and reporters keep reminding us of.

Hope all at home are well. Assure you I'm fine and can almost feel myself getting fat from the good chow we have been having lately.

Love,

Richard

May 10, 1945

Unit History

Company billeted in town—regular guard and outposting town. Weather fine and morale high. 2nd Lt. William Wallace joined

---

91   Winston Churchill, King George VI of England, and the Prime Minister of Canada. —Ed.

92   Richard is referencing the famous World War I song "Over There" written by George M. Cohan. These are the words of the last verse of the song: So prepare, say a prayer / Send the word, send the word to beware. / We'll be over, we're coming over / And we won't come back till it's over over there. Duffy, Michael, "Over There," *FirstWorldWar.com*, http://www.firstworldwar.com/audio/overthere.htm (June 22, 2014).

company and assigned principal duty as Armored Infantry Unit Commander.

Headquarters Combat Command "A"
14th Armored Division, API #446
United States Army 10 May 1945

SUBJECT: Commendation
TO: Commanding Officer 68th Armored Infantry Battalion, API 446, U.S. Army, Germany

The actions and accomplishments of the 68th Armored Infantry Battalion during the operations of the approach to and the breaching of the Siegried Line by Combat Command "A" from 15 March to 24 March 1945 were most outstanding. The Battalion pursued the withdrawing enemy with a fine dash and elan from Surbourg through Niederroedern and to the Bienwald Forest north of Salmbach in Alsace. It then, on 20 March, attacked and secured a foothold within the organized Siegfried defenses at Steinfeld, Germany. Passing through other elements of the division, it attacked early on the morning of 23 March 1945 to capture Schaidt. Strong defense by an alert enemy threw the battalion back with severe losses. Reorganized, it again attacked to capture Schaidt on the morning of 23 March 1945. Exhibiting an outstanding determination and an unusually well coordinated action by its A and C companies, the battalion advanced over 3000 yards through an area completely covered by numerous enemy concrete bunkers and, as the friendly artillery fire lifted from Schaidt, rushed into the town and, after a period of about 5 hours, completely cleared the enemy therefrom. Immediately reorganizing, the battalion sent its 3rd Platoon C Company, riding the tanks of B Company 25th Tank Battalion, into the town of Freckenfeld and cleared out the remaining enemy elements from the town, thus completing the penetration of the first belt of the Siegfried defensive system. It is with great pleasure that I commend every member of the 68th Armored Infantry Battalion.

KAREN BERKEY HUNTSBERGER

C.H. Karlstad

Brig. Gen. U.S. Army, Commanding

Claud Wilson to Richard

Dear Berkey,

I'm finally well enough to write and thank you. I've been out of the unit for five weeks now, but I will never forget the day of April 4th.

We were on one of the prettiest little roads running thru the countryside near Lohr, east-northeast of the bigger town of Aschaffenburg, east-northeast of Darmstadt. A little brook ran eight feet below the road to the left. Telephone wires crossing the road were seen by the lead half-track. Our convoy stopped and some GI went, on foot, to check them out. How he knew, I'll never know, but I remember his calling back, "they're alive!"

About that time a couple of rifle shots rang out. One round hit the shell container of the 30-caliber machine gun on our half-track, making it unusable. One of the boys tried to swing it around to rake the direction of the shot, but it jammed. The next bullet hit Temple next to me in the center back. The sound was traumatic. He fell over forward as the Lieutenant told us to get out. And then the rest of us saw some big gray-green over-coated figures to our right, up a slight slope.

We knew we were sitting ducks, so we piled out of the half-track and lay on the sloping bank of the road to our left. Why we weren't fired on at that point, I'll never know. I looked once more, and fired at the lower part of a big guy walking away from the group. And that was when a shell struck either the tree over my head or the half-track. I never knew. I only saw blue and my ears went out.

I looked from where I was blown backward and here you came, bent low, but coming on. When you got to me, I had felt the front of my helmet torn and I bent down and couldn't see out of my left eye too well. I recall the first words I said: "Berkey—see if my left eye is gone!"

You said, "No, it's a cut over your eye and the blood is in your eye." Then you cut my left shirtsleeve open and found the biggest wound on my upper arm and bandaged it after putting sulfa powder on it.

My right knuckles were all messed up and I said, "Reckon I'll ever get to play the piano again?" "Sure," you said, "come on, I'll help you back to the rear and the ambulance will come get you and the others." You put your arm around me, my left arm around your shoulders, and we crawled back.

There lay the body of Temple who was hit in the back before we got out of the half-track and several other wounded guys, some walking and some on litters. I later learned that the half-track was destroyed. My duffel bag was hanging on the side of it—oh well!

The ambulance tenders got lost on the way back to the field hospital. And once they rode down a railroad track—the bump, bump, bump made it clear. We finally were directed by MPs in Lohr to the field hospital. By that time I had gone from a "sitting" patient holding a plasma bag over a guy, to a litter case because I began to shake and get dizzy—loss of blood, I guess.

In the hospital I learned this strange medical fact—with sulfa powder, wounds that are flesh wounds stay open, clean looking, pink, and non-bleeding till one is driven or flown to the hospital. I spent a few days in the cot-lined tents of the field hospital. Under doctor's care, we were taken to Frankfurt and then flown by a DC-6 to the general hospital in Reims. Big, tall, blond Afrika Korps German prisoners handled us as if we were their brothers unloading us from the plane.[93]

---

93   Afrika Korps: German troops in the North African Campaign in World War II. —Ed.

Your calm manner helped me handle that day and the days since. They say I can probably be back with the unit in another couple of weeks. Being 38 years old, I guess I'm taking longer to heal than you younger guys! We're all glad it's over now. I know the unit had it really rough near the end. Sorry to ramble on. Just wanted you to know how very grateful I am!

Claud

May 11, 1945

Unit History

Company left Aspertsham at 1300 hours on mounted march of 11 miles and arrived at Egglkofen, Germany, at 1430 hours. Company billeted in town outposting, regular guard and awaiting orders.

May 14, 1945

Richard to Folks

Dear Parents,

I've been so lazy the last few days that I've almost forgotten what letter writing is. Finally received some mail today, Mother's V-mail of the 28th, and at last a line from Buster who seemed to be quite all right and very pleased with his work.

There seems to be a scarcity of American flags around this place. I was wondering if it would be possible for you to send a flag of a size that could be placed on a pole. I would be very pleased if you could get hold of one for us. Thanks!

Love,

Richard

May 15, 1945

Mother to Richard

Dear Richard,

I want to write a little to each of you who are away tonight, to tell you that Jonas and Mildred have just been here. Jonas called us Friday night saying he had just reached Jeffersonville. He said they would stay there until Sunday afternoon and then come up here. We were going to see Grandmother Sunday afternoon, as it was Mother's Day, so they met us there and came home with us.

At Key West Hospital they gave Jonas insulin, which helps the body utilize fats and carbohydrates. He also took strychnine to counteract the bad effects—and ate all he could hold. In two weeks he gained 15 pounds. He was not allowed to be in bed at all. He has been assigned to the recruiting station at Huntington, West Virginia, just across the Kentucky line, and on the Ohio River. It is only 200 miles from Louisville so they ought to get home once in a while. He is to be at Huntington five months. Mildred is going to visit at home a little while, getting some dental work and some sewing done, and maybe by that time Jonas can find them a good place to live. Both of them look just fine. Jonas weighs 165 and seems full of energy again as he used to. They are both so brown from the Florida sun that they make the rest of us look sick. Monday afternoon we went to the farm and planted a little more stuff, dug some sassafras, and roamed around. We found over a quart of strawberries (our first) and came home and had short cake and ice cream for supper. We *did wish* you were here.

We had a nice big letter from David on Sunday. He had returned from a trip and found 22 letters, seven of them from home. Most of his letter was commenting on those letters. He seemed to be quite all right. We got the week's copies of the *New York Times* in which he had said there would be an article about one of their operations, but we can't find anything we are sure is the one he meant.

We got your letter of April 25 and are hoping you were still all right when the firing stopped. So you had to join the Third Army and work until the very last! What are you doing now? Logan Martin's son Russell wrote that he was guarding prisoners. I know you are all anxious to get away as soon as possible, but I don't want you in a place like Okinawa, so there's no hurry, after all. Jack Etzler is on Okinawa and his folks are so worried.

The point system, which has recently been made public, does not give you much chance of getting out of the Army soon. About 45 points would be all of yours.[94] Here's hoping you get out before you wear long white whiskers.

Love,

Mother

May 16, 1945

Unit History

1st Lt. Edward Gosselin, from missing in action 13 Jan 45 to killed in action 13 Jan 45.

---

94   The points system awarded soldiers a number of points based on their years of service, each month served overseas, combat awards, and number of dependent children under the age of 18. Initially, the number of points needed to get out of the army was 85, but that was quickly amended when the war in Japan ended. The points required for demobilization were reduced several times, reaching 50 points on December 19, 1945. —Ed.

Castle Egglkofen

May 17, 1945

Unit History

2nd Lt. Joseph Charles joined company and assigned principal duty as Armored Infantry Unit Commander.

May 18, 1945

Unit History

Company left Egglkofen at 0630 hours on mounted march of 16 miles and arrived at Oberbergkirchen, Germany, at 0715 hours.

Rodman to Richard

Dear Richard,

I got your letter yesterday, over a month old and no doubt at present we are somewhere within a radius of 250,000 square miles of each other anyway. By the time you get this, I'll probably be moved and you will, too, but what the heck—here goes, anyway.

It looks as though I followed you all the way across Germany and maybe a few times passed you along the road and didn't know it. At present I'm at a village named Kauns down in the hills of Austria. This morning, after getting your letter, I journeyed back to Imst on a little business and while there I inquired a little concerning the whereabouts of your company. Replies were mostly unsatisfactory so the best I could get was, "It's 60 miles back," which puts it in Germany. Of course I found no one who knew of the 68th AIB. It will be interesting to know where you were anyway. If I ever get my jeep repaired I may have some time for reconnaissance before going back to the States—er I mean the CBI.[95]

Whatcha doing mostly now? Guess you're happy it's all over with. I'm about the luckiest man in the ETO not to have had any more of it than I did.[96]

I'll write more later. I know what you mean when you speak of those crappy German classes back at school.

Yours,

Rodman

Eska Bush to Richard

Dear Richard,

Thanks so much for the letters we have rec'd from you. We should have answered sooner but it's so hard for me to write a letter, it reminds me so much of the many hours I have spent in writing to Dee. He was in the Army almost three years and I wrote every day except about five or six. It's so hard for us to

---

95   CBI: China Burma India Theater, the general term used for the war in the Pacific. —Ed.
96   ETO: European Theater of Operations, the general term used for the war in Europe. —Ed.

realize that all we have left of him is just a memory. So many times I think "if he only had not went into the Air Corps," then I have to banish that thought from my mind. I think that it was just his time and God's will. If so, it must have been best but only those that have traveled our road before we have knows how hard it is to see it that way.

I don't know whether Dee ever told you or not but if all would have went well no doubt he would have been married by now, for he told me X-mas when he was home he might get married before he went over. He gave his girl a diamond for X-mas. Her name is Marilyn Thompson. She lives at Cedar Rapids, Iowa, she seems to be mighty nice. I have rec'd many nice letters from her, they have helped me lots. I am sending you a picture. Sure hope it reaches you.

We are glad to know you are okay and hope this will soon be over and you as well as all the rest will be back. That time of course when it comes will be mighty hard for us but some way some how we will be able to carry on for that is what Dee would want us to do. This letter I know won't be much of a morale builder but I am sure you will know why and be able to overlook it. Suppose you have never seen Lee Henry, so far they have only had two letters from him this year.

The weather this spring has been in accordance with our hearts, dreary and gloomy, which hasn't helped us much. We don't have any plowing done yet all our work is going to come at once but I guess "Where there is a will there will be a way," but for the first time in our lives we don't have much will to work. In a way the things of this world seem so immaterial to us, but for Mary's sake we will have to try and look forward to brighter days to come.[97] Arthur Lee is still here.[98] His deferment is up again June 1. We hope he will be left for a while longer. We are looking forward in a few weeks to having a grandson. Maybe

---

97   Mary was Dee's sister. —Ed.
98   Mary's husband, Arthur Lee Maudlin. —Ed.

in a small measure it will help to take Dee's place. He thought that would be a wonderful experience to be called Uncle but that now is like so many other things "just so much water over the dam." We wish you lots of luck, let us know if you receive the picture. We are glad to hear from you anytime, bye.

Love always, your foster parents,

Claude and Eska

May 20, 1945

Unit History

Company still billeted in town patrolling area and posting regularly and following schedule.

Richard to Folks, from Ampfing, Germany

Dear Folks,

Finally censorship has been lifted a bit and I can tell you exactly where I'm at now. You probably can't find this town on the map, so 'tis about 70 km east and slightly north of Munich. A larger town than Ampfing, just east a few kilometers, is Mühldorf. We are in a large valley and can see easily the Bavarian Alps. When the sun shines on them they are very impressive with the snow. Yesterday I had the occasion to visit them and in particular Hitler's own Berchtesgaden, quite some place and well taken care of by the Air Corps.[99] Hitler's house was strictly kaput, and I do mean kaput! What wasn't blasted by bombs was gutted by fire. His famous living room with spacious window, and snow-covered mountains in front, was intact but all burned out. He sure had what looked to be quite a ritzy joint. We weren't

---

99   Berchtesgaden was the common name for Hitler's vacation home near the town of Berchtesgaden. The home's real name was "The Berghof" and was owned by Hitler for 10 years. In late April 1945, it was bombed by the British, set on fire by retreating Nazi troops in early May, then looted by the many Allied troops who visited it right after the end of the war. —Ed.

permitted to visit the tunnels beneath. I got a few souvenirs, which were few and far between due to the destruction and GIs who had captured and visited the place. Enclosed is a very suitable one to send in a letter. Obersalzberg is the town below Berchtesgaden.

Received Mother's letter of the 6th today. Thanks for the stamps, I can use 'em. I'll send one back to you on this letter. Suppose you have read concerning the point system for discharge. Seems as if very few have 85 in this outfit. I have 50, 28 for months served and 7 for overseas service, making 35. I have 15 for combat credit—5 for Bronze Star Medal, 5 for Bronze Battle Star (participant in major battle), and 5 for Purple Heart Medal, and that makes 50. Having no kids—ha! 12 points are given for kids under 18, up to 3 kids. That points stuff doesn't worry me anyway, not now anyway. I figure I'll be in quite a while longer anyway like most everyone else. Guess the rest of the kids in the Navy don't have to mess with point stuff. Guess when the war's over is the time to start figuring points.

By the time you receive this letter you will probably have received the commendation I sent. In particular on that paper I'd like for you to notice Freckenfeld. C Company's 3rd Platoon was the one I've always been attached to and was so attached during the taking of said town. It really wasn't half so bad as others before, the worst being Steinfeld and Schaidt. We rode tanks halfway and after running into a tank trap walked the rest of the way. We got a few Jerries but had to contend mostly with civilians. It was the first time I'd ever experienced a feeling of being a conqueror. But I was so darn tired after patching up about a dozen Krauts,[100] all I could do was eat some good ol' Jerry ham and eggs and black bread and go to bed in some big shot's house, who we had previously run out—ha!

---

100 U.S. and German medics sometimes worked together to treat and evacuate the wounded, particularly if a company was captured. Men were wounded, disarmed, treated, and organized into litter teams to carry those that could not walk back to where they were transported. —Ed.

On second thought I think I'll enclose the souvenir in another letter with a paper telling about why I got a Bronze Star. I never did tell about the day I got it, but maybe I'll get round to it in a couple of days.

Am okay these days. Got a terrific sunburn about a couple weeks ago, as usual, but am very well now and played some softball today. Got two letters from Buster last week. He seems okay, but as yet haven't found out where he is. Hope you are all well at home.

Love,

Richard

May 22, 1945

Richard to Folks

Dear Folks,

I've been so lazy today I've only managed to do laundry and finally at 11:45 got started on this letter. It's been cool and rainy all day and tonight 'tis cold and very bright out like fall.

Enclosed is our battalion newspaper, a new and recent publication which more or less stinks, but since there is an article about yours truly in it I thought I'd give you a preview. The article is not so correct, as they usually are. I was playing around with a kid yesterday and in the midst of an entanglement a mirror was smashed in my shirt pocket and thus the back page headlines.

Censorship seems to be completely out and thus I get to lick my own envelopes now. How nice of the government.

My trip to the Alps Saturday was my second visit. In November we were in our first action in the Maritime Alps on the Franco Italian border, near Nice, thus my short visit to Nice on Thanksgiving Day, November 30. Nice is a beautiful "American" type city. The Army has a huge rest center there now. Guess I'll go to bed.

Nite,

Richard

From the battalion newspaper *Allus Kaput* (22 May 1945):

Superstitious?

C Company's Medic, T/5 Dick Berkey broke a mirror today: Looking down at his hand, he solemnly chanted, C-B-I—seven years of it. The mirror obligingly broke in three neat triangular pieces. Three other Armored Divisions, no doubt.

Softball Result

Behind the fine pitching of "Bugs" Bogdovitz, the terrific hitting of "Tiny" Griswold, and the tight fielding of "Speed" Carlysle, HQ Company nosed out A Company in an opening day thriller, 7-7. Tiny banged out a homer, triple, and a single in four trips to the plate, knocking in the winning run in the 8th. "Hardrock" Gregory hit two homers for the losers and Gray was the losing pitcher. With T/5 Berkey on the mound and top fielding by his teammates, C Company was able to take B Company in their first league tilt, 5-2. Berkey held his opponents to a few scattered hits while his men collected several extra base hits from S/Sgt. Paul Schlesinger, the losing pitcher.

All in a Day's Work

In the process of exploring the castle in Zanberg, T/5 Elrod came across a surprise package—a newly born infant bundled up in a blanket and coat. Company Commander Capt. Lamb was rushed to the scene and dispatched his men in what proved to be a futile search for the mother. In the meantime, he moved the six-pound infant to a private room and cared for it until help arrived in the form of a young lady—not the child's mama. Capt. Lamb won the admiration of his men by his coolness and efficiency in executing the duties of a mother during the crisis.

I Dood It

Mike (I hate guard duty) Mattiace was frantic. For the first time in his Army career it looked like he was going to pull guard. Detailed to guard one PW, the C Co. barber was seen desperately using every ruse in the book to get rid of the Kraut. Mike offered him a bottle of beer to run away, was prepared to give him a bike so that he could ride, and even tried to get him to make a false move so that he could shoot him. He finally convinced him that he was sick and carted him off to the medics several miles away. You beat the rap this time Mike, but there'll come a day!

May 23, 1945

Richard to Folks, from Kraiburg, Germany

Dear Folks,

Guess I'll finally get around to telling you what I promised about the parade when I received my medal. Got the Purple Heart when in the hospital, supposed to be given to all soldiers by a colonel, but some sergeant from Indiana (Fort Wayne) gave (handed) mine to me, so it was just as appropriate, him being from Indiana—ha! The hospital was in Dijon, France, by the way, quite a large town but rather old and musty, on Rhône River, or is it?—Ha!

Anyway I returned from the hospital and rejoined the outfit February 22 at a town by the name of Ringeldorf. We were on the line then at a town about a mile up, La Walck or Pfaffenhoffen—some name. I went out as aid man again in about four days with C Company third platoon, have been ever since. We pulled back to a rest area in a couple of days to Saessolsheim, France, about 20 miles north of Strasbourg near Hagenau, where the 14th had a couple battles. We were billeted in French homes. On March 5 we had a battalion review. Naturally, 'twas cold and rainy and a freezing wind. There were about 12 of us receiving medals and we marched out together after the rest of the battalion. We marched outside of town and up on top of a hill in a wheat field. To our front were a couple old men plowing with two cows. We marched to the side of the rest of the men and then after the general made his appearance we did another maneuver and ended up about 20 feet in front of the general. As an adjutant read a name and citation we stepped forward, saluted, and the general pinned on the ribbon and said a few words. He said to me, "I sure pin a lot of stars on medics, more than anyone else. They sure do get around," and then said something else I don't remember and "Congratulations" and then shook hands, saluted, about-face and returned to original position. And that's that, I didn't say nothing, as usual!

Two of our other medics got medals along with me, and funny enough for the same action at Oberotterbach, Germany, near Wissembourg, France, on the border. Oberotterbach is about 5 to 6 miles inside Germany and is a Siegfried fortification. It is near Freckenfeld, Germany, where we later stayed a while before pushing into Germany. When we were resting at Freckenfeld I went over to Oberotterbach and looked the place over. Saw where I was wounded, in a grape vineyard, and what a terrible looking place it was after quite a few months battling. The town itself is nil, completely destroyed except for a few remaining houses. The dragon teeth are just on the hill beyond.

I believe I was going to tell you about the two other medics that got medals. One from Gary, Indiana, I mentioned before (originally lived in Elwood), Glenn Scott. He got a Silver Star and a battlefield commission later for gallantry in action at Oberotterbach. He was there 7 days. The other kid, Elvin Mude, pronounced Moody, from Iowa, got a Bronze Star for going through an open field to help a platoon sergeant who had been shot. We were all aid men for C Company. I think they indeed appreciated us medics in that action and they showed their appreciation by rewarding us.

I keep wishing I were home so I could tell you all the little things that happened and are indeed interesting and some quite funny. I keep rambling on in this letter and after reading it I find it quite incoherent. Think I'll stop for now. A kid just got a nice box of homemade cookies and we're enjoying them, sure good. Am okey-dokey.

Love,

Richard

May 24, 1945

Mother to Richard

Dear Richard,

This week we got your letter of May 6. Glad you were still okay that near VE day, and trust you still are. We are anxious to know whether or not you will get a furlough home. There is still so much unrest in the world that real peace seems a long way off—although it's so peaceful here that it's hard to realize it.

We are still housecleaning and did the living room yesterday. Virginia is fine help. She is going to work in conferences again, so she will be gone most of June. School will be out next week. Every class and club is having a picnic, and it usually rains. The class play is Friday night. We are going to the farm this afternoon. Our garden has been put out in mud so far. It will be hard to tend. We get a quart or so of strawberries every time we go. Strawberries are eight dollars a crate this year and Aunt Fannie doesn't have many, so we won't be canning them! Write us more about things, if not so censored now.

Lots of Love,

Mother

L-R: Richard, Pettit, Smitty (Kraiburg, Germany)
Courtesy of Bill Rutz

May 26, 1945

Richard to Folks,

Dear Folks,

I've lost track of the days this week, guess this is Saturday. Have been piddling around the past few days getting all my stuff, including clothes and souvenirs, straightened out. Still have dirty fatigues in my duffle bag that I wore over here on the boat—ha. By the way, I never did say anything about the boat trip, except getting sick.

Sailed from New York, Staten Island, October 14 on the USS *LeJeune*, a captured German vessel, and a very nice boat, too. Passed Gibraltar on the morning of the 25th and 'twas most impressive, a beautiful sunny morn. The coast of Spain was brilliant and then the Moroccan coast loomed up with jagged peaks, then came Gibraltar, indeed a unique formation of gray rock, then the big rocks of Hercules on the right which were to my notion the most impressive. In the morning sun, they were the softest gray color I've ever seen. The water was a blue-green and many fish and dolphins darted about. "Spitfires" darted overhead, too. Later in the day we saw Oran, Algeria, and then that night and the remaining time the sea was so rough that seeing anything but foam and spray was impossible. We came into Marseille Bay on the afternoon of 28 Oct, another very impressive sight. Got off the boat the next day and marched through the outskirts of the city to a troop assembly area. Later I went to Marseille on pass, 3 or 4 times, once with Buster, and what a city—Wow! Most all the people, every nationality, looked like rats and spoke practically any language regardless of what it was. Later on I went through Toulon and on Thanksgiving Day hitchhiked to Nice and enjoyed a few hours in that city. The French Riviera is indeed beautiful with all sorts of tropical plants, palms, etc.

Today and tomorrow the Battalion is sponsoring another trip to the Bavarian Alps, this time to Innsbruck and possibly Brenner Pass. I didn't go today, don't know whether I will or not tomorrow. I've seen about as much of these Alps now as I want to see—they're beautiful. Rodman is near here in the Alps somewhere with the 7th Army. Saw Mack Moss's outfit roll past the other day but didn't see him naturally, or at least the outfit he was in at Camp Campbell.

You probably read in the paper about the 14th taking Moosburg and liberating the big prison camp. The 68th did that! I was going thru there May 1 and witnessed quite a spectacle. General Patton came by in a peep, plus a couple other generals, and one of the liberated prisoners got in his way while riding on a bicycle. Naturally his driver stopped and Patton jumped up out of his seat waving his arms and said, "Get the hell out'a the way"—ha! So I now believe all the wild tales about Patton. This all happened right beside the half-track I was riding in, indeed quite an interesting incident for a 4-star general.

The sight of liberated prisoners was indeed a pathetic one, especially seeing our own troops. One of our boys liberated in Moosburg was standing by the road as we passed and evidently had found a bottle. He waved his arms and said, "Get 'em boys, make 'em *good* Germans, dead Germans." I've learned that most of 'em are only good when they are dead, especially the SS troops.[101] That's about all we fought this side of the Rhine. I saw SS troops shoot three Wehrmacht troops who had surrendered to us and were coming to us with their hands up,[102] nicht sehr gut.[103] We got the SS'ers. Am okey dokey.

Love,

Richard

---

101 Headed by Heinrich Himmler, the SS was founded in 1925 by Hitler to serve as his personal bodyguards. They grew in power and numbers over the years and were regarded as the most vicious of Nazi troops for their intense racism and lack of regard for human suffering. There were three subgroups: Hitler's bodyguard, administrators of concentration camps, and thirty-nine divisions of elite combat troops. —Ed.

102 Wehrmacht: name for the unified military of Germany from 1935-1945. It included army, navy, and air force. —Ed.

103 "Nicht sehr gut" translates as "not so good." —Ed.

May 30, 1945

Richard's Journal

As usual I've neglected writing and that's bad since much history, of which I was an intricate part, was made. But guess I can remember the main points of interest, although some should be recorded, others possibly, and some but definitely, should be forgotten. I see the last time I wrote we had just cracked the Siegfried Line. And did lots of sweating, and we got a citation for that, too, or rather a commendation, in particular my 3rd Platoon for taking Freckenfeld.

April 4 we got ambushed in the evening near Langenleiten, wherever that's at, and lost quite a few men and HQ half-track. We really sweat that little episode, think I kinda got grazed on my right hand by a bullet, got a couple smack thru my pack while riding on the half-track. Dunn was shot thru the throat, died later.[104] Strowbridge, Claud Wilson, Sgt. Robb, etc., got it. Some affair that was.

April 7 we got a rest at Unsleben where we stayed until the 11th. I sent home a Jerry flag, a Jerry medic's knife, and some beads to Julia. I picked wildflowers and enjoyed the spring weather for a change. On April 14, at or near Neuhaus almost got it. Our column got fired on by Jerries as we were entering a town. I was riding with my squad and we got one in the back end right where I was sitting, 3 men killed and anti-tank squad lost 2 half-tracks. Scotty and I took care of 'em and it was pretty bad. My ear bothered me for a couple three days or so. The next day or so was the "Champagne Campaign," about Pottenstein, and something well to remember. The liberated Russian prisoners and their striped suits. They ran all over the place with bottles of stuff, and how! Truthfully, the first taste of champagne I ever had! On April 17, we got in Hausheim after an over the valley and hill route from Altdorf, sweat another town the next morn. Rangold shoots a woman Jerry SS, some place, B Co. takes Pölling. April 21 we sweat Neumarkt, a big town, and have big time. Hospital, canal,

---

104 Pfc. Richard J. Dunn was from Baltimore, Maryland, and had enlisted in the Army on March 20, 1943. He was 22 years old at the time of his death and is buried at the Lorraine American Cemetery in St. Avold, France. —Ed.

got picture taken crossing the canal under sniper fire. 3rd Platoon fires tank in Neumarkt and we pull out about 4 bells on morn of 22nd. Later read an article in a Jerry newspaper that said the SS drove us out—ha! The Air Corps took care of 'em that morning on the 22nd. We take Mörlach across 3 miles of woods and fields the night of 22nd and 23rd. Clear woods all day of the 23rd and pull back to Mörlach that evening and take off to another Sector, being transferred to Patton's 3rd—III Corps. We move to Pettling by the Danube and stay 2 days waiting to cross the river. We cross the Danube at Ingolstadt the 28th by pontoon at 14:35 and shack up in Meilenhofen that night.

April 28 was a sad day. Late in the evening we ran into SS at a small town near Mainburg. Billhymer gets killed by a Panzerfaust,[105] and Ringeisen of my platoon gets shot in head by SS buzzgun.[106] Sure lost two of our best soldiers that day! Ringeisen is from Milwaukee, Wisconsin and Bill from Northern Indiana. Walked into Mainburg and stayed the night after blastin' the Jerries. In that little town the SS shot 3 Wehrmacht soldiers as they were walking towards us with hands in air—some stuff. On the 30th, we ran into trouble at Altdorf and had to sweat woods, etc., and finally took Altdorf by night. Early in the morning before light, we started an attack on big Landshut under a most terrific artillery barrage. We got in an open field and had to hit the dirt, they got so close. I crawled in a big bomb crater and Bunnel alongside. Sizzle and a big piece of shrapnel goes right between us and hits in the water—red hot—boy! We looked at one another and I could just see he was thinking the same thing as I, when's that one going to drop on us—ha! The whole trouble was

---

105   2nd Lt. Robert M. Billhymer was from Pendleton, Indiana. He is buried at the Lorraine American Cemetery in St. Avold, France. —Ed.
106   Pvt. George J. Ringeisen was from Milwaukee, Wisconsin, and enlisted in the Army October 20, 1942. He was 22 years old at the time of his death and is buried at the Lorraine American Cemetery in St. Avold, France. In *Memories of the 14th Armored Division*, Staff Sgt. William Rutz wrote that Ringeisen was killed by a German soldier who was only 3-4 yards away. Ringeisen was shot through the neck and died instantly. The German soldier who killed him was captured and turned out to be just a boy, maybe 15-16 years old. The boy was not killed in exchange for providing information about the enemy. —Ed.

the Air Corps had removed the houses we were supposed to stay in during the barrage. Well, afterwards all went well and we cleared the muchly banked joint, to the river, looted a big chocolate factory of cookies, chocolate, champagne, and about anything else you could think of, moved back that evening to Altdorf being relieved by the 99th Infantry Division. They later took the town and got lots of American prisoners in a Lager.[107]

May 1—Altdorf to Moosburg, crossed Isar River at 15:00 by pontoon bridge. The day before B Co. liberated 100,000 prisoners there and what a sight, made tears come into my eyes. We gave GIs about all we had including champagne. Heard a gruesome story told by a Canadian Ranger who was liberated. He was dragged out of the English Channel by the Jerries 3 years before. And too, the most important item of the day!!! While sitting in our half-track waiting for the column to move, Old George (hell raisin') Patton comes tearing up with his 4 stars, 6 peeps, 3 armored cars, and a couple 2-star generals. A prisoner just liberated got in the way of his jeep while he was passing our vehicles. He (Patton) jumps up in his seat and throws up his arms and says, "Get that thing the hell outa' the way!"—ha!—what an exhibition! I now believe all I've read about him. That night we shack up out in some barnyard, and it snows. I sleep in the stables with the cows, lots warmer there.

May 2—Geislbach to Irl to Aspertsham, a little village in the Inn River valley overlooked by the beautiful snowcapped Alps of Hitler's Redoubt,[108] which never materialized. We moved 3rd Platoon to Söllerstadt on May 7 where we were on patrol and where the war ended officially. Listened to Churchill's speech that afternoon and the king, etc. We did a little celebrating and Petit got tight and he and the old man, the Romanian we picked up to cook for us and who sleeps with Vedee (the puppy) and who we have as yet still cooking

---

107 Lager: German for camp. —Ed.
108 Hitler's Redoubt was the feared establishment of an inner fortress in the Alps. Korte, Jeff, "Eisenhower, Berlin and the National Redoubt," *Gateway: An Academic History Journal on the Web*, http://grad.usask.ca/gateway/archive22.html (Jan. 26, 2014).

for us, had a great time until Petit got sleepy and sick and went off to bed. Now know that May 2 was the last day of this war for us. I even baked some chocolate cake and biscuits. We got Vedee and Snowball, the puppies, a couple of days ago. Had fun leading the comfortable lazy life not believing it possible that we don't have to get shot at by Jerries anymore.

May 11 we move to Oberbergkirchen above Ampfing. On May 19, got to see famous Berchtesgaden and Chiemsee on a conducted tour with HQ Company's Medics. Roamed all around the entire afternoon over Hitler's once proud retreat but now another Air Corps mess. Got lots of junky souvenirs and picked some wild flowers in Hitler's backyard to send to Mrs. Phillips and home. Some guys swam in Chiemsee, but was too cold for me. Got some pretty little rocks there, however. On the 28th, I delivered a baby with aid of midwife across the river from Kraiburg, 7 lb girl to Polski refugee.

Nazi flag and German medic's knife sent home by Richard

KAREN BERKEY HUNTSBERGER

View looking at The Berghof from neighboring hill. Photos taken fourteen days after The Berghof was destroyed on May 5, 1945. Courtesy of Norman Eliasson

Richard standing in front window of Hitler's bombed-out home, The Berghof.
Courtesy of Norman Eliasson

KAREN BERKEY HUNTSBERGER

Looking out from inside The Berghof.
Courtesy of Norman Eliasson

May 31, 1945
Mother to Richard

Dear Richard,

We were lucky today. We got letters from you and Lucy, both of which we had been watching for. Your letter was dated May 9. Lots of people have had letters from the boys in Europe that are a week or 10 days more recent than that, but at least you wrote after VE day. Yes, as you said, we were all thrilled to know the war in Europe was over, but nobody felt like noise and jollification. There was too much still to be done, and too, many families were sad because of their losses. Dell Strain blew a blast on the factory whistle, and that was about all.

Now the question is—what is to be done with you? Daddy said he talked to Ford Smith this morning. He thought Lee Edward might be transferred to the 15th Army and stay over there. He said they hoped that he would, as they do not want him to go to the Pacific. We feel about the same way, though we hope you can come home on furlough before too long a time.

Lucy said she got the Nazi insignia you sent her, and we got the Jerry flag and knife. The flag is on such a nice piece of red material and is so fresh and clean. You must have washed it or had it cleaned. It is a good souvenir and we are glad to have it.

Daddy and I are about frazzled. We spent yesterday, Memorial Day, at the farm and went back this afternoon because it was Thursday. Our garden is so hard to work because so many rains packed it down. We have been a whole month just getting things to come up. This afternoon we planted two rows of big fat lima beans and preparing the rows, hoeing, and plowing up that hard dirt was a big task. We have no help, for school is not out until tomorrow, and Virginia is away, getting ready for conference work. She will be gone off and on through June, and Eleanor will be gone for two weeks.

On Memorial Day, we took Aunt Fannie to the cemetery as usual with her flowers and ours. We put a bouquet on Dee's grave this time. Johnny Ingram has been home again and came to see us. He had been all the way to the Philippines. He was on a communications vessel. He will be at Treasure Island in school again for a month.[109] Hap Hinds is at home now. Still has a paralyzed foot but thinks they can patch the nerve. Leroy Clark has written that he is in a hospital in the South Pacific with a broken leg. He caught it between the big ship and a little boat. Bob Hoke was killed down south when a train struck his car. His funeral was here Sunday.

I wish you could see the roses on the arbor now. They are gorgeous this year, especially the red.

Lots of Love,

Mother

---

109 Treasure Island Naval Station was a Works Progress Administration (WPA) project in the 1930s. It was built on the sandbars of Yerba Buena Island and was used for transporting soldiers and equipment to the war in the Pacific. "World War II in the San Francisco Bay Area," *National Park Service*, http://www.cr.nps.gov/nr/travel/wwiibayarea/qua.htm (Feb. 9, 2014).

CHAPTER TWELVE

Looking Back and Moving Forward

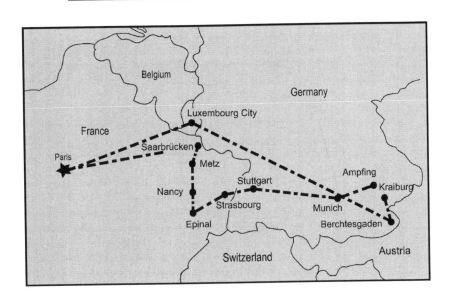

June 1, 1945

Richard's Journal

We took off for Paris on the 30th. Skillman takes Bohn and me to Wasserburg to dinner. About 6 that evening we take off in GI trucks for Luxembourg. It hails and rains, biggest hail I ever saw, likely to freeze all night. Arrived in Luxembourg at 11 on the 31st after 400-mile ride. Have a chicken dinner in the rail station, see city, change money and eat ice cream, the 1st since the States. Boarded train for Paris at 7:00 and arrived in Paris at noon. Ate nice chow in station and go to hotels. Bohn and I stay at Pavillion Club. After cleaning up and getting oriented and chow, we start our sightseeing tour. Saw Champs-Élysées, Arc de Triomphe, Eiffel Tower, and what a place. The Arc is most impressive.

June 2, 1945

Richard's Journal

This morn tried looking up Buster and Carroll Moore. Found they were in Mailley-le-Camp and no response so that's that. In the afternoon I sold some cigarettes, loot, etc. for 1500 francs. Tonight Bohn and I enjoyed a show at French Stage Door canteen and then took off in a northerly direction. Hit a street carnival and I rode on the electric "bump" cars and had a big time. Then we accidentally run onto famous Pigalle and saw how the prostitutes operate for 500-1000 francs.[110] That's some place but actually none to be seen in by your best friends—ha!

June 3, 1945

Went to Folies ticket office and got reservations for matinee, Bohn, Kneeland, Slim, and myself.[111] Got front row seats and saw the show that afternoon. Pretty swell show and gals, too—okay. Sunday night we puttered around Rainbow Corner canteen,[112] and this and that. Took in the hotel dance and messed around in general. Ended up eating ice cream near our hotel, raspberry sherbet.

June 4, 1945

Richard's Journal, Paris

Kneeland and I got to PX and got rations, cigarettes, candy, toilet articles, perfume, billfold, etc. Sent perfume to Virginia and billfold to Dad. In afternoon I went on conducted tour of city and really

---

110 Pigalle: area of Paris frequented by servicemen in World War II for sex shops, adult shows, cabarets, theaters, and prostitutes. —Ed.
111 Folies Bergère: famous cabaret music hall in Paris. —Ed.
112 Rainbow Corner: Red Cross club in Paris for servicemen. —Ed.

enjoyed seeing all the sights and hearing the history of each. Wish I had gone the first day. I would have appreciated my stay a little more maybe, but all was really nice. At 8 bells we boarded train and took off for Luxembourg. Stopped for doughnuts and coffee in Reims, saw Verdun and then Luxembourg in the morn. Our trucks were waiting and we took off for home.

AMERICAN RED CROSS

PAVILLON CLUB
HOTEL PAVILLON

SIGHTSEEING around PARIS

ITINERARY

OPERA — GRANDS BOULEVARDS — MADELEINE CHURCH — CONCORDE SQUARE — CHAMPS-ELYSEES — GRAND PALAIS and PETIT PALAIS — ARCH OF TRIUMPH — AVENUE FOCH — BOIS DE BOULOGNE — TROCADERO — PALAIS DE CHAILLOT — EIFFEL TOWER — MILITARY SCHOOL — INVALIDES — Visit of the TOMB OF NAPOLEON — QUAI D'ORSAY — CHAMBER OF DEPUTIES — SCHOOL OF FINE ARTS — INSTITUTE OF FRANCE — LUXEMBOURG PALACE — PANTHEON — LATIN QUARTER — SORBONNE — CLUNY MUSEUM — NOTRE-DAME (Visit) — TOWN HALL — PALACE OF JUSTICE — CONCIERGERIE — LOUVRE PALACE — CARROUSEL SQUARE — RUE DE RIVOLI — PLACE VENDOME — OPERA.

Bus leaving every day at 9.30 a. m. and 1 p. m. and 3.15. p. m. from the Pavillon Club.

FARE: 60 Frs.

EXPLANATIONS GIVEN by COMPETENT ENGLISH-SPEAKING LECTURER.

Tours organized for our account by « Vendôme-Tourisme », 14, rue de Castiglione - Paris.

*In front of Arc de Triomphe—Richard is in back row, second from left.
Photographer unknown*

Richard in Luxembourg Garden. Courtesy of Norman Eliasson

KAREN BERKEY HUNTSBERGER

June 6, 1945

Got to see practically all the Siegfried Line front—Kaiserslautern, Saarbrücken, Metz, Épinal, Nancy, Strasbourg, and saw cathedral, Ulm, Stuttgart, Munich. Arrived back at aid station at Ampfing on morning of 6th—what a trip and most enjoyable.

June 7, 1945

Richard to Folks

Dear Folks,

I've just returned from Paris and a very nice 8-day vacation. Boy is that Paris a place! Everything is there except good old home and family. Spent three days and nights there and sure did enjoy myself. I never realized that so much history etc. is connected with the city until I took a tour of the city with a French (English speaking) guide.

Guess the best way to tell you about the trip is to just start from the first. Road from here to Luxembourg in a truck, some odd 400 miles. Went thru much battered Munich and up the autobahn and Siegfried Line to Luxembourg. We started from here the morn of May 30 and arrived in Luxembourg the next afternoon in time for a big chicken dinner, which was much appreciated since it rained during the night and was cold and even hailed outside of Munich. The ground was white and hail was enormous, 1-2 inches in diameter, believe it or not. We also passed through the Saar Basin and Moselle River section where the 3rd Army did a lot of fighting, Saarburg, Saarbrücken and Sarreguemines, and Metz to name a few cities.

Stayed one afternoon in Luxembourg and finally after running all around to get my money changed to Belgian francs I was able to purchase the first ice cream I'd had since leaving home. Not real ice cream though, just watery sherbet, but good! Walked around the town a while and is indeed a very beautiful place, not damaged at all in main sections.

Caught a train for Paris about 7 and arrived in Paris at noon on the 1st. Went through historic Reims where the peace was signed and where SHAEF, Supreme Headquarters Allied Expeditionary Force, is located and through Verdun.

We received another chicken dinner in a very nice dining room at the terminal, then proceeded to our hotel. I stayed in the Pavilion Hotel, American Red Cross Pavilion Club, taken over by the Army for combat soldiers on leave and run by the Red Cross. This hotel is located in the center of town near the opera. Had another chicken dinner in the evening. A very nice hotel with all sorts of things to do right in the hotel—ping-pong, pool, dancing, all sorts of reading material, artists to draw a profile, musicians playing the piano, etc., during the day and an orchestra at night, a photo place and a wonderful dining room with black haired, and very good-looking, French waitresses and an orchestra playing while you eat. And the violinist played request numbers and would come right over to your table and play what you requested—okay! Ha! Staying in that place makes one feel like a big shot.

After receiving our pass and room and eating dinner, another kid and I went sightseeing. Doesn't get dark till about 10:30 or 11:00 due to the time change, two hours ahead of regular time. So we took off down Boulevard Montmartre and down Italiens to the Opera. Passed Rainbow Corner, famous Red Cross canteen center, and boy is it a super duper place all for U.S. soldiers. Down to Place de Madeleine and to Place de la Concorde, and the Champs-Élysées and what a street, really impressive! Walked up this avenue to the Arc de Triomphe. I was most impressed by this memorial, more so than any other thing in Paris, including the cathedral. The flame was burning and a big array of flowers below. French unknown soldier is here, flame burns at his head. The wreath was sent by the New York City Legionnaires, the day before being Memorial Day, and said on a piece of ribbon—"To our Buddies." The wreath is changed every day by French war veterans and the fire renewed with oil.

We went on over next to Eiffel Tower across the river, the big theater opposite across the river and the other way the military school, all indeed very nice and impressive. 'Twas getting about dark by this time and our legs were rather tired so we went over to the Paris Stage Door canteen on the Champs-Élysées below the Arc. They had for entertainment a band and stage show. We ate ice cream and drank real Cokes and proceeded to see how the French do things, which knowing the French, anything can happen, and does. They had a couple of acts, acrobats and then Annabelle, Hollywood movie star, made an appearance and spoke mostly French and I didn't understand most of it. Then they danced a while and had a gal sing. She was evidently not very well enjoyed for all the Frenchies started booing and she stopped singing, put her hands to her face and ran off the stage—ha! More fun, first time I ever saw that happen. By the time we got back to our hotel that night we were pretty tired and 'twas only about 2 bells so we decided to go to bed. Not that there wasn't anything to do, just be rested for more tomorrow.

Saturday morning I ran down to Base Headquarters and attempted to look up Carroll Moore. Had a letter from Buster before I left saying that Carroll had called him up from Paris but found out he was in Mannheim on the Rhine many miles away. Also looked up Buster and found he was in a town about 50 to 75 miles east of Paris, so I didn't get to see anyone in Paris I knew.

Saturday afternoon was spent messing around in North Paris and indulging in the black market. Sold 2 cartons cigarettes for 30 bucks (1500 francs) to sorta reimburse my pocketbook. Everybody does it and there sure is a demand for cigarettes. Everything is extremely high in Paris and one needs plenty of francs to get along, of course in accordance to what one does—ha!

Saturday night we decided to hit the northwest part of town which we did after spending a couple hours at the French canteen being entertained by an old French babe who seemed to be trying to be a good hostess. We passed by one of these street carnivals on our journeys during the night, just like back home, and I had to amuse myself for about an hour riding the electric "bump" cars. More fun! I'd just go bumping into everyone. Almost broke my neck and arm once when I attained a great speed (5 mph—ha!) and crashed into a couple of girls who crashed into another car. They sort of flew out like birdies and settled back with a big thud—ha! Big laugh for the whole gang—ha!

After the carnival we ended up on Pigalle Avenue (famous?) by mistake, but proceeded to take it in anyway and did so and ended up at the hotel in the wee, wee hours.

Got reservation Sunday morning for the famous Folies Bergère and paid 200 francs for front row seats. Went to the matinee and what a show—wow! Lasted about three hours and really enjoyed it. Spent Sunday night partially "uptown" and at the dance we had at the hotel. All the girls were English-speaking, to a limited extent, and all went very well.

Monday morning the 4th was spent in shopping. Bought my PX rations including 7 packs cigarettes, 6 candy bars, can of tomato juice, bar of soap, toothbrush, etc., best PX rations I received since being over here. Bought a bottle of perfume and sent it to Virginia and a wallet and sent to Dad. Maybe all you women folks at home can share the perfume. I paid no meager sum for it and knowing nothing about perfumes, I just guess it's okay. There were perfumes priced at unimaginable figures—whew!

Went on tour of city and 'twas the most enjoyable afternoon I had spent. We went to all places of interest, namely Notre Dame and Les Invalides where Napoleon's tomb is and where a few more of that family are buried. What was most remarkable about Notre Dame to my notion was its age and how it was built and lasted all these years.

Caught train at 9 Monday night for Luxembourg, arrived next day at noon. The poppy fields between these two towns are really beautiful. Never saw anything like it, they even cultivate them.

Monday afternoon we boarded trucks and had a very interesting trip. Went through Metz, Nancy in Lorraine, Saar Basin, Saverne and Strasbourg in Alsace. Got to see the old cathedral in Strasbourg and 'tis indeed a work of art. A shell hit the back part of the building during the fighting and knocked off a cupola. Crossed the Rhine, passed thru the Siegfried fortifications, cities of Stuttgart, Karlsruhe, Ulm, Augsburg, and Munich. All these towns might now be termed "ghost towns." The French were mostly in the sector and they really believe in tearing up towns.

Arrived here the morning of the 6th, which was a holiday, and caught up on a little sleep, etc. I sure was fortunate in being able to go to all these places that were so bitterly fought for. The last big battle I was in was at Landshut, north of here. We "looted" a chocolate factory—ha! About our toughest fight this side of the Rhine was at Neumarkt. Got my picture taken in action there. We had a footbridge across the canal which was under sniper fire and as I ran across a photographer took my picture. We almost lost him later when he was left in the town all by himself after we withdrew, but his buddy rescued him in a peep. He was in a big hospital asleep—ha! We later flanked the town and another division took it.

Today I received your box, Mother, with the pancake flour and baking powder. Thanks loads, now I can have some fun. Also thanks for the recipes. I think I'll try some of them. Also received your V-mail of the 24th along with a letter from the Bushes, the first since Dee was killed, a very nice letter indeed.

A letter from Buster today also says that Frank Richard is starting to walk. He'll soon be a year old—can't believe that hardly.

Played a couple of games of softball and am sore as can be. This morning we beat a team 18 to 1 for the first medic victory. Must have been my appearance, first time I'd played. I got two doubles, a single and out once, scored three runs. Played short field and got my back sunburned again—ha!

Think I'm going to Innsbruck tomorrow, the famous summer resort down in Austria above Brenner Pass. I've really been sightseeing deluxe here lately.

Am okay but haven't got any strawberries to eat yet. They are just now getting ripe. This section of the country has the most beautiful grain fields I ever saw, and they cut it by hand!

Love,

Richard

June 9, 1945

Richard's Journal

Go over to Kraiburg with C Company and set up a Company aid station with Ladd. Bohn relieves Ladd. Kraiburg is on the Inn River. Beaucoup of fraternizing, ha and plenty of good-looking women here. Sat around doing nothing much. Here they are making the town Nazis dig up about 30 Jews that were killed and buried a couple miles from here near Jettenbach.

Dad to Richard

Dear Son,

HAPPY BIRTHDAY. We will be thinking of you on your birthday, June 24. Got your letter this morning asking about the cake. Will let Mother read it at noon. Yesterday got your letter about the American flag. Got one from Howard O. Pick-elheimer that is 3 x 5. Will send it as soon as we can fix it up. Going to put your name on it so when you get through with it you can send it back and keep it. That is just a thought. Thanks for the German flag and knife you sent and also the flowers. Keep telling us where you've been, etc. Of course, a German

Luger pistol would be a good one to keep.[113] I'll pay the postage if you want to send one. It would look nice in the office window. Hope you get to see Munich and Paris, and other places. Looks like you have a chance to see many historical places. Some pay big money to see those places.

Wrote Lucy for her birthday—June 12. David is now in Philippines. By the way, your picture was on the front page of the *Indianapolis News* yesterday. Real good. The one receiving the Bronze Star. Jonas is now at recruiting station, Huntington, West Virginia. Mildred is with him. You can write him at that address. He will be there until October 5 unless he gets orders changed which is not likely. Virginia and Eleanor were at McCormick's Creek Camp with Girl Scouts all this week. Just got back last night. All week has been rainy and cool. Both have colds. Virginia will be away week after next at church conference. Too wet this week to make garden. Will issue you a war bond on the 24th and put it with the others. I am getting the 10 each month and adding it to your building and loan fund. So the bond will be for your birthday. Again, Happy Birthday and good luck. Keep writing.

Your dad,

James G. Berkey

Mother to Richard

Dear Boy,

We got another of your most welcome letters today. It was the one that enclosed flowers from Hitler's retreat. I have mounted them on three cards and certainly want to keep them for a souvenir.

You also requested a cake. I rather doubted the wisdom of sending it, as it will be so stale, but it's on its way! Virginia baked the

---

113 Luger: semi-automatic German pistol heavily used during World War I and World War II. —Ed.

layers, I cracked some nuts and put on chocolate icing and we packed it in oiled paper and popcorn. Virginia took the package to the post office and tried to send it by airmail, but they wouldn't take it that way. Said it wouldn't get there for a long time—about six weeks at the least. Poor cake! Oh, poor boy! We also have your request for a flag, in a delayed letter dated May 14. Daddy got a nice one, 3 x 5 feet, and we'll send it the first of the week. Only one package a week, you know. Maybe by the time you get it you won't be needing it. You don't even venture a guess as to what is to be done with you. Suppose you don't know. Oh yes, a little more about the cake package. The icing is made from a frosting mix that Mildred got in Miami and put in my Mother's Day package. The heavy paper and string are from Lucy's package mailed in Washington. Quite a cosmopolitan package!

Got a letter from David. He told about a monkey they have. Its name is Atabrine! Today Mrs. McBride sent us a letter from Mildred describing the lovely apartment they have in Huntington. She says it's so nice she should have her sterling and crystal and best things along, to live up to it. The only trouble is the too small kitchenette, and not a very good gas stove. Virginia got an announcement tonight about Virginia Hutto's baby. Its name is Darcy Kit. We guess it's a girl but are not sure.

Leroy Clark called his folks last night from the West Coast. He has lost a leg. It developed gangrene and had to be removed.

Lots of Love,

Mother

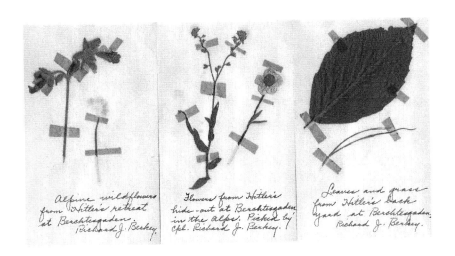

Alpine wildflowers from Hitler's retreat at Berchtesgaden. Richard J. Berkey.

Flowers from Hitler's hide-out at Berchtesgaden in the alps. Picked by Cpl. Richard J. Berkey.

Leaves and grass from Hitler's back yard at Berchtesgaden. Richard J. Berkey.

David with "Atabrine," the monkey
Courtesy of Nina Seven

June 11, 1945

Rodman to Richard

Hello Richard,

I received your letter a few days ago. I was happy to hear of your location and all your adventures. I just returned from a three-day leave in Brussels, Belgium, and I'm a little worn down yet but still livin'. Brussels is a swell town but the trip is too much for only three days. We traveled 647 miles one way in a jeep and 2½ ton truck—all in two days! The babes in Brussels speak English, too, the universal language. "I come wiz you, babe; you zig zig?"[114] Not me though, nix; I don't touch the stuff. Brussels is the nicest town I've hit yet though. It has felt the war very little compared to places like Paris, London, etc. I even bought some of this famous Chanel #5 perfume that the gals back home all go nuts over.

When you all going back to the U.S.A.? As for me I don't know what the hell the score is here. Our colonel is in Paris or London all the time but he never brings home any dope. I think he only stayed with us two days last week. You ask about fraternizing. Well, everybody fraternizes here from the colonel on down, all but me; I never touch the stuff!!

Congratulations on that extra stripe. I forgot to mention it in my last letter. And how about some of these citations I hear you have? Let me hear about them and what they are. My platoon medic got the Bronze Star, the only decoration in my platoon. The company had some but not so many. You see, we weren't in the show very long.

In that short time I must say I picked up a few things myself. Right now I have an Austrian painter painting pictures of the Alps for me. He's really a character but does some nice paintings. Now I'm wondering how the hell I'm going to get them home.

I'm in a little village of Prutz down here in Austria. Have been here ever since the war ended. We were with the 44th Division

---

114 This was a common expression prostitutes used to solicit soldiers. —Ed.

but they have gone so we are with the 103rd now. They are all over here. If you ever get the chance, hop the mail truck, ration wagon, or something and come down. We'll put you up for a while and even take you back. It's pretty hard for me to get that far in our own vehicles for this chicken shit battalion thinks the office has to stay around. I'll keep my eyes open however, I may get around yet. I was at Augsburg about two weeks ago at a 7th Army supply meeting. At the time I wasn't sure where you were. In case you can't find Prutz on the map, just look at the border of Austria, Switzerland, and Italy—that's us! We have guards in three countries now! And there's only one road down here.

Well, old man, it looks pretty bad back home so far as women are concerned for us. These *old* veterans are moving in and how! I was surprised to hear of Betty Nell and Pauline Mead. Next it will be big Jim Huffman and Martha I suppose. Oh yeah, did I tell you Eddie Alberding is in the Marianas and is engaged to Margaret Persinger? I figure when Eddie starts operating like that, it's time old Rodman should be startin' too. I saw your picture plus write-up in the January issue of the alumni magazine. Very nice! Have you seen it, or do you get the alumni magazine?

You asked me about points! Well, that is sort of a laugh to me. Here I am single, young, a little weak from Brussels but still going. I just didn't have enough kids and I only got 31 points. Oh well, the Japanese war will be over in a few months anyway. All that inactive service I had in ERC didn't count on my points.[115] That wouldn't have helped much anyway.

Well, I'll bring this to a screaming halt here. Hoping this finds you well and happy and all packed for a trip to the U.S.A. Write soon.

Yours,

Rodman

---

115 ERC: Enlisted Reserve Corps. —Ed.

June 15, 1945

Mother to Richard

Dear Richard,

You have written us so many interesting letters since censorship was lifted that it keeps us busy passing the news along to the relatives. Twice I've typed letters, making two carbon copies, to send to Jonas, Lucy, and David, getting extracts from your letters. I thought it was hardly likely that you would write all that again, to either of them.

It is certainly thrilling to hear you tell about visiting all those places mentioned in history and literature. I'm so glad for you to get to see them. On the other hand it is heartbreaking to know you have had to witness the horrors of war. I hope it will not make you hard and unsympathetic. After all there are *some* good Germans who are not dead Germans and I hope you'll have an opportunity to find some of them, if you have to stay in the Army of Occupation. The church is still alive in Germany, even though it has had to work underground at times. But, from what the papers tell us, you're going to meet problems, problems, and problems.

As your letters come, you are answering many of the questions I asked you, even before you got the letter asking them. We were glad to get that commendation at last. Your picture was in the *News* last week, I think I told you, and today it was in the *Louisville Times*. Myrtle Esther called up to tell us she was proud of you. Several people have called.

Bob Crockett has been home on furlough again this weekend. I see that Camp Campbell, which was closed for a while, is to be opened as a reassignment center. Camp Atterbury is now discharging about 300 soldiers a day.

We had a letter from David. He said he is now entitled to wear the Liberation of the Philippines badge with one star. He was in on the invasion of a part of Mindanao. They went up the

Mindanao River. Don Anderson is at home but has to go to the Pacific. It's still showery, like April. Nearly every day is partly cloudy. Sorry this is so terribly disconnected—I keep listening to Eleanor and Virginia chatting in the next room!

Love,

Mother

June 16, 1945

Richard's Journal

Moved to Frau Lager across the river from Kraiburg and 3-4 kilometers from Ampfing. Frau Lager is women's hospital for Hitler's children, nice and modern. Went to dance tonight at aid station. Polish gals, 20 of 'em, came from nearby Lagers and we had a big time, plenty to eat and drink, good music and all. I liked to dance my legs off.[116] We even did a Polski dance that is like our American square dancing. A big time was had by all and how!

---

116 The end of the war was not the end of the suffering. There were many displaced people all over Europe. In Germany, many had been freed from prison camps but had no food, money, or transportation and were often not well enough to travel. Many displaced people found shelter wherever they could—abandoned factories, army barracks, and even concentration camps. Many displaced people also did not wish to return to the newly formed Communist regimes in their own countries. "European Refugee Movements After World War Two," *BBC History*, http://www.bbc.co.uk/history/worldwars/wwtwo/refugees_01.shtml (Jan. 27, 2014).

Richard with Claud Wilson (Kraiburg, Germany).
Photographer unknown

From back of Photo: "R.J. Berkey, Claud C. Wilson, and little German girl who
refused to have her picture taken with her cute hat on. She was rewarded with two
sticks of chewing gum and ran home delighted to no end."
Photographer unknown

June 17, 1945

Richard's Journal

Pruett Field dedicated in honor of Pruett of B Company. Pruett was Buster's buddy, killed at Rittershoffen where Buster got hit. [117] Had ceremony and then we won game from 25th Tankers 6-4.

June 18, 1945

Richard to Mother

Dear Mother,

Received your letter of June 5 and since you ask all the questions, I decided that for once I'll answer them. So here goes—

This town of Ampfing is a few miles west of Mühldorf, which you should find on the map. Oberbergkirchen is not Oberkirch but only a few miles apart. By the way, a large town near here is Haag, 20 miles west, and Wasserburg, 30 miles southwest. Kraiburg is 4 miles southeast of Ampfing and across the Inn River. The town of Pfaffenhofen you found is north of here, I think, a little south of Ingolstadt near the Danube River. However, not the one I mentioned—it is in France north of Hageunau. Other towns near there are La Walck, Bitschhoffen, Ringeldorf, and Saverne. We came through this Pfaffenhofen in Germany a few days before the war ended.

Crossed the Rhine on a pontoon bridge at 2:30 a.m. near Worms in a motorized column. The moon was very pretty on the water and was more or less unimpressive other than it was the Rhine. Of course I've crossed it a few times since but it

---

117 Pfc. Luster Pruett died at Rittershoffen, Germany, on Jan. 13, 1945. Luster Pruett was from Vandalia, Illinois, and entered the army March 2, 1942. He is buried at the American Cemetery in Épinal, France, and was 23 years old at the time of his death. He was a minor league ballplayer who had signed with the St. Louis Cardinals in 1941. He was named to the Ohio State League All Star Team in August 1941, and was sold to the Meridian Eagles of the Class B Southeastern League the same month. "Luster Pruett," *Baseball's Greatest Sacrifice*, http://www.baseballsgreatestsacrifice.com/biographies/pruett_luster.html (Jan. 29, 2014).

seems that 'tis just another river. The "blue" Danube was much more impressive.

At Oberotterbach the aid station was not in the vineyard. It was in the next town back and I was with an infantry platoon advancing on foot through the vineyard when it became light and we got shelled and small arms fire, too.

I think I've already written about being at Berchtesgaden. I didn't get to take the trip to Innsbruck last week. By the way, Rodman is at Prutz, Austria, where Italy, Austria, and Switzerland meet. The Alps are very near here and visible except on extremely dark days. This valley leads right up to them. Yes, I'm inclined to believe Hitler is dead. Of course, there is that something in the back of my mind that says maybe he isn't.

When the war ended we were just north of here about 10 miles at the town of Irl and the other one I forgot, but is written on the back of the snapshots I sent. We relieved the 4th Armored Division during their famous drive and continued till the war was over, however we turned south during the last days when other 3rd Army outfits continued on into Czechoslovakia. Our last big battle was at Neumarkt, way north of here, and too, Landshut. And at Moosburg, B Company and some tankers had a fight and then liberated the 100,000 prisoners. That was indeed a pathetic sight for the most part. Have seen "beaucoup" emaciated prisoners and quite a few atrocities. Up the valley here in a camp the bodies of political prisoners were stacked up like wood and what a smell! Awaiting burning and also some were lined with something to eat them up. Just last week over at Kraiburg we made the civilians dig up about 30 Jews that the SS shot some few months ago and place in caskets and give them a decent burial. They had been thrown in a big hole and covered with about 6 feet dirt, and they also stank—ugh. Right here in this camp where I'm at now they shot six Jews just before our recon peep got there.

We have no camps like back home, we live in German homes, make 'em move out since it is unlawful to live in a house with them. However, at present I'm in this camp called "Frau Lager," a woman's hospital and labor camp. 'Tis in a fine forest beside the Inn River across from Kraiburg. The hospital was for mothers bearing Hitler's "children,"[118] and this place we are in was regular living quarters for women prisoners who worked in the nearby powder factory, mostly Polish and Russian laborers. Our division hospital now occupies the hospital. 'Tis all very modern and new with modern plumbing and electric. Also a large airport on the other side of the woods, many German planes destroyed, quite a mess. Another medic and myself take care of the ailments of C Company, approx. 250 men. Seems kinda funny to hang out our Red Cross flag beside a German Field Hospital—ha! However, we only take care of minor and emergency things and if we don't know what ails one, we send him to the aid station in Ampfing.

We have never lived in tents except a few weeks at Marseille, always billeted in French homes or confiscated or liberated German homes. Oh yes, I can always find a place to cook! Made some Aunt Jemima pancakes the other night. I used an alcohol burner and a mess kit and got grease and butter from the Company's kitchen across the court.

---

118 The "Lebensborn" (Fountain of Life) was part of Hitler's plan to create a master race. Approximately 10,000 German babies and 9,000 Norwegian babies with blond hair and blue eyes were born between 1935-1945. Hitler encouraged "affairs" between SS soldiers and women with Aryan features. Ten homes (hospitals) were provided in Germany and nine in occupied Norway where these unwed mothers could give birth. All SS soldiers were ordered to father as many children as possible. Some women applied to be in the program and had to pass a racial purity test, even though unwed pregnancy was considered immoral. It has been implied that many other women were abducted for this purpose due to their appearance. Many of these children were adopted by families supporting this program. Many of these children are alive today. Bissell, Kate, "Nazi Past Haunts 'Aryan' Children," *BBC News*, http://news.bbc.co.uk/2/hi/world/europe/4080822.stm (Jan. 26, 2014).

I've had a touch of catarrh lately,[119] but Doc Battenfeld fixed me up okay with Argyol packs.[120] So that is okey-doke. 'Tis about the same as back home. My ears are okay, only a couple times did I get much concussion so they are okay. My arm is very well. I have some scar tissue underneath the muscle that causes a slight bump where the piece stopped and was cut out. Not visible and causes no trouble whatsoever. Have a scar on either side of my arm, the one on the front side about 1 inch and on the back side about 2-3 inches. They are not bad at all, so my arm is okay, can play ball all right.

I hope this answers most of the questions. If it isn't sufficient I'll enjoy writing more later and answer as much as I can. As you know, some things I don't wish to say anything about and some I'm not supposed to, such as our casualties and the like.

Love,

Richard

Richard to Folks,

Dear Folks,

Enclosed is the program sheet from the dedication of our ball field. This boy Pruett, who the field is named after, was in Buster's squad, also the boy who I bunked with when I was in B Company those few weeks last summer. He was the left fielder on our team last season when it won the Division Championship at Camp Campbell. He was second in Division batting, and a very good ball player, he comes from Illinois. He was one of Buster's best friends and one of mine, too.

At the dedication ceremonies before the game, a color guard from B Company presented the flag, the chaplain said a prayer and the short dedication speech, "Taps" and "The Star Spangled

---

119 Catarrh: nasal congestion with excessive mucus. —Ed.
120 Argyol: Medicine used to clear infections of the mucous membranes. — Ed.

Banner" were played. The flag was raised on a staff in center field during the latter playing, then General Smith threw the first ball, said he'd pitch the game, but his arm was a little sore.

We won the game 5-4, very scrappy playing. The field was slightly muddy. All scores were made in the first 2 innings. Played the 25th Tank Battalion who were runners up in last year's competition.

I sent Buster a program and told him all about it. I also send him all of our *Allus Kaput* papers, and I hear from him about every week now. He's at Mailly-le-Camp France, east of Paris. Am sending some pictures in another envelope.

Love,

Richard

June 20, 1945

Richard to Folks

Dear Mother and Dad,

I see that today is your wedding anniversary, so thought I'd drop a line and say Happy Anniversary. Hoping you are both well and fine, and assuring you that I am.

Today I puttered around doing nothing much in general. This afternoon I put on some Kraut shorts we liberated and played softball and got some sun. Also this afternoon we gave the company shots, typhus and typhoid. I took both and naturally my arms are a wee bit sore this evening.

Tonight we have been playing a dart baseball game. We lost the darts so I took surgical needles and put stick matches in the ends and they sure worked fine. I beat my buddy finally, after getting the bases loaded with two out and walking a run in—ha!—more fun.

The mail situation has been rather pathetic the last couple weeks, seems as if I haven't been getting much. I think the transportation system is rather messed up.

As yet don't have any idea how long I'll be here or just what will happen. I think there's an equal chance of staying here a while or going to the Pacific, at least that's the way I figure it.

Yesterday I picked some wild strawberries and at least got to see how they taste this season. They were small, sweet, and tasted much like the ones at the farm. The nights are cool here near the mountains but gets rather warm during the middle part of the day.

Again, Happy Anniversary, and hope I'm around for the next one.

Love—your son,

Richard

June 23, 1945

Richard's Journal

Rodman dropped in unexpectedly this afternoon. He's with the 96th Chemical Mortar Battalion in Prutz, Austria. Boy was I glad to see him, had big time talking, fried Aunt Jemima pancakes before bed.

June 24, 1945

About 11 Junior Berkey (Maurice) calls up from Wasserburg and says come over. So Rodman and I get in his peep after chow to see Junior at Wasserburg. Big time we had. Rodman took off soon, wanting to go to Berchtesgaden before dark, so Junior and I shot the breeze till about 4 and then I parted with some medics passing by and he takes off for Munich where he is stationed with Special Troops and Army HQ. He's got it made. All in all a very unexpected but wonderful birthday. I don't feel a day older.

Richard to Folks

Dear Folks,

Had a most wonderful birthday today, visited with both Junior Berkey and Gene Rodman. I really didn't expect anything so nice.

Yesterday afternoon I looked out the window here and there was no one other than Rodman. He and some of his boys were out on a weekend visit looking up friends and he by chance found me. We had a regular old time get-together and talked about most everything, mainly home, of course, and finished off the evening by frying some Aunt Jemima pancakes. That was 2 this morn—ha!

Before noon I was called to the phone and the voice said, "Hello Berkey, this is Berkey." I couldn't quite get it for a minute and finally I understood it was Junior. He was calling from Wasserburg, about 20 miles from here and our division headquarters.

So, after chow Rodman's boys came back with his peep and we all go to Wasserburg and see Junior at the Red Cross. Had a big get-together, but Rodman left pretty soon, having quite a distance to travel by way of Berchtesgaden before dark this evening. Junior and I talked for 2-3 hours and had a big time. So about 4:30 this afternoon he had to start back to Munich where he's stationed and I, by chance, got a ride back here with some of our medics, so we said farewell in hopes of meeting again sometime. Munich is only 70 km from here, some 45-50 miles. He's with HQ 3rd Army, which is okay for the 3rd Army.

Haven't been doing much lately, just lying around my little dispensary here and patching up some dozen guys a day, etc. The mail situation is still very poor. Think I've received 2-3 letters in the past week. Did receive a birthday card from Martha Neal today. She really guessed the correct day for it to arrive.

Have been playing quite a bit of softball and volleyball lately just outside in the courtyard. Also have a dart baseball game here in the dispensary. Sure beat Rodman this morning at that. In fact no one around can beat me, guess I practice too much for 'em.

Some of Rodman's buddies took pictures of us together and also of the three of us together, so maybe if he gets 'em developed you will be able to see the results of our historic Bavarian meeting—ha!

I provided a wee bit of entertainment for Rodman last night by showing off my "loot." I have a very interesting stamp collection. A few Berchtesgaden souvenirs, including a "prize" package address card sent from Kaiser Wilhelm Strasse in Berlin to Hitler's famous mistress, Eva Braun, at Berchtesgaden. Also we both refought our personal battles again plus what we did participate in. I brought out my maps and all and we refought day by day as far as we could remember. I still have my diary of most of it.

With Junior too, we refought the war, he telling me his angle, etc. He's sure grown by the way, much taller than I and rather plump. He also showed me quite a few pictures he'd taken both here and back home. Indeed I sure had a good time today. Am well and fine and I believe, some twenty-three years!

Love,

Richard

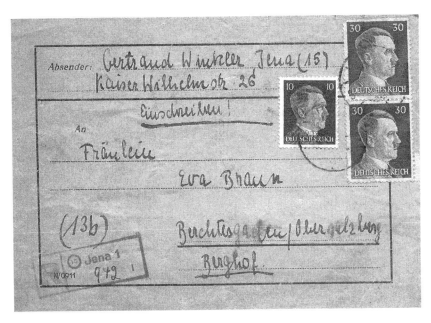

This postal label Richard found at The Berghof was actually sent from Eva Braun's cousin, Gertraud Winckler,[121] who lived in Jena, Germany.

June 29, 1945
Richard to Dad

Dear Dad,

Have received your letter of the 9th and thanks for the birthday wishes. Indeed I had quite an enjoyable day, getting to see both Gene and Junior. Sure thanks for being able to get a flag to send. I'll be looking forward to receiving it.

I didn't know you were interested in getting a Luger, etc. They are not supposed to be sent thru the mail, so I never bothered

---

121 Gertraud Winckler was an only child and her parents had strong anti-Nazi feelings. In the summer of 1940, she spent a month with Eva Braun in Munich. Gertraud was invited to The Berghof in the summer of 1944 and her parents refused, but allowed her to met Eva in Munich. When Gertraud arrived in Munich, an SS soldier escorted her directly to The Berghof, against her parents' wishes. She spent the next six months there and lost all contact with her family. Lambert, Angela, *The Lost Life of Eva Braun*, (New York: MacMillan 2008).

about it. Most guys around here are taking them home with their other equipment. I don't happen to have one at present. I think all I have now is a .25 special. I had a beautiful 6.75, 32 in our guns. I found it on a Jerry bicycle one day and was offered 100 bucks for it after the war was over but I traded it for a stamp collection and another pistol. At one time I had all kinds of pistols, but gave them away, etc. So many fellows shot themselves with them, accidentally, that I was rather afraid of 'em. Anyway I'm more interested in stamps and other stuff. I have a really wonderful stamp collection, most of it I acquired thru trades. I'll see if I can get hold of a Luger or P-38 and bring home. However, they are rather scarce these days since the war's over. All the SS troops carried 'em and we got beaucoup of them. They are more or less distributed now for souvenirs.

Thanks too, for the war bond. Thanks also for Jonas's address, think I'll drop a line some of these days. I'm just taking it easy now, have a small dispensary I operate and patch up a few guys now and then. Again thanks for the bond and your letter.

Love,

Richard

CHAPTER THIRTEEN
JULY 1945

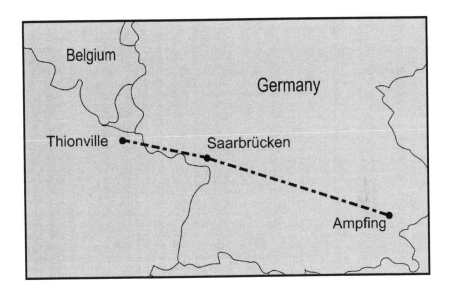

July 1, 1945

Richard's Journal

Went to church over at the 60th French Hospital both this morn and evening. Actually, the first time since Dec. 17, 1944, the day before I got wounded, that was at Oberseebach, France. But after all I guess 'tis what one thinks, believes, and does that counts. This afternoon played some terrific games of softball and volleyball. Got a slight sunburn. The weather here is rainy and cool all the time. Much ado about sinuses, which I had a couple of weeks ago. And the latest, they are bustin' up the old 68th and as well possibly the 14th Armored Division. Yeah, some guys leave tomorrow, in fact today few are left. I expect to go any day now.

Richard to Folks

Dear Folks,

Have great expectations of being home by fall, at least that's the latest. Whether that will happen or not I don't actually know, but here's hoping. Went to church up at the hospital this morning, had a very poor meal, better for supper, and played a couple of games of softball this afternoon as well as 6-7 games volleyball. Haven't been getting much exercise lately and I'm rather tired this evening.

Last night I saw *Rhapsody in Blue* again and enjoyed it thoroughly. The night before we had our division band over here and they put on a very nice musical show. Picked some red raspberries today and they were sure good. Lots of wild ones around here, more so than strawberries.

Finally got all my equipment in shape, that is all I have. Washed all my clothes and everything else that would wash the other night. The last couple of months of the war I didn't even own a set of ODs.[122] Couldn't get supplies so everyone shared what they had. After wearing our clothes three or four weeks they weren't good for anything else but to throw away, so we did, and "bummed" some off of a fortunate fellow that had an extra pair. When the war ended I had a pair of windproof green pants that were 6 inches longer than my legs and would reach around me an extra half turn, and also a shirt that was so small that I could hardly move. I've rid myself of those critters.

Got the *Leader* of May 31 yesterday and noticed in the alumni article that Win Berkey was listed as one who died in the past year. I never knew that he died or else forgot about it completely, if you did tell me.

July 2—was interrupted and didn't get to finish this yesterday evening so will do so now.

---

122 Olive drabs. —Ed.

Has been such terrible weather these days, rain and cool, that everyone is in a dreary mood. Laying around like this the jitters have caught up with a good many. I'm pretty well occupied with this dispensary and so on, so I'm faring well.

I think I sent the negative of a picture of me holding two little puppies. We got them on VE day. The one with the black eyes is mine and another kid's, the other belongs to Company Headquarters. I call ours "Vedee" for VE Day and the other one is called "Snowball." Most think mine is named after VD—ha! They are both much larger and very cute and fight all the time.

I've been to the aid station most of the day today getting supplies and mail. Received an awfully nice box from Lucy and see that I shan't go hungry for a day or so. Think I'll catch up on my correspondence tonight.

Love,

Richard

July 2, 1945

Richard to Virginia

Dear Virginia,

Happy Birthday! And here's hoping you have a good time on that day. Received a letter from you some time ago, but didn't answer because I figured you read all I sent home. Mother tells me you are jumping around all over the place these days, as usual. On the contrary, I'm taking it easy and expect to for quite a while.

I suppose you're still contemplating taking nurses' training. And you still have your mind set on going to Yale? 'Twould be nice I expect to be able to go there.

'Tis raining like cats and dogs out tonight and I'm getting sleepy so think I'll hit the hay. I can't think of anything to write about anyway that would be of interest. Anyway this is a birthday greeting and I want you to know I'll be thinking about you on the 24th and hoping you have a good time. So again Happy Birthday!!!

Love,

Richard

July 4, 1945

Richard's Journal

Rained all day and cool tonight. C Company had a dance at Frau Lager Auditorium with beer, hamburgers, Polski gals, and dancing. Had a swell time, danced much with the same gal I had at our medic's dance some 2 weeks ago. In fact, I took her home and even kissed her goodnight. Imagine that? Ha!

And so today is the 4th of July. The only noise is the workers blasting a bridge over the way that they are repairing. Got up at 10:30 after going to bed about 2 last night. Saw off a bunch of guys at noon going to 45th Division. Capt. Miller and Capt. Lorimer left Monday for the 20th AD. [123] And so here I sit on this rainy, damp, and chilly afternoon finishing up what I should have done each day or so for the past couple three months and so I'll stop till sumpin' happens, and it ain't going to be far off—HA!

July 6, 1945

Buster to Richard

Hello Richard,

Today I received the Battalion papers from you and I was really glad to get them. It's given me some idea of what they are doing in their spare time. Are you doing any training now or not?

I also got my notice that I would be leaving here in the next few days, to where, I don't know. I'm sending you a picture of

---

123 Capt. Miller was the 68th AIB dentist and Capt. Lorimer was a 68th AIB surgeon. —Ed.

the folks' new trailer and also a picture of you. You probably have one but I'll send it anyway. Bob got married and is going to be an instructor on a B-27.

Frankie is walking and Helen sent me a picture of him and I couldn't realize that he was that big.

Paul Tackett got wounded on Luzon and died later. Dad said to tell you hello and I'll send you my new address as soon as possible.

Your pal,

Buster

July 9, 1945

Richard to Folks

Dear Folks,

Enclosed is a letter from our C.O. Excusing the profanity, I think it's really swell and know you'll enjoy it.

Some of our guys left the other day and we really lost some good men and soldiers. What few of us that are left really hated to see 'em leave, and too, are wondering when we may go. Latest dope is that we'll be home in September, at least it said in the *Stars & Stripes* today that the 14th was slated to be home in September. I hope I'm still with it then, but guess I'll be home around that time anyway.

Love,

Richard

Enclosed Letter

July 1945

To the Officers and Men of the 68th Armored Infantry Battalion:

I'd like to have a chance to get you all together and say a few words to you this morning, but with Company A in Munich and the rest of us scattered all over "Hell's Half-Acre," the most practical way to tell you this is to just write it like I'd say it.

It's pretty hard for me to put my thoughts and feelings into words, but to put it simply—I sure hate to see 'em bust up our team. We've been through a lot of hell together—one hell of a lot, and, although I am not a fighter by nature or choice, if I do have any more fighting to do, I'll never find a team I'd rather do it with, or one that could do the job better than the 68th AIB. Never was there a better time to say, "Here today and gone tomorrow." I don't know what my next job will be, or how much longer I'll be here, neither do you. Over 500 of you are leaving today or tomorrow. But I do know that the outfit you go to will get some damned good fighting men and be proud to have you. I consider it the greatest honor of my life to have commanded this battalion for the past year and five months, and through six months of the most vicious fighting in Europe. I feel like I know each one of you personally—I wish I did.

I have seen you in the States near your wives and loved ones; I saw you go up the gangplank at the port; I watched you drag up the Marseille hill to our first foreign bivouac; I saw you in the Maritime Alps entering battle for the first time; I remember your gallant attempt to break the Siegried Line at Oberotterbach last December; I saw you in the foxholes with the icy water knee deep; we went into Rittershoffen together and I saw you slug it out with 'em for nine days —seldom out of hand grenade range with the enemy; I saw you attack bravely, kill savagely, and die heroically; I saw you wipe out the enemy bridgehead in the Ohlungen Forest and I do mean wipe out! I saw the deep snow, dyed red with the blood of enemy paratroopers—Hitler's best—and they couldn't stop you; I saw you "batter the Boche"[124] at

---

124 Boche: derogatory French term for Germans and in particular soldiers during the two World Wars. The 68th AIB beat the Germans badly at Oberhoffen, hence the expression, "batter the Boche." —Ed.

Oberhoffen; I saw you smash through the Siegfried Line at Steinfeld, Schaidt, and Freckenfeld; I remember you crossing the Rhine, the Main River, the Sinn, the Saale, the Main again, the "beautiful blue" Danube, and the Isar. We saw the war end near the banks of the Inn River! Yes, Company B crossed the Inn. We sweated it out together. That's why I say I feel that I know each of you personally because we lived together, died together, fought together, and won together. We have a swell team—you played your part well, and I just want to say I'm proud of you.

When we finish taking care of the Japs like we did the Krauts, I don't know what you plan to do. I'm not sure what I plan to do. I may go back to Hiwassee, Arkansas, and cut the sassafras sprouts off my farm with a dull grubbin' hoe; I may end up working for you—you may end up working for me. But seriously, wherever we meet again and whatever the circumstances, I'll be proud to shake your hand and say to myself, "Here's one of the finest soldiers that ever fought in any man's army."

Good luck to you from your Battalion Commander and friend,

Bob E. Edwards, Lt. Col., Infantry

Mother to Richard

Dear Richard,

I have a sore throat and need my medic at home to doctor it. Eleanor said she saw Bill Lester today. Guess he is going to the Pacific. Billy Seat has been to Salem. They say he looks fine after regaining the 35 pounds he lost in a German camp. We saw in the paper yesterday that the 14th Armored Division is supposed to come home in September.

Aunt Minnie's family is all upset because Frank C. is out of V-12 and is being put into active service. He got back to Purdue Thursday after a 12-day furlough and found he had failed his physical exam because of eyes. They have to be so perfect that they require an 18/20 test, and his is 10/20. They threw out seven boys for the same reason. Four were sent to Great Lakes, not having had boat training, and Frank C. was one of three being sent to Treasure Island. He sent home for his sea bag and Frank, Francis, and Helen drove right up. Martha is in Delaware visiting her aunt. Frank C.'s transportation was not to be ready until today, so he got a weekend pass and came home with the folks. Last night they *all* started back to Lafayette with him. They were going to leave the truck in Scottsburg and go on the train. He may not go overseas for a while. May be reclassified and get some special training.

Kent brought over a big mess of green beans from the Wakefield garden tonight. Don't know what I'll season them with—am out of bacon and it's hard to find. Also other meat, at times. Blackberries are ripe and I have started to can.

Had a letter from David today. He sent some pictures taken with natives when he was on Luzon. He said going up the river in that Mindanao invasion was hard on the nerves but he is perfectly safe now. Talks all the time about coming home in another four or five months.

Am too sleepy to write more. Awfully thrilled over your visit with Junior and Rodman. Both mothers called me.

Love,

Mother

July 10, 1945

Rodman to Richard

Dear Richard,

Another change of scenery and it was on the exact date I told you, too. Still no change in my status but I won't give up until I see the jungles. Right now I'm in Camp New Orleans about 40 miles south of Reims. I can't say that the setup here is really the best but it isn't bad. The joint reminds me of Camp Hulen,

Texas, where I went to machine gun school last summer, not a tree in sight, white sand, and the sun hot as hell. Entertainment, beer, etc. are good though. Tonight we had Ella Logan here for a show. Quite a girl that Ella! Tomorrow the Jane Froman show is coming here.

Camp Miami is just across the pasture. When we go to the latrine, we walk halfway from New Orleans to Miami! I'm sweatin' out a few trips to Paris, from here only a hundred miles. Boy, how I love that place!

I sort of hated to leave Austria. Fraternizing is excellent there. In fact to take everything as a whole, weather, women, work, etc.—it's got it all over this place. It looks like I'm going to start working again. I drew the job of packing officer for the company again. I hate the job; I did it at Camp Swift. I have requisitioned eight PWs to help; boy will I ever give those guys a workout!

Anything new coming from your department? I sure was glad I got to see you the other day. You and Junior Berkey are the first two guys I have met over here that I knew. Oh yes, I got those pictures printed that we took. They aren't bad, good souvenirs to look back upon anyway. I'll try to have some printed up on some of that printing paper you sent me and send you some.

Just read in the *Leader* that Ernie Bundy got married. I'll swear, Richard, you and I are out of luck! Dammit, I think I'll get married by proxy. Have you ever thought of it? The only thing is I have no one to marry.

Say, old man, if you move sooner or later, chances are you'll hit one of these camps around here. When you arrive, let me know which one. I'll probably be around here seven or eight weeks so maybe we can get together again and you can meet some of the characters in my outfit. Two guys in my platoon took clap[125] just before I left Austria. See what I mean? Can't beat that country!

---

125 Clap: venereal disease gonorrhea. —Ed.

I got a letter from Eddie Alberding the same time I heard from you, two days ago. He's on Guam now. He is building radios, developing pictures, and trying to decide whether to major in optics or electronics when he gets back to school. Quite a character, that boy!

Well it's getting dark. No electricity so I'll write more later. Drop me a line soon and tell me the latest.

Yours,

Rod

P.S. Saw Berchtesgaden on the way back from Kraiburg—some joint!

July 11, 1945

Richard to Buster

Dear Buster,

How's things in France these days? When you going home? I read in the *Stars & Stripes* yesterday that we are scheduled for the September movement. I hope so anyway. I'm going on a pass to Brussels tomorrow. I hear it's about like Paris. If it is I imagine I'll have quite a time, at least I hope so.

About broke my neck trying to ride a horse a while ago. The damned thing bucked like a Wild West bronco. I said finis for me and quit that stuff before I did get hurt.

Mother said in a letter that Bob got married, surprising to me.[126] I guess he did plenty of sweatin' over here, too, from what I hear. But I still believe we had it rougher, don't you?

You ever heard anything about Russ Fultz? I see that the 47th tanks are in this vicinity, but have never seen him. I think I'll try to look him up some of these days.

---

126 Bob was Buster's brother. —Ed.

Our newspaper is kaput—they ran out of paper. I'm enclosing the last issue. Our baseball team isn't doing so hot. They took some of the best players and put them on the division team, especially Gregory and Beal and Homestead. Write—

So long,

Richard

Richard to Eleanor

Dear Eleanor,

Whatcha say kiddo? Working hard? You evidently aren't, from what mother tells me. I hear you've been attending lots of conferences, etc., right?

Maybe I'll be seeing you before long. I read in the newspaper yesterday that this division is scheduled to go home in September. That's good!

Went horseback riding tonight, but the horses were rather excited for some reason and had quite a time controlling them. Finally gave it up after one almost threw me off. Lots of fun, however.

I hope you don't mind, I'll answer a question or two that was in Mother's letter I received yesterday. Most anyone fraternizes that wants to, although not so publicly. There are many Polish girls around here the guys go out with. The fraternizing law is rather silly indeed. The German girls are much nicer looking and have better clothes to wear, naturally. All the Germans in this vicinity are very well off because of this rich valley. Well, bye for now—

Love,

Richard

July 12, 1945

Olive Wilson (Claud Wilson's wife) to Richard

Dear Richard,

Claud asked me to write you and explain that they couldn't develop these negatives in Paris, so he sent them home and I had them developed. This was the best they could do with them, but I'm very proud of my set.

I was so glad Claud mentioned that you "grabbed him when he was hit." We had often wondered how long it was before anyone got to him. Thanks so much! He seems to be well now, but I guess I won't be sure until I see him again myself. We are hoping they will let me come to Paris.

Claud makes such nice friends and he says you're one of his best. He's such a cut up but a great guy. He told me to keep the negatives of him alone. I enclose the rest. Thanks again and good luck!

Very truly,

Olive Wilson

July 13, 1945

Richard's Journal

Went on pass to Thionville Rest Center, XX Corps, with Swientko. Drove all day in 6 x 6,[127] and arrived in France about dark and they had started the Bastille Celebration in each little town. Quite a colorful occasion. Arrived at Thionville at 2 bells in morn, up at 8:00. Missed ride to Brussels, so we decided to stay and rest, 3 days of it and all very nice. Swimming, sunning, played basketball, saw a French soccer game, had good eats, nice looking waitress, etc. Last night was spent in a Polish home at Hayange, some 5 miles from Thionville.

---

127 6 x 6: cargo truck that came in many configurations. The one Richard rode in probably had a canvas top and sides over the truck bed with wood slats for the floor. —Ed.

We went by trolley. They had lots of kids and I played with them lots. Also played the game "Home" with a gal and a priest. Had a great time. Swientko spoke to 'em in Polish and I in German and we had quite a time. Hitchhiked back about 2 in morn. Rode back to here in 6 x 6. Spent one night in Saarbrücken.

July 19, 1945

Mother to Richard

Dear Richard,

We are doing about nine things at once this week, so I haven't written any letters. This morning I'll dash off a short note to each of you, as this afternoon is farming time again. Blackberries are about at their best now. I've already canned 21 quarts and made some jelly. I'll bet you'll be picking wild blackberries in Germany!

Yes, Win Berkey died at Veteran's Hospital at Marion about the time you left. Was diseased since other war. Went to pieces all over. Mind was bad.

We are all fine and this has been a perfect week, with regard to weather. Claude Bush is a grandpa. Mary has a baby boy, Irvin Dee Maudlin. *So glad* you are due to come home before long.

Lots of Love,

Mother

Eska Bush to Richard

Dear Richard,

Sorry to have waited so long before answering your letter but I am rather dilatory along that line yet I don't guess I will ever enjoy writing as I once did. Thanks for the picture you sent us, it was you all over only like the rest of us you look a little older, yet when I come to think about it guess I couldn't expect you to look any other way. If I'm not mistaken you are now 23. Dee would have been 24 tomorrow, July 20.

Now for a bit of news, we have the finest grandson ever, he came July 14, his name is Irvin Dee. He weighs 9 pounds. I have been down helping to care for him for the past few days. Claude's mother is at home doing the cooking there. We are hoping in time this baby can help to fill some of the empty spaces, but I realize I shouldn't worry you with troubles on this side of the globe for no doubt you have plenty of your own. Do you know how much longer you will be over there? Hope you'll soon be coming home.

We will be moving to our new home about August 1. Did I ever tell you we had bought the James Highful place just across the road from Dr. Coffman's farm? I am so forgetful these days I don't remember one day what happened the day before, old age creeping on I suppose for in one more year I'll be starting on the downward slope. We have our harvesting about all done except threshing, then will be straw baling. Do you think you'll make it home by then? We have had a cool pleasant summer so far with plenty of rain. Looks as if everyone will have good crops this year.

Well this isn't much of a letter but anyway I have answered, hope you'll enjoy it just a little anyway while I'm on the job. I'll write a few lines to Dee's girl in Iowa. She seems to be so nice. She has written me lots of nice letters this spring. They have sure helped. Well bye and as I used to tell Dee be a good boy, or guess I should have said a *man*. Answer soon.

Your lifelong friend,

Eska

Richard to Folks

Dear Folks,

Just got back from my pass last night. I'll have to take it back about going to Brussels. I missed the truck at the rest camp outside of Luxembourg and so I stayed there three days and really did rest, went swimming every day, played basketball, boxed, ran, and had lots of fun. The fellow I was with spoke Polish and we spent one night with a Polish-French family. They spoke German, too, so I could get along just fine. They had six of the cutest kids, and I played with them most of the night. Had nice blue plums to eat, like at the farm. I've really got a suntan now, first one. It's finally warmed up over here and is rather hot, yet cold at night. The last six days I've been out in the sun and only got burned once. Received Mother's letter of the 10th today. Am okey-doke.

Love,

Richard

July 20, 1945

Richard's Journal

Today is Dee's birthday, July 20th. I've been thinking about him lots today. I received an American flag from the folks a couple days ago and hoisted it this afternoon. When I salute a flag now I have some friends to salute. In particular today Dee, and lots more guys, too, that aren't here to be sad with me.

The flag Richard received from home

KAREN BERKEY HUNTSBERGER

July 21, 1945

Dad to Richard

Dear Son,

Thanks for the billfold. Just about needed a new one and this one will come in handy. If you send me your picture I will put it in the place for one.

We are glad you had a good birthday with the other boys. Learn and see all you can over there and it will be useful to you when you get back. An old saying was that travel was equal to an education.

Virginia got your letter for her birthday. She also got the perfume. Oh my. She and Eleanor went to the farm with us Thursday. Worked in garden and picked some blackberries. They are fairly good this year. Mother is canning and making jelly. The cucumbers are doing well and also beets. I have been making blisters hoeing potatoes. Eleanor set out sweet potato plants and they are doing very well.

Virginia got a letter from David this week. Lucy has not been home. Glad you got her box. Jonas is doing okay. Mildred has a job. She is the secretary to the Christian preacher at Huntington, West Virginia. Likes it. About time to close office so will say good luck and write us. Enclosed is the new three-cent Roosevelt stamp for you.

Your dad,

James G. Berkey

July 24, 1945

Richard's Journal

Virginia's birthday. Had a battalion track meet yesterday, am I sore today—wow! I was the only medic entry and garnered 3rd place in the meet with 11 points. A Company and one man got 2nd with 19.5 and HQ Company, 56.5—they had all the men. Service Company got 4th with 8. Got 1st in discus and high jump, 3rd in shot and 4th in broad jump, 400 meter run, and softball throw—quite a time and lots of fun. This afternoon attended a baseball game at Pruett Field and it was lousy. We lost to the 125th Engineers, 9-12. I stayed only to get some sun. I'm acquiring quite a tan now, most I've ever had. Got 2 bottles of good old American Coke today in rations, sure tastes good. Capt. Lorimer and Miller went to 20th Armored Division some 3 weeks ago, Biener, Bohn, and Martin went to 45th Infantry a couple weeks ago. We are sweatin' out leaving. Am at aid station now, no longer aid man. I am scheduled to go home in September.

July 26, 1945

British election results: Churchill's party, Conservative, out. He and Eden won seats in House but Attlee will be Prime Minister and return to Big Three conference at Potsdam in place of Churchill.[128] Such a distinct trend to the left was surprising to all politicians.

July 29, 1945

Have been doing exactly nothing today. Received some mail from home yesterday. Irvin Dee Maudlin born to Mary Bush and Art on July 14, news in letter from Mrs. Bush. They are also moving to a new home they bought across road from Coffman's farm east of home. Said they would move about Aug. 1, won't seem the same going to see them there. They are still much upset about Dee and expressed much hope that Irvin Dee could fill in the empty spaces. Received a letter from Dad, always an inspiration, witty and subtly newsy. This time he enclosed the latest Roosevelt stamp. Went on 3 calls today with Scotty to see civilians, interesting as always. Here one usually receives eggs for one's due reward—ha—eggs and Germany!

July 30, 1945

Richard to Dad

Dear Dad,

Received your letter of the 21st and enjoyed thoroughly. Thanks for the stamp of Roosevelt. Glad you received and can use the billfold. Reminds me that I should have purchased one for

---

128 The "Big Three" were the leaders of The United Kingdom, United States, and Russia: Clement Attlee, Harry Truman, and Joseph Stalin. They met at Potsdam, Germany, near Berlin from July 16 to August 2, 1945 to work out postwar arrangements for Europe. An important part of this meeting was the request that Japan immediately surrender or face "prompt and utter destruction." "Big Three' meet at Yalta," *WW2History.com*, http://ww2history.com/key_moments/ Eastern/Big_Three_meet_at_Yalta, (Jan. 28, 2014).

myself. I still have one Jonas gave me for his wedding. It sure was a good one and still is, but rather worn. It's had a rough time all through my Army career. I'm enclosing some negatives of pictures I sent a couple of days ago. I hardly think they would be appropriate for your billfold however. I don't have any that I could send you otherwise.

Wish I was home to eat some blackberries. It's rather odd but there seem to be no blackberries in the vicinity, although strawberries and raspberries are abundant.

I'm expecting to go to some other outfit possibly this week. Seems as if they are replacing the division with 85-point men so they will be able to go home next month. Probably means I'll be delayed in getting home, which maybe after all isn't too bad, a good break for staying out of the CBI Theater.

Played a little basketball this afternoon and as usual have a sore arm now—ha! Yesterday our division beat the 9th Infantry Division in a game down the road here 7 to 3. Our team is plenty good, all big men. I'll bet the team averages 6'1" and 200 pounds. Makes an opposing pitcher rather leery about throwing the ball at all, and they can sure hit it, too. The 9th had a big league Boston Braves pitcher who previously had 2 no hit, no run games to his credit.

Got a letter from Buster the other day and said he was moving. So's Rodman. Haven't heard from Junior recently. Should go to Munich and see him I guess.

Thanks again for the letter.

Love,

Richard

July 31, 1945

Richard's Journal

Ol' Pay Day again, and naturally the vices—oh! Played craps this morning and lost about a hundred bucks at the little poker game tonight.

CHAPTER FOURTEEN

AUGUST 1945

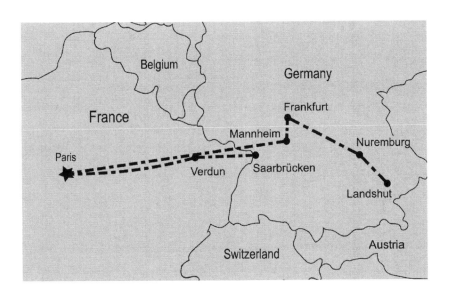

August 1, 1945

Richard's Journal

This morning some of the boys left for 80th Infantry Division—Ladd, Kerr, Swientko, Zientarski, Skillman, Benish, Costello, and Steinmann. Sorry to see 'em go. Some pretty good guys in the bunch. This afternoon I may have made another fatal mistake. I practically volunteered for CBI Theater. Signed up for CIC, Counter Intelligence Corps, up at Division—direct deployment they say. Eliasson, Coe, and I went along, were interviewed and filled out a history, ate doughnuts and coffee at Red Cross. Then over to Mühldorf and Altötting to see if we could pick up some better shirts, no soap, home at 3:00.

Richard to Mother

Dear Mother,

August reminds me that your birthday is coming up the 15th. Wishing you a very Happy Birthday!!! Hope you'll relax and enjoy yourself that day. I have an antique beer stein I picked up and will send to you tomorrow as sort of a present. You'd sure enjoy seeing all the old relics one sees over here. I hope it will get to you in one piece some time. I'll try to pack it well.

I have saved all the letters I've received since being over here and will send them also. Guess you can find someplace to tuck them away among some of my other junk. I would almost be tempted to send my stamp collection, too, but my better judgment says no. I expect that the customs officials would not allow it. I may also send my German aid kit and contents. I threw mine away and used the German one during the last of the war because it was much better for convenience sake.

Some more of our men left this morning and few of we originals remain. It's come to the point that we are next in line, which isn't bad at all. It has become cool and rainy again. I was on a trip again, too. Two other fellows and myself visited surrounding towns this afternoon in our peep. Saw many interesting Bavarian towns and things. Tonight 'tis cold and rainy and the lights are out, so I'm reading and writing by candlelight in my room.

Again I wish you a most Happy Birthday and to let you know I'll be thinking about you that day, as every day.

Much love—

Son Richard

August 2, 1945

Richard's Journal

Sowell and Shufrin left this morning for 4th Armored Division. Both Class D men. Messed around today, nothing much doing, washing and ironing.

August 3, 1945

Supposedly accepted for CIC, according to Battalion—good! Got in another poker game tonight. We retired at 3 bells and I finally came out on top with about 10-15 bucks for a change. Rainy and cold. Sent some boxes home today with old letters, aid kit, junk and beer stein for Mother's relic collection. The postage was tremendous—$9.80—wow!

Saturday, August 4, 1945

Accepted for sure for CIC. Will be leaving in next few days they say along with Eliasson, Goldstein, and a guy named Harris from A Company, good deal, I hope. Rainy and cold.

August 5, 1945

Richard to Folks

Dear Folks,

Not much happening tonight, so thought I'd drop a line. Sent those boxes off the other day, one with Mother's beer cup, one with my aid kit, one with my letters, and one with junk in it. Boy did the postage set me back. A couple of boxes had to go first class and all four cost $9.80, I think. But I think all is well worth it, nothing so much to do with one's money over here anyway.

In answer to Grandmother's wondering where I got the flag, 'twas in a small town by name, Burgsinn, probably not on the map, but somewhere north of Nuremberg a few miles.

Still am anticipating leaving this outfit soon. By the way, what's David's address now? I haven't heard from or written to him for months.

Love,

Richard

August 6, 1945

Richard's Journal

Supposed to leave this morning but nothing happened so still hanging around. Went to ball game this afternoon, 10 innings. Got a little suntan. Poker tonight.

August 7, 1945

Leaving in morning at 8 for CIC. Captain Battenfeld came back yesterday from U.K. We all sat around and talked from 9-1 tonight. Goldie, Eli, Scotty, Capt. J.L. (Battenfeld), and Schneider. Got P-35 from Scotty.[129] Played a few hands poker and 2 bells now, packed, bushed, so to bed.

August 8, 1945

Read about atom bomb dropped on Hiroshima. Bid farewell to what's left of the 68th AIB Medical Detachment. Eli, Goldie, and I, along with 5 other men from Div., piled in a ¾ ton truck and took off for Frankfurt. Had flat tire on trailer at Landshut, delay in fixing, got to look around Landshut a bit. Saw what was left after bombers got it the day after we pulled out, all beat to hell. The arch is gone. The old bus station remains and a bridge is across the canal. Got in Nuremburg late and decided to stay all night, got supper at a transient mess and billets. We three roamed around in the ruins until dark taking pictures, all so torn up, yet so remarkably scenic. Had a drink in a little bar that was unusual, the beer tasted like lye water.

---

129 P-35: Semi-automatic pistol. —Ed.

*Flat tire at Landshut, Germany, Aug. 8, 1945. L-R: Richard, driver, Ehlert, Harris,
Goldie, Cayce, Sheehan, Kavalus, assistant driver, boy. Courtesy of Norman Eliasson*

Max Platz, Aug. 8, 1945 (Nuremberg). Courtesy of Norman Eliasson

Hefuers Platz, Aug. 8, 1945 (Nuremberg).
Courtesy of Norman Eliasson

August 9, 1945

Richard's Journal

Rainy today, up at 7, chow and out to Frankfurt. Arrived in mid-aft. Had Coke at Red Cross and went to USFET headquarters where all the big shots are.[130] Finally got a guy to take us to CIC HQ, outside of Frankfurt some 10 miles. Had wonderful meal this evening.

---

130 USFET: Headquarters, U.S. Forces European Theater. —Ed.

August 10, 1945

Rainy and cold, slept all morning, the chow here is terrific, best since Cincinnati. This afternoon listened to the whims and woes of Eli and Harris. Heard Allies sent Japan a peace offer and are waiting acceptance. Russia declared war on Japs and attacked from the north. Another atomic bomb, with more potency, dropped on Nagasaki by U.S. B-29s. Must be a hell of a thing, 4.1 square miles of Hiroshima vaporized. All this should make the Japs give up.

Saturday, August 11, 1945

Up at 6:00, chow, we eight and another guy left for Paris at 7 in ¾ ton truck. Went down to Mannheim and across. Arrived in Paris at 8 tonight and finally found our place of billets on Avenue Victor Hugo—WOW—the big shots' neighborhood. A few blocks from the Arc, had chow, to bed on an innerspring. Bedroom overlooks Place Victor Hugo.

Richard and Norman Eliasson in hotel room overlooking Place Victor Hugo.
Courtesy of Norman Eliasson

Near Bad Dürkheim en route to Paris, Aug. 11, 1945. Courtesy of Norman Eliasson

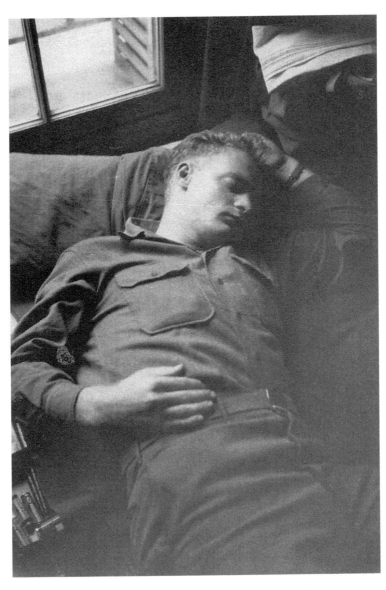

A much needed rest in Paris. Courtesy of Norman Eliasson

August 12, 1945

Chow and slept late. This afternoon and night we three ran all over Paris, and am I tired—ugh!

August 13, 1945

Expecting Japs to surrender anytime now. These damn Parisians must be on a holiday all the time. Their weekends are from Friday to Tuesday. So today everything closed up. Messed around over around Eiffel Tower, etc., meant to go out tonight but slept instead.

August 14, 1945

This afternoon papers came out with the announcement that Japan had surrendered—good! We three went shopping this afternoon down around Avenue Rivoli. Went in the Louvre and saw Winged Victory and Venus and some paintings. Eli and I went to show tonight, Goldie being on CQ.[131] Beforehand, sat out on Champs-Élysées and had a couple drinks, Paree style. Saw the show *Rage in Heaven* with Robert Montgomery, George Sanders, and Ingrid Bergman, a very fine show! Afterwards went up avenue to a bar and had dry vermouth, Tom Collins cocktail of the house, and ended up with a very fine liquor (grain). About that time quite a few GIs had a VJ celebration going up and down the avenue.[132] So we joined in a while, great time, finally ended up here at Vic Hugo and to bed—WOW!

---

131 CQ: Charge of Quarters, meaning the Commander's representative at the barracks in his absence. Duties included police call, answering phone calls, and other details. The CQ implemented rules and guidelines set forth by the commander. —Ed.

132 VJ: Victory in Japan. —Ed.

Goldie and Richard, Notre Dame. Courtesy of Norman Eliasson

Goldie and Richard, Tomb of the Unknown Soldier.
Courtesy of Norman Eliasson

Richard and Goldie in the Eiffel Tower.
Courtesy of Norman Eliasson

KAREN BERKEY HUNTSBERGER

Richard and Norman Eliasson in the Eiffel Tower.
Courtesy of Norman Eliasson.

Richard and Goldie outside the Ritz.
Courtesy of Norman Eliasson

Richard and Goldie sampling Parisian cocktails.
Courtesy of Norman Eliasson

August 15, 1945

Mother's birthday. Theoretically VJ Day! Japs have yet to send peace envoy and MacArthur is awaiting them in Manila. Having party here tonight and I'm on CQ. A hell of a job. Champagne and cognac floating around, bed this morning at 4:00, and party is still staggering on.

Richard to Folks

Dear Folks,

Finally getting around to a line. Have been having such a good time here I've almost forgotten writing. Have been here in Paris for a few days now and I'm attached to headquarters for present. Really live in an exclusive place, by name, Villa St. Honore d'Eylau, 84 Avenue Victor Hugo, a most wonderful location where all the big shots of Paris have their homes. Am a few blocks from the Arc, my bedroom here overlooks Place Victor Hugo. The statue itself is long ago removed, for the bronze in it. The subway across the street makes it convenient to go anywhere in Paris and I've been using it. Distances are so great it takes all one's energy to walk.

Went shopping yesterday afternoon down on Avenue Rivoli, which is the exclusive shopping avenue of Paris. Also visited the nearby Louvre Museum and saw *Venus de Milo, Winged Victory* and lots of paintings. Last night helped a few parading GIs celebrate VJ Day by going up and down Champs-Élysées on any transportation available. Am getting to see lots of things now that I didn't have time to when here before.

Headquarters here is having a victory party tonight but I'm on CQ so will have to look on I guess.

I'm still hoping, now again, to be home in September. I'm sure glad this thing's over, maybe I can get out in another year or so!

Hope all are well at home, assure you I am, weighed 207 yesterday—ugh.

Love,

Richard

August 16, 1945

Richard's Journal

Up at 7, finished off CQ and to bed, up at 12—WOW. On motor pool detail this afternoon, worked till 5. Went down to Champs-Élysées tonight and had a drink with wine. Home at 10 and hungry. Goldie had candy bar and orange to spare. Zeli on CQ at garage. Looks as if I joined the CIC to do their details.

August 17, 1945

Messed around all day, slept, went to a show tonight with Goldie, *Weekend at the Waldorf*, pretty good—ha!

Saturday, August 18, 1945

Went up in Eiffel Tower this morning and had a look around. Went to aquarium also. Had a little talk by *the* Major Doyle after chow. We had all been screwing off work so he politely informed us that we would have to do the "housekeeping" around here for a while and naturally we all ended up on detail this afternoon at the garage. We three went to Casino de Paris tonight, fairly good show but nothing superb. Caught last métro and sack at 12:00.

August 19, 1945

Detail at garage this morn, slept this aft. Went to Folies Bergère tonight and found much more interesting and better by far than the casino, very good show.

August 20, 1945

Slept this morn and worked this afternoon, rewarded with a bottle of hot beer by Lt. Krojeski. Went to show tonight at Artistic, *Naughty but Nice*, fair. Caught cold.

August 21, 1945

Slept most of morn, got bad head cold. Visited Les Invalides this afternoon and also museum, enjoyed muchly. Don't feel well so didn't go out tonight. Wrote letters to Julia, Bushes, and Folks. Jap surrender envoy finally came to Manila yesterday and returned with orders some 13 hours afterward. MacArthur says he's going to Japan shortly for occupation and surrender signing.

Richard to Folks

Dear Folks,

Decided to stay home tonight and catch up on a few letters. Besides I've acquired a nice little head cold. The weather took a turn for the chilly side yesterday and I was swept in, probably because I quit taking vitamin pills a couple weeks ago—ha! Could be the effects of gay Paris, however!

Still enjoying being in the "city of light" but find one can't afford it by any means, the prices of everything are beyond all reason. I read in the paper today that the French government is going to give us 17 dollars a month. Sounds crazy to me, but I'll take it being it probably comes from our government anyway. Example of how silly some things are: I needed a comb so I go into a 10 cent store and find the cheapest common ordinary comb in the lot is 30 francs, 60 cents, no sale. Tomatoes on the market are almost a dollar a pound, fresh pears dollar 20 a pound—ugh! I'll be glad to get back to dealing in dollars and cents. Almost the opposite thing is happening in Germany. Even at the exchange rate of one mark to 10 cents one gets more than his money's worth, and in dealing in old German marks one makes 30 cents if he spends 10, most unusual.

Am still enjoying revisiting various places of interest, spent the whole afternoon at Les Invalides, visiting Napoleon's tomb, the museum, etc.

Still don't know how long I'll be here. I'm no longer with the 14th Armored but with the CIC, Counter Intelligence Corps.

Hope all at home are fine, maybe I'll get there in not too long. The sudden end of the war may have changed my status, but I hardly think so.

Love,

Richard

Richard at Les Invalides. Courtesy of Norman Eliasson

August 22, 1945

Richard's Journal

Slept all morn and worked at garage this afternoon making and packing boxes. Got cold yet and feel bad, slept tonight.

August 23, 1945

Slept all morn and as that goes most of day and tonight.

August 24, 1945

Slept most of morn. We three went to Versailles on Red Cross tour from Rainbow Corner, left at one. Went to palace, had pictures taken, went thru the palace, very beautiful and nice. Hall of Mirrors and gardens were very impressive as well as paintings. Went to Marie's garden and saw old chariots used by Napoleon III, etc., all very wonderful to me. Returned at about five, had big flat tire about a couple blocks from Porte Dauphine Métro. We rode the métro the short distance home. Tonight went out in south town to look up a gal Eli knew for a Kraut soldier in Ampfing. Found her house but no gal. Took subway and went to Pigalle and about 11 while sitting at a sidewalk café who comes up but Scotty and Lt. Thraff! Scotty had been to the Riviera and Thraff stayed here. They say the 14th Armored Division is going home by September 13. Thraff took us home in his peep. Tonight started the liberation ceremonies, the Place de la Concorde was floodlit.

Tour to Versailles—Richard: back row in front of statue;
Norman Eliasson: to Richard's left; Goldie: second from right in front row.
Photographer unknown

Mother to Richard

Dear Richard,

We've not heard from you this week and have an idea that you may have been moved. It would be nice if you were left with the 14th after all and were coming home in September, but that is hardly possible. Grandmother has just been here three days to help can peaches and she said to tell you she was counting on you to kill rabbits this fall. Daddy killed one nice squirrel last week, and I fried it. He got a box of shells and a box of cartridges from Uncle Omer.

Speaking of Grandmother, what she wanted to know was not where the flag came from but whether you ever got the pair of khaki colored socks she knit for you.

Otho Trueblood is at home and I heard that he said only a little over 400 men came on the big ship that brought him home. There was a misunderstanding about it, and no more were ready to sail. He saw the mess sergeants throw overboard crate after crate of perishable foods, just because they were not going to need them. Said he remonstrated with one of them, and told him to leave the nice apples on the deck for fellows to eat, but they went on dumping them. Otho saved 16, by stuffing his pockets. Later, on the trip when eating them, boys would ask, "Say, where did you get apples?" Sample of waste. There has been a wave of articles in the papers recently about the awful immorality in European countries now, especially the cities. I am glad you happen to be in that rich valley where the people are not so poverty-stricken and desperate.

We had a letter from David this week, delighted because of the war news. He said he wished the crew could bring the PGM-5 home, but it won't be done that way, you can guess.

Lucy had a big time the night victory was celebrated in Washington. She was in a wild mob and finally got in front of the White House. There she saw one of her instructors from Hunter College. She said it was funny that after two years, they met in Washington in front of the White House, celebrating victory. She said their preacher said, "Sailors were kissing old maids, and they were enjoying it."

Lucy thinks she will be out in six months. They only have to have 29 points and she has 24. She called us up last Sunday night but we were not home from the farm. We also missed

Buster! He got home, called his folks at Louisville, and they came out. He went back with them Sunday night but will surely be out again this weekend. He stopped and talked to Virginia and Eleanor. They said he looked fine and his eye didn't show badly at all. Radio says Jap occupation will begin tomorrow.

Love,

Mother

Saturday, August 25, 1945

Richard's Journal

Paris Liberation Day, parades and crap. Up for breakfast for a change and to garage to gas up a peep for use tomorrow morn, going to drive to Frankfurt. This afternoon went with Eli to Pantheon and St. Chapelle and very nice trip this afternoon messing around. Pantheon very beautiful inside. All glass taken from St. Chapelle to protect it. Messed around Pigalle again tonight and didn't do much and had to walk home. Hell of a walk. Actually had 2 bananas on corn flakes this morning, simply wonderful!

August 26, 1945

Up for pancakes for breakfast. Read *Stars & Stripes*. MacArthur supposed to go to Japan tomorrow. Slept this afternoon. Tonight went to GI movie *Don Juan Quilligan*, very interesting. Packed my musette bag for tomorrow. Been here 2 weeks and no mail for beaucoup ages . . .

Richard to Folks

Dear Folks,

This is the picture of the group I went on tour with Friday to Versailles, the palace in the rear and statue of Louis XIV. Of course, I can be seen with my usual unpleasant facial expression. The boy to my right and also the one second from right (squatting) in the front row are from the medics, too. We three came here together.

Am now getting over my cold and feel much better. Have been here two weeks now and still don't know what's to happen. Hope all are fine, haven't had mail for three weeks now.

Love,

Richard

August 27, 1945

Richard's Journal

Up at 6 this morn, had powdered eggs and bread, off at 7:30. Ten peeps in convoy and they ain't so hot, so the guys are driving like mad, that's wide open. Got to Verdun for chow and ate in transient mess and had goat. Refueled there and got mixed up and lost a couple hours. Drove like mad till we got to German border and dragon's teeth in particular and Norman almost put fini to himself.[133] Just outside Saarbrücken he hit a large hole going pretty fast and his trailer caught on the iron gate and pulled it off and smashed it up while he miraculously ended up on the other side unhurt and only a flat tire. Sure a scare. We proceeded to Hamburg and had hot transient chow. Got to Mannheim about dark and refueled. Stopped at CIC and I called up, or tried to, Carroll Moore at 57th QM. Had to leave a message, proceeded on to Frankfurt up autobahn and to Oberursel, Germany. Arrived about 11:30 after wide open all the way. What a relief to hit sack.

August 28, 1945

Richard's Journal, Frankfurt-on-the-Main, Germany

Slept this morn till 11, shaved and showered and chow. Eli went to Bad Homburg to see some people and Goldie and I took a walk

---

133 Norman Eliasson. Richard generally refers to him by his last name or as "Eli." —Ed.

and then I took a sun bath for an hour or so in back yard. Sure hot here. Tonight Goldie and I went down the street and had a refreshing drink at a place. Upon arrival home, Eli was back and told us all about his visit which turned out wonderful he said. Marty Blumenthal is here and so completes our detachment. Maybe we can take off for home now. Sack 12 after bull session.

August 29, 1945

Big day today. Slept this morn and had good chow for noon as is always the case here. At 3 bells we packed and left for airport. Got on a C-47. Very calm and enjoyable ride, sure enjoyed it. Didn't get sick for a change. Arrived in Paris 2 hours later at 6:15. Flew right smack over Eiffel Tower. Had transient chow at airport while waiting for transportation. Also saw "Schoolboy" Hanhart who was going back to Germany from U.K. Got big kick out of Eli on his first plane ride, he was all over the place—ha! Got back here at 7:30 and had beaucoup mail, 4 from Mother, one from Virginia, Julie, Imy, M.J., DeJeans, Ellie, and Rodman. Mother included picture of Virginia, Eleanor, Mother, and Dad taken at Virginia's commencement. Very nice! DeJeans included a photo of their offspring and themselves. First mail for a month and was I greedy—wow. Wrote letters to home, Julia, and Rodman. Rodman said he was out at Camp New Orleans, near here, maybe can see each other again.

Richard to Folks

Dear Folks,

Had big time today, including 11 letters, first time in a month including four from Mother.

Quite an experience today, was in Frankfurt-on-the-Main at 4 o'clock this afternoon and here in Paris at 6. Had a nice fly in a C-47 and surprisingly enough I ate a very hearty meal a few minutes after landing here. Drove a peep to Frankfurt Monday in a convoy. We had 10 peeps to take there and then the proposition to fly back today. The boy who was standing beside me in the picture I sent was driving a peep and tried to crack the Siegfried Line with it—ha! His peep got out of control as we were going through the teeth and his trailer smacked on one of 'em and tore it off, the trailer. Surprisingly enough, he didn't turn over and wasn't hurt. He was quite calm about it all, more excited with his first plane ride today.

Rodman is in a camp near Paris he says and comes here often. I dropped him a line and maybe I'll be able to see him this weekend.

Monday night I stopped in Mannheim and tried to call Carroll Moore. He was stationed there last I heard from Buster. I didn't get him, but left a hello message for him.

The DeJeans sent me a picture of themselves with Davey, very good. They both wrote lines in the letter, Ellie told me all about the offspring, slobbers and all!

Still have no idea when I'll leave here, soon I hope. Thanks for the picture—it's swell! I'm proud of my good-looking family. Saw, incidentally, at the airport this afternoon the lieutenant whose platoon I was attached with. He was returning from a pass to England but he's no longer with the 14th. They are on their way home now I guess.

Bye and love—

Richard

August 30, 1945

Richard's Journal

Slept this morn and worked at garage with Eli this afternoon stenciling boxes, stayed in tonight, still prep for big surrender Sunday.

August 31, 1945

Lay around all morn and this afternoon we went up on hill to big church and overlooked Paree, wonderful view and beautiful church. Tonight went to Opera, *Boris Godunov*, simply wonderful. First opera

I'd ever been to and I was thrilled actually. We had good seats, too. Most luxurious opera house.

CHAPTER FIFTEEN

SEPTEMBER 1945

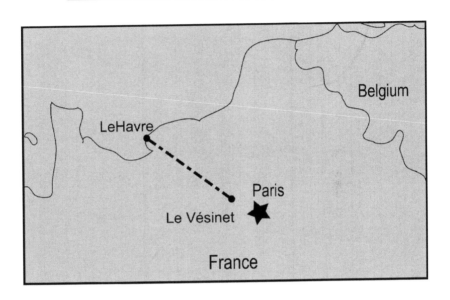

September 1, 1945

Richard's Journal

No payday yesterday. Sent all the finance people home or some big excuse, so what! Worked at garage this morn, shoveled sand, and worked in supply room, acquired a couple of pairs pants, jacket, and shirt outa the deal. Got PX rations this aft and of course slept. Some guy back from Lisbon, Portugal, had a couple bottles, scotch and cognac, and opened 'em up and we had drinks. This evening Eli and I walked down the street to see the house that the duke and duchess are to occupy shortly according to papers, nice little square four-story affair, white stone and iron fences, no garden, no yard, just a nice look-ing little stone house sitting on the corner of the Paree elite district. What they got on me—Ha! I'm living in the elite, too—ugh! Also went up on Champs de Le Lido, a real dive and we took a dive in and then right out again after a one drink, 280 franc bill, had a show which proved enjoyable in spots. We proceeded to spend remainder of evening in Bar Americain and home at 12.

September 2, 1945

Up for chow and *Stars & Stripes.* Japs signed surrender terms at 3:30 Paris time on the Battleship Missouri in Tokyo Bay. Truman immediately proclaimed VJ Day. On CQ tonight after uneventful day, writing letters, listening to radio. Rodman didn't show up.

September 4, 1945

Slept all morning. About 2 bells Rodman popped in and we started another reunion. We talked till about 4:00 and we walked over to the Trocadéro with Eli and Goldie and took pictures. Had chow and went to Olympia Theater and saw a show. Pretty good. We had a few drinks in a bar afterward and Rodman had to leave at 12:00. He rode up back home and took off. He's a 1st now, proud boy.

Rodman and Richard at the Trocadéro.
Courtesy of Norman Eliasson

September 5, 1945

Slept all morn and afternoon and Goldie and I saw *Christmas in Connecticut.* Then we went to Eiffel Tower Club and hit the champagne till about 1 o'clock—WOW!

Richard to Folks

Dear Folks,

Had another visit with Rodman yesterday. He's stationed at Camp New Orleans about a hundred miles from here. He came yesterday afternoon and left last night at midnight. We had a big long talk, took some pictures, and went to a GI variety show last night. We had quite a time. He's been out at that camp some two months and still doesn't know what's to happen to him. He hasn't got many points and is likely to stay here a while but nothing definite. He brought the picture of Junior, him, and myself taken at our last meeting and you'll find it enclosed. I look almost like an old man—ha! Two other snaps enclosed, also.

I'm still hoping to be on my way home soon, maybe this month. With the new VJ readjustment of points I'll have over 60 and that at least assures me of remaining in the States if I ever get there, and too, maybe a not too distant discharge, I hope.

Just finished doing a little laundry. We have our own laundry in the hotel, but my methods are more expedient. Chow time—zip!

Love,

Richard

September 6, 1945

Richard's Journal

Worked at garage this morn. Came back at noon and found I was on 10:15 shipping order for Le Vésinet,[134] ate and packed, left at 1:30, arrived about 2:00, just 30 miles from Paris. Got billets, etc. chow. Ehlert and Blaman are with me from 14th, a kid named Whallon from Cincinnati, Hanover boy. Strolled around tonight, went to a dance up in the little town. Beautiful place this little town, NCO Club and chow house are near here.[135]

September 7, 1945

Richard's Journal, Le Vésinet, France

Went down to CIC HQ at 9:00 and got processed etc. Ehlert and I went to town for business reasons. Made about 40 bucks on the black market, etc. Got 1000 francs for a 25 pistol—ha! Came back on train tonight at 10:20. Saw Eli and Goldie this aft at HQ here.

September 8, 1945

Some more processing and had to work all day in Paris at HQ Victor Hugo on detail pay vouchers, at least got some good chow. Went to NCO Club tonight with Eli, Goldie, and Ehlert, beaucoup stuff.

September 9, 1945

Report at 8:00, no breakfast since I been here, too lazy to walk half mile, slept rest of morn. Went with Marty to NCO this aft and had again beaucoup stuff and also went tonight with Eli, Goldie, and Marty.

Richard to Folks

Dear Folks,

---

134 Le Vésinet: Municipality in the western suburbs of Paris. —Ed.
135 NCO: Non-Commissioned Officer. —Ed.

Moved to the little town here in the suburbs of Paris a couple of days ago, otherwise my first step towards home. Have already been "processed" and just waiting to go to Le Havre, should be there in less than a week. Have spent most of my time in Paris the last few days, worked all day today at HQ typing the payroll for detachment. First day's work I've done for ages. This little town here is beautiful, evidently a residential district for the wealthier Paris aristocrats. Most houses are made of coral and stone and extremely modern with big gardens, yards, and lots of trees, very nice. I'm no longer in the same detachment with the two boys I came here with from the medics. However, their new detachment moved out yesterday and will probably go home together. 'Tis raining this evening and I'm tired so think I'll go to bed.

Love,

Richard

September 10, 1945

Richard's Journal

Report at 9:00, typed another voucher, got PX rations. Slept this aft. Went in to Paris with Marty and Ehlert. Met Eli and Goldie at Pigalle, sidewalk café at Clichy and show, *That Certain Woman* at Artistic. Home 12 bells.

September 11, 1945

Up at 8:30 and check at HQ at 9 as usual, took it easy this morn. This aft visited NCO Club a few minutes and went into town and met Eli, Goldie, and Ehlert at Rainbow Corner at 4:00. We ate chow at Arcade Club and walked up to Pigalle and messed around all night.

September 12, 1945

I did lots of laundry this morning. Went to town this afternoon and got paid finally, also got the French 17.15 donation. Went swimming with Eli, Goldie, and Marty at Columbia Club, water swell, ate chow at Arcade Club and then came back here and went to NCO Club and had beaucoup stuff. Very nice evening spent in usual arguments with impossible Eli.

September 13, 1945

Up at 8:30. Messed around repacking duffel bag, expecting to go to Le Havre tomorrow. Spent this afternoon at the NCO with Eli, Goldie, and Marty, another terrific argument ensued. On CQ tonight here at billets. Wrote letters, V-mail to Folks, Bushes, and Julia. Very wonderful weather last few days, sure glad to go home soon.

Richard to Folks

Dear Folks,

Found out today that I would probably be leaving here tomorrow for Le Havre. So there is no reason for you to write this address anymore, for I'll probably be home in a few weeks.

I have yet to receive mail from you at this Paris address. I did get some forwarded from the 14th. Otherwise it's been over a month since I've heard from anyone. Have been spending my time here just lounging around. Usually go into Paris, for something good to eat and entertainment. Yesterday afternoon I went swimming at the Columbia Club. Tonight I'm on CQ again and have a chance to catch up on correspondence. Hoping to see you all soon!

Love,

Richard

September 15, 1945

Edgar DeJean to Richard

Dear Richard,

Since I'm dental OD this afternoon it seems that I shall have some time in which to send a few letters.[136] That is I hope to have some time if too many emergencies don't come up.

So you and Rodman are both in gay Paris! Naturally I know you go to the U.S.O. for any nightlife you might desire, but I have my fears for old "ladykiller" Rodman. I'll bet he has at least five women all convinced that they're the only one for him. You certainly got a break being stationed right in the heart of the city although the prices must be terrific from what I gather. It is now time to mail Christmas boxes, in case you could use some cigarettes just let me know, perhaps they are even more valuable than chewing gum.

We are now back here in Valley Forge after a month at Camp Lee. This time I'm here for permanent duty and like you I believe I have a good deal. A private office and work by appointment with all the comforts of a civilian practice. This is really a wonderful hospital, mostly plastic surgery, neuropsychiatric, maxillofacial, and work with the blind. I just now treated a tooth for a fellow with a plastic eye. You'd never know the eye was artificial unless you were right on it. They can do some very remarkable things in the way of plastic surgery.

We're moving into a small house October 15 so that David can have a little more room. He has two new teeth and we expect him to crawl any day now but then he may take after his father and just be too lazy to crawl. At six months he weighs 24 pounds and is 30 inches so you can see he has no deficiency when it comes to size.

Elly's sister Dot married some soldier the other day. These Army men must have some attraction for the females, ask Rodman about that next time you see him, boy, Rodman in Paris, that's really putting him in the height of his glory! Course, I must repeat I know that your presence there is of no import to you and that you stay home and read Shakespeare every night.

---

136 OD: Officer of the Day. —Ed.

Yes, we had a letter from Julia, she must be having herself a time out in California. There are more people I wish I knew the whereabouts of, maybe two years from now when I get out of the Army I will catch up with them. Be careful and write soon.

So long dong,

DeJinx

September 17, 1945

Richard's Journal

Still awaiting shipment. On guard tonight, 2-3 hour shifts, not bad. This life is getting boresome, no mail, no nothing, no soap. Only fun is dealing in the black market—ha!

September 18, 1945

Finally got mail this morning from Mother and Lucy, first news from home in over a month. Buster is at home now, all my packages got there, still awaiting shipment, NCO Club, etc.

Richard to Folks

Dear Folks,

Received Mother's letter of September 8 this morning and first news from home for exactly one month. So you can see I've got more coming someplace. I think in my last V-mail I said I'll be leaving here. Well I'm still going, but when? I actually expect either today or tomorrow.

Glad to learn all my packages got home. The box contains only my old letters, it was my old stamp box and I failed to take the label off. I still have all my stamps in my duffel bag and will carry them along with me. I'd rather not risk sending them.

The letter brought first news of Buster being home. Please give him all the histories about the Battalion and medics for I have more. However there is a book, *Now It Can Be Told*, that I'd enjoy keeping, but if he wants it please give it to him. I felt quite bad about not being able to get the forthcoming Division book for him. I found out after it was too late that I could order two. I hope Helen gets one, otherwise they can have mine, if they ever get printed.

A letter from Lucy today revealed her address and present well-being, very interesting letter all around, about VJ celebrations, etc.

Met a guy here who is Charlie Bush's brother-in-law, a flyer. He knew a lot of people from Salem, etc. His name is Snead, also a boy in my detachment here is from Hanover. His mother is Dean of Women at Hanover College, his name is Whallon. Another boy in the detachment is from Whiting. We agree with most everyone about Indiana.

Love,

Richard

September 19, 1945

Richard's Journal

Same old stuff today, got job for tomorrow as billet sergeant, last a few days, supposed to leave next Wednesday for home.

September 20, 1945

Walk, walk, walk today, this billet is miles away and I got beaucoup distance to walk, nothing to do, just lie around, NCO Club tonight with Eli and Goldie and Marty and Ehlert.

September 21, 1945

Same stuff, having time with women at the billet, show up in the morning and find them all over the house—ha! NCO tonight.

September 22, 1945

Laid around all day, tonight went to a dance at Quasi just a short walk from the billet, some dance, lasted till 5 o'clock and wow! What a time, bed about 5:30.

September 23, 1945

Up at 9:00, was going into Paris with Eli to see a service at the White Russian church, but he never came and finally called at 11:00 rather hungover from the night before. NCO Club tonight.

September 25, 1945

Got rid of my billet Sergeant job today. Spent night at NCO Club, last night here.

September 26, 1945

Eleanor's birthday, sweet sixteen, and I'll bet she is, sent her 5 bucks for a present. Shipped tonight at 7. Rode thru Paris, past Arc to St. Lazare Station, last look at Paris for a while I hope. Left Paris at 10:30 for Le Havre.

September 27, 1945

Richard's Journal, Le Havre, France

Got here at 4:30 a.m. after slow ride.[137] Got out to Camp Wings at 7:00, chow and tents, left for Camp Home Run at 1:00, and am here tonight and about to go to bed. Really feel lucky being this far toward getting home. Saw the good ol' Atlantic again. Le Havre is really beat up.

---

137 Le Havre is only 122 miles from Paris. —Ed.

At Camp Home Run. Courtesy of Norman Eliasson

September 28, 1945

Up for chow, better than Le Vésinet, had some ice cream and Coke this morn, PX rations. Processed today, etc. Sold some cigarettes for 3 pounds and thusly acquired some pounds as souvenirs from a bunch of Air Corps guys going back to Germany.

September 29, 1945

Slept till 9, went out on point and saw harbor. Watched a beautiful sunset this evening from the top of this old fort. Expecting to leave soon, got a haircut this afternoon and ice cream and coke. All processed except physical.

September 30, 1945

Didn't realize this was Sunday. Went out on point and sunned myself. Am reading *Forever Amber* by Kathleen Winsor. Spent all my time doing that this afternoon and evening and finished before bed. After supper went out on point and watched some boats come in and sunset. Saw the USS *LeJeune* come in, the boat I came over here on.

CHAPTER SIXTEEN
WAITING TO GO HOME

October 1, 1945

Richard's Journal

Up for fresh eggs for breakfast. Did laundry this morn. Watched a ping-pong exhibition this afternoon at 1 between Sol Schiff, 4-time World's Ping-Pong Champ, and George Lott, 5-time World Doubles Tennis Champ. Very good. Spent from 1:30-5:30 on the point overlooking the harbor. Watched the USS *LeJeune* leave for home, the boat I came over here on, very nice-looking boat. Went to movie tonight, still laying around here and expecting to leave any time.

Watching the LeJeune going home.
Courtesy of Norman Eliasson

Richard to Folks

Dear Folks,

Arrived here five days ago and expected to be gone by now, but still here. Hoping to be going homeward way in a few days. This afternoon I went out on the point overlooking the harbor and watched the USS *LeJeune*, the ship I came over on, leave for home, very stately ship and large. I wish I was on her again.

I was looking over my diary a moment ago and find that I was last home exactly a year ago today, seems only yesterday now. Before the war was over, it seemed like years.

Am doing nothing here, just waiting. Have been reading, watching ships go in and out of the harbor etc., went to a movie tonight. This afternoon saw a couple of ping-pong champions give an exhibition at the Red Cross. This camp is called "Camp Home Run," very nice.

Hope to see you all very soon.

Love,

Richard

October 2, 1945

Richard's Journal

Slept till 10:00, had ice cream for breakfast, and then a volleyball game before chow. The Cubs and Tigers clinched the pennant in respective leagues. Series starts tomorrow. Went to movie this afternoon.

Richard jumping to hit ball at Camp Home Run
Courtesy of Norman Eliasson

Goldie and Richard at Camp Home Run
Courtesy of Norman Eliasson

WAITING *for* PEACE

Richard, Norman, and Goldie at Camp Home Run.
Courtesy of Norman Eliasson

October 3, 1945

Buster's Birthday (23), up at 9:30, slept all afternoon, listened to Series game from 7:15 till 9:30. Cubs won over Tigers 9-0. Won a buck off Marty. Got a boat today finally, a Victory,[138] Coaldale, for the 7th. Got something to look forward to, oh yeah, seasickness. Watched ping-pong exhibition after listening to game.

October 4, 1945

Movie this afternoon *Along Came Jones*. Listened to Series tonight, Cubs 1 Tigers 4, lost 2 bucks—ugh! Dance at dayroom, had coffee and doughnuts, and then sack at 10:30. Eli and Goldie leave the 6th, I think on a different boat, being in a different detachment now. Eli

---

138 2,710 mass-produced "Liberty" ships were quickly built in the United States to respond to the urgent need for ships in World War II. They were too slow to quickly deliver the tons of supplies that were needed to win the war and were replaced by a faster, larger series of ships called Victory Ships. "Liberty Ships and Victory Ships, America's Lifeline in War," *National Park Service*, http://www.nps.gov/nr/twhp/wwwlps/lessons/116liberty_victory_ships/116liberty_victory_ships.htm (Jan. 28, 2014).

is so childish, Goldie so mum. Had big volleyball game before chow this evening.

Rodman to Richard

Dear Richard,

I suppose you are wondering why I didn't get to Paris to see before you left, and I assume that you did leave as you had hoped. I had hoped to get to Paris again before you left but the big movement came up the day after I got your V-mail saying you were going home that weekend. The big movement was all of 50 miles to this camp which I must call my home for the next few months. And I'm working, too, like a son of a gun! And in an office of all places! God, the Army will do anything to a guy. I'm Station Complement here acting as a closing out force. And I'm processing records for guys going home. You can imagine how screwed up things are with me doing it. Anyone that gets home now via Camp Boston is extremely lucky!

And speaking of lucky guys, you were just that! Only fellows with 70 or more points can go home now, and what a screwed up mess. Every outfit is transferring men in and out therefore delaying their shipment. The port is screaming because they have ships waiting to sail and no men to fill them, typical Army red tape.

Seeing any football games? IU looks better than average this year. I got in a bit of the Autumn Classic about two weeks ago when I saw a couple of GI teams play in Reims. 30,000 GIs were there to see it. I enjoyed it but it lacked a lot of things like speed and good ball handling. I haven't had time to see more. The World Series is in full swing and looks as if my Cubs may make the riffle. Hope so.

How's everything at home? I assume that you are there. Been squirrel hunting any? I've been running across several Salem boys' names in this job. Howard Morgan is in my outfit now.

Beaucoup guys from New Albany, Scottsburg, Seymour, and all around. I ran across Sherald Baker's name just last night. Cecil Murrell is in here with the 106th Division.

What do you expect as your immediate future in the Army? You said you were sort of volunteering for Japan. Is that still the deal? I think I should volunteer for something like that. The way it looks now, I'm stuck over here perhaps for a long time. The setup isn't too bad but it sure is cold. No stoves and no fuel yet. Boston is about the best camp over here.

Well, let me hear the latest from you and all about things at home. I haven't been to Paris since that day I saw you. I'm holding out for another leave now. Hope it's Switzerland this time.

So long and be good,

Rodman

October 5, 1945

Richard's Journal

Slept most of morn. Show this afternoon, *Standing Room Only*. Listened to ball game, Cubs 3, Tigers 0.

October 6, 1945

Up middle of morn and did some laundry. Eli and Goldie left at noon, show this afternoon—*Nob Hill*. Series game tonight, Tigers 4, Cubs 1. Got physical today, flu shot.

Richard to Folks

Dear Folks,

Finally got a boat the other day and I'm supposed to leave here tomorrow night for New York. My other two friends from the 68th Medics left today for Boston. The ship I go on is a Victory ship and thus I expect it will be rather rough. The name is "Coaldale Victory."

Have just listened to the Series game and of course was disappointed in Chicago losing their second game.

I've been occupying the time here by sleeping, reading, movies, and volleyball. Best of all we can buy ice cream, but it always runs out in the mornings. The Coke isn't good. Hope to see you all in about three weeks at the most.

Bye and Love,

Richard

October 7, 1945

Richard's Journal

Up at 9:00, got money today, $100 plus the French 17.15. Show this afternoon, *Captain Eddie*. Have been playing volleyball every night for exercise. Tigers 8, Cubs 4. Leave for boat at 3:30.

October 8, 1945

Richard's Journal, at sea

Got out to boat at 4:30, sailed at 8:17. Passed southern coast of England. Saw lighthouse and chalk cliffs, good chow, naturally expecting to get sick. Cubs gone in 12 innings, 8-7. Ties Series at 3 all.

October 9, 1945

Could only eat apricots for breakfast and threw them up later on deck. Decided to return to bunk and have been here rest of day! Ate an apple today.

October 10, 1945

Still krank,[139] lay in bed all day, finally got an orange to stay down. Tigers beat Cubs 9-3 and won, and I lost 18 bucks—ugh!

---

139 Krank: "sick" in German. —Ed.

October 11, 1945

Better today, up and around and ate a couple meals. Some "musicians" are occupying my cot or I'd be in bed now, pretty tired. Chow at noon was first in last 6 meals. Have been moving watch back one hour each day. This thing makes about 18 knots, 4th crossing and was launched in Baltimore in February. Rocks like a tub. Maybe I'll get to bed after a while.

October 12, 1945

Got round to a little chow each meal today, spent greater part of afternoon on deck, in Gulf Stream now, notice seaweed and moss on water. Today's paper, *The Coaldale Tale*, says we reached the halfway point last night at 2000 hours, so that's nice.

October 13, 1945

Ship's Log
As of 1200, 13 Oct 45
Distance from Le Havre - 2,279 miles
Distance from NYC - 904 miles
Distance last 24 hours - 427 miles
Average speed last 24 hours - 17.8 knots
Position: 42 degrees 18 feet North Latitude
53 degrees 17 feet West Longitude

Expect to arrive in NY Harbor sometime Monday night and dock Tuesday morn, above info sounds and looks good, oh boy! This morning this little tub was sure rocking around a bit and I thought I was in for another spell, but took a seasick pill and stayed in bed till 11, and fine afterwards. Had noodle soup, quart of frozen fresh milk and apple for dinner and for supper my first big meal since sailing, really enjoyed it—steak, corn, potatoes, ice cream, bread, butter, coffee, and apple. Feel much better tonight, spent this evening reading and talking, morale is greatly improved. Got on the *LeJeune* one year ago today heading the other way.

October 14, 1945

'Tis now 11:15, I figure we are some 276 miles from NYC. Should be getting into NY Harbor tomorrow afternoon. Moved watch back the last hour. One year ago today at 4 bells sailed from NY going in opposite direction. Rather a coincidence, out of continental limits exactly a year. Did nothing whatsoever today. Read in August *Reader's Digest*, shaved, and ate a couple rather hearty meals and a light lunch for dinner. Be glad to get off this boat, my head's a constant roar and my stomach's a swirling dervish.

October 15, 1945

Richard's Journal, Camp Shanks, New York

BROTHER...............! 10:30 p.m. called home and talked to Mother and Eleanor—boy! Everyone okay. Sighted land at 16 minutes after 12 this afternoon. Pulled in Harbor at 2 and proceeded all the way up Hudson to pier point opposite Camp Shanks. Really a wonderful afternoon, a boat met us with gals and a band, then the Statue of Liberty and skyline. Up the Hudson under the Washington Bridge and got off boat at 8:10 tonight and hit solid good 'ol U.S.A. soil. One of my most wonderful days, especially calling home. Had a big steak dinner here tonight after arriving. Best meal I'd had since leaving here a year and a day ago. Cold here, took nice hot shower and sack, nice soft sack. 12:30.

October 16, 1945

Up at 6:30 for big chow. Ran around here this morn. Got pass at 2 for NYC, got off at Columbus Circle and looked up Eli's friend, Mr. Parmelee. Talked with him for ½ hour, very interesting character, manager, Columbia Concerts Corp., 113 W. 57th. Walked down 7th St. and over to Times Square, quite a sight, Empire State Building, RCA, Duffy's Tavern, Madison Square Garden, and all. Quite a thrill! Saw a Roy Rogers Rodeo at Madison Square Garden after a turkey dinner at Childs, had a pineapple soda at Walgreens, ate beaucoup hot dogs and ice cream. Kinda chilly tonight. Came back to camp at

3 this morn. Pretty tired after so much walking. The trees are colored and the view down the Hudson is most enjoyable. The French shot Laval yesterday, big dock strike here in NY.[140]

October 17, 1945

Went with O'Conner this afternoon into NYC. Went up in Empire State Building, toured Rockefeller Center and Music Hall, Radio City, really a wonderful deal. Messed around Broadway and Times Square, ate a halibut dinner at Lyons, went home 2 bells, cold.

October 18, 1945

Up at 6, chow, moved out of barracks, ready to ship. Left for train at 1:40, walked to train, down same hill I walked up one year ago struggling under duffel bag. This time didn't carry a thing. Walked thru "States" Avenue, left Camp Shanks at 3:30, up Hudson River on NY Central RR. Really beautiful, no Pullmans so folded up some seats and had rather comfortable bed. Went to bed in Utica, NY, after buying some ice cream from a boy. Expect to reach Camp Atterbury tomorrow night.

October 19, 1945

Richard's Journal, Camp Atterbury, Indiana

Woke up this morning in Cleveland. Rode to Columbus and then arrived in Indiana at 3 bells this aft. Then to Richmond, Indianapolis, and Camp Atterbury at 7:00, a little processing, doughnuts and chow, ate pint of ice cream before bed. Expect to leave tomorrow, have high hopes for getting a discharge after hearing things here, expect to go on 45 days leave tomorrow. Sack in a sheet. Good old INDIANA! YEAH!

---

140 Pierre Laval was a French politician and had been the prime minister in 1931-1932. After Germany's defeat of France in 1940, Laval became a puppet for Hitler and signed orders allowing the removal of French Jews to Nazi concentration camps. Found guilty of treason, Laval was executed by firing squad after attempting to commit suicide by ingesting poison on the morning of the execution. "Vichy Leader Executed for Treason," *History.com*, http://www.history.com/this-day-in-history/vichy-leader-executed-for-treason (Jan. 29, 2014).

October 20, 1945

Up for chow at 7:00, read my first *Indianapolis Star* while in line. Lots of processing this morning, done about 3 and took off for home. Got on bus at 3:20 and rode to Scottsburg and hitchhiked HOME. Home at 6:05. Walked in front door, Mother, Dad, Eleanor, and Grandmother, what a greeting! Just in time for chow, meatballs, and Mother's swell yeast biscuits. Spent evening showing off loot and souvenirs to Folks. Went to town at 11 and saw Aunt Minnie, Frank, and Martha. We all went to Greeks and saw Julia, Betty, and Imy. What a day—home at last!

EPILOGUE

Prior to the war, Richard had been training to become a doctor. After his experience in World War II as a combat medic, he lost interest in pursuing medicine as a career. He arrived home in October 1945 and went back to school at Indiana University in January 1946. He graduated from Indiana University in June 1947 with a B.A. degree, focusing on psychology. In July of 1948 he was inspired by a minister at a revival meeting at church and made the decision to become a minister. He married Martha Barrett in August of 1948. They moved to Indianapolis and enrolled in Butler University/Christian Theological Seminary. Richard and his brother Jonas were ordained in 1950 in the Christian Church, Disciples of Christ.

Richard and Martha served churches in Indiana, Michigan, Washington, and Arizona. They had three children. Richard's optimistic attitude and joy in life made him a very successful and loved minister and counselor. He particularly enjoyed working with youth groups and was involved with The Institute of Cultural Affairs. As a result of his war experience, Richard became a pacifist and worked to promote peace throughout his life. During the Vietnam War, this included helping draft-age men prepare their applications for Conscientious Objector status.

Richard passed away in 1991 at the age of 69. Martha passed away in 2008 at the age of 85. James G. Berkey (Dad) passed away in 1961 at the age of 80. Lennie Berkey (Mother) passed away in 1981 at the age of 87. Lennie's daughter-in-law, Carol (David's wife), reported that Lennie could never pray for just her own sons during the war. So many people's sons worldwide were involved that she felt it was selfish to pray for the safety of her own boys. Instead, she prayed for everyone's son to be safe and return home. Richard's brothers returned home safely from the war.

Mother – Lennie Martin Berkey – Lennie was born in 1893. She first met her future husband, James (Jim), in 1912. He was twelve years her senior. She agreed to his marriage proposal, but said she must have a college degree first. She majored in journalism at Indiana University and while there served as a staff writer and reporter for the *Indiana Daily Student.* To help finance her education, she took a short teaching course and taught three short winter terms at her hometown school between semesters at IU. She graduated in June 1917 with an A.B. degree, cum laude; a Phi Beta Kappa membership; and election to Kappa Tau Alpha, a journalism honor society. She and Jim were married one week after her IU graduation and settled in Salem, Indiana. Between 1918 and 1929, they had six children. Lennie was a scholar, historian, genealogist, writer, teacher, and homemaker.

Father – James G. Berkey – James was born in 1881. He graduated from Hiram College in 1904. He attended Michigan Law School, graduated in June 1907, and was admitted to the bar that same month. After a short time in Montana, he came back home to Salem, Indiana, and opened his law practice in 1907. In 1914, the Salem Building Loan Fund and Savings Association selected him to be their legal attorney and elected him secretary of the association. He became general manager of the investment and collection operations. The law practice, the Building and Loan, and his own insurance agency kept Jim busy six days a week. He kept up this pace for 47 years.

Jonas Berkey – Richard's oldest brother. Shortly after Pearl Harbor, Jonas enlisted in the U.S. Naval Reserves. He was a second year law student at Indiana University when he enlisted. Jonas completed his basic training at Notre Dame in August 1942 and then went to Columbia University for technical naval studies. In March 1943, he began serving aboard the USS SC-1039, a sub-chaser that was patrolling the northern coast of South America. The ship later escorted merchant vessels around Guadalcanal and other nearby islands, protecting them from Japanese submarines. He had many harrowing experiences. Jonas became a lieutenant and for a time was captain of the USS SC-1039. Unfortunately, he contracted malaria in Panama and was hospitalized five times.

Mildred Berkey – Jonas Berkey's wife. At the time of her marriage to Jonas on December 4, 1942, Mildred was Supervisor of Music in the Elementary Schools of Jeffersonville, Indiana. She did return to teaching but resigned in early 1943, as Jonas was to go overseas. Because she had gotten married, Mildred would not be rehired at the end of that school year.

Lucy M. Berkey – Richard's oldest sister. Lucy graduated from Indiana University in 1942 with a degree in Fine Arts. She taught art in Columbus, Indiana, for one year prior to enlisting in the WAVES in August 1943. After training at Hunter College, she was assigned to the Hydrographic Office, Damage Control Section, in Suitland, Maryland. As a Specialist X, 2nd Class she worked on ship diagrams as an engineering draftsman.

Virginia F. Berkey – Richard's younger sister. After graduation from Indiana University in 1945, Virginia attended the Yale School of Nursing where she was accepted into the last class of the Cadet Nurse Corps, graduating in 1948. She had wanted to serve as a nurse during the war, but the war was over at the beginning of her training.

David B. Berkey – Richard's youngest brother. David was drafted into the Navy shortly after he graduated from high school. He trained as a radioman and began service in July 1943. He was first stationed on the island of Bougainville and then on a Patrol Motor Gun Boat. Aboard this vessel he took part in the shelling of Luzon and the invasion of the Philippines.

Eleanor L. Berkey – Richard's youngest sister. Eleanor was a high school student during World War II and the only child living at home with her parents during the time Richard was overseas.

(Frank E.) Buster Crockett (Crockey) – Richard's best friend from childhood, Buster was drafted in December 1942 and was originally a cook with B Company of the 68th Armored Infantry Battalion. Quoting Buster, "I went AWOL because I wanted to go home to see my first born, Frankie. I was busted from a sergeant to a private. They took my skillet and handed me a rifle and I was sent straight overseas into combat."

Harold Bush (Dee) – Richard's high school friend was drafted in July 1942 and first served in the Medical Corps. Later, he requested to be transferred to the Air Corps and was in training at Alexandria, Louisiana, as a radioman on a B-17, Squadron S, 329th Army Air Force, when he died.

Edgar DeJean (DeJinx) – Richard's high school and college friend. While in dental school, DeJean was drafted into the Army Specialized Training Program. After receiving his D.D.S. at age 21, he served in the Army Dental Corps in the United States.

Maurice E. Berkey (Junior) - Richard's cousin. Junior served in World War II as Acting Accounting Sergeant Major for General Patton's U.S. Army Headquarters, Special Troops Detachment, 3rd Army in Europe.

Eugene Rodman (Rodman) – Richard's high school friend. Rodman served with the Army in the European Theater of Operations as a lieutenant. Near the end of the war he was with the 96th Chemical Mortar Battalion in Austria.

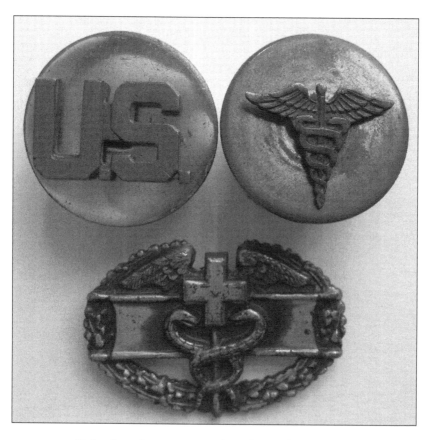

Richard's uniform insignia and Combat Medical Badge.[141]

---

141 The Combat Medical Badge was awarded to members of the Army Medical Department assigned or attached to an infantry unit of brigade, regimental, or smaller size, or to a medical unit of company or smaller size, organic to an infantry unit of brigade or smaller size, during any period the infantry unit was engaged in actual ground combat on or after December 6, 1941. Battle participation credit alone was not sufficient; the infantry unit must have been in contact with the enemy. "Military Awards," *Dept. of the Army*, http://armypubs.army.mil/epubs/pdf/r600_8_22.pdf (June 22, 2014).

"Every gun that is made, every warship launched, every rocket fired, signifies in the final sense a theft from those who hunger and are not fed, those who are cold and are not clothed."

—Dwight D. Eisenhower, Commanding General of American forces in Europe during World War II, and later 34th President of the United States

"I hate war as only a soldier who has lived it can, only as one who has seen its brutality, its futility, its stupidity."

—Dwight D. Eisenhower

"The soldier above all others prays for peace, for it is the soldier who must suffer and bear the deepest wounds and scars of war."

—Douglas MacArthur, Supreme Commander of Allied Forces in the Pacific during World War II

"To me the real heroes of the war were those who very seldom get medals—they're the medics. Whenever a man is injured, he very seldom calls out for his sweetheart or his mother. The first thing he calls out for is the medic. He always says, "Medic!" Whenever that word is heard, the medic rushes over. And to rush over he is just dodging bullets. That takes guts."

—Daniel Inouye, Former United States Senator, World War II Medal of Honor recipient

BIBLIOGRAPHY

"AIA Report, 68th Armored Infantry Battalion, 14th Armored Division, Jan.-Feb. 1945," *Record Group 4307, Records of the Adjutant General's Office*, 1917-, Entry 427 WWII Operation Reports, 1940-48, 14th Armored Division, 68th Armored Infantry Battalion, 614-Inf-(68)-0.3 through 614-Inf-(68)-3.1, Boxes 13248 and 13249, Stack Area 270, Row 58, Compartment 30, Shelf 3, National Archives II Building, College Park, MD, Box 13248, 14th Armored Division, 614-Inf (68)-0.1 to 614-Inf (68)-0.9, Folder 614-Inf-(68)-0.3.

"American servicemen and women gather in front of Rainbow Corner," *National Archives, Picturing the Century*, http://www. archives.gov/press/press-kits/picturing-the-century-photos/gallery1.html, (Jan. 20, 2014).

"Army Operational Rations – Historical Background," *U.S. Army Quartermaster Foundation*, http://www.qmfound.com/army_rations_historical_background.htm#The%20K%20Ration (Jan. 21, 2014).

"At the 36th General Hospital, Dijon, France, April, 1945," *Yumpu. com, Marshallfoundation.org*, http://www.yumpu.com/en/document/view/19091231/at-the-36th-general-hospital-dijon-france-april-1945 (Jan. 20, 2014).

Batens, Alain and Major, Ben, *WWII U.S. Medical Research Center*, http://www.med-dept.com/index.php (June 17, 2014).

Baumgardner, Randy W. (ed.), *Memories of the 14th Armored Division*, (Paducah: Turner Publishing, 1999).

Berkey, Jonas M., *The Christian Berkey Family in America: the Salem, Indiana Lineage*, (Louisville: 1994).

"Big Three' meet at Yalta," *WW2History.com*, http://ww2history.com/key_moments/Eastern/Big_Three_meet_at_Yalta, (Jan. 28, 2014).

Captain Joseph Carter, *The History of the 14th Armored Division*, (Atlanta: Albert LoveEnterprises, 1947), Chapter V p. 1, Chapter VII p. 17.

Cooke, James, "Chewing Gum, Candy Bars and Beer: The Army PX in World War II," *49th Parallel,* http://www.49thparallel.bham. ac.uk/back/issue26/Gomez-Galisteo_review.pdf , (Jan. 26, 2014).

"Death Photo of Icon from WWII Surfaces", *Boston.com,* http://www. boston.com/news/nation/articles/2008/02/04/death_photo_of_ icon_from_wwii_surfaces/, (April 10, 2014).

Deighton, Len, *Blitzkrieg,* (New York: Alfred A. Knopf, 1979).

Duffy, Michael, "Over There," *FirstWorldWar.com,* http://www.first-worldwar.com/audio/overthere.htm (June 22, 2014).

"Ernie Pyle," *Indiana University School of Journalism,* http://journal-ism.indiana.edu/resources/erniepyle/, (Jan. 23, 2014).

"European Refugee Movements After World War Two," *BBC History,* http://www.bbc.co.uk/history/worldwars/wwtwo/refugees_01. shtml (Jan. 27, 2014).

"Forty and Eight Boxcar," *Skylighters.org,* http://www.skylighters.org/ encyclopedia/fortyandeight.html (Jan. 1, 2014).

Fox, Myron, "Censorship," *PBS.org,* http://www.pbs.org/wgbh/ameri-canexperience/features/general-article/warletters-censorship/, (March 27, 2014).

Hazelton, Ken, *Unit History, 68th Armored Infantry Battalion Medical Detachment, from Port of Embarkation to V-E Day,* Booklet (1945).

"German Weapons – Landmines," *Blanco County WWII Museum,* http://ww2blancomuseum.com/german_weapons/german_weap-ons_-_landmines, (May 31, 2014).

"Great Lakes Naval Training Station," *Encyclopedia of Chicago,* http:// www.encyclopedia.chicagohistory.org/pages/543.html, (Jan. 27, 2014).

Grossman, Zoltan, "A Briefing on the History of U.S. Military Inter-ventions," http://academic.evergreen.edu/g/grossmaz/interven-tions.html, (March 16, 2014).

"Hazel Pearl Maxey Karnes," *FindaGrave.com,* http://www.findagrave. com/cgi-bin/fg.cgi?page=gr&GRid=68732828, (Jan. 29, 2014).

Johnston, Wesley, "American WWII Association Historians Consortium," http://www.7tharmddiv.org/awahc/mrs.htm, (Feb. 20, 2014).

Johnston, Wesley, "Dad's War – Finding and Telling Your Father's World War II Story," http://www.wwjohnston.net/dadswar/ (Jan. 19. 2014).

"Join the U.S. Cadet Nurse Corps," *The U.S. Cadet Nurse Corps*, http://uscadetnurse.org/sites/default/files/RecruitmentBrochure. pdf (Jan. 24, 2014).

"Journal 68th Armored Infantry Battalion, 14th Armored Division January 1945," *Record Group 4307, Records of the Adjutant General's Office*, 1917-, Entry 427 WWII Operation Reports, 1940-48, 14th Armored Division, 68th Armored Infantry Battalion, 614-Inf-(68)-0.3 through 614-Inf-(68)-3.1, Boxes 13248 and 13249, Stack Area 270, Row 58, Compartment 30, Shelf 3, National Archives II Building, College Park, MD, Box 13248, 14th Armored Division, 614-Inf (68)-0.1 to 614-Inf (68)-0.9, Folder 614-Inf (68)-0.7. Journal 68th Armored Infantry Battalion, 14th Armored Division January 1945.

"Journal and File, 68th Armored Infantry Battalion, 14th Armored Division, Feb. 1945," *Record Group 4307, Records of the Adjutant General's Office*, 1917-, Entry 427 WWII Operation Reports, 1940-48, 14th Armored Division, 68th Armored Infantry Battalion, 614-Inf-(68)-0.3 through 614-Inf-(68)-3.1, Boxes 13248 and 13249, Stack Area 270, Row 58, Compartment 30, Shelf 3, National Archives II Building, College Park, MD, Box 13248, 14th Armored Division, 614-Inf (68)-0.1 to 614-Inf (68)-0.9, Folder 614-Inf (68)-0.7.

"Journal 68th Armored Infantry Battalion, 14th Armored Division, April 1945," *Record Group 4307, Records of the Adjutant General's Office*, 1917-, Entry 427 WWII Operation Reports, 1940-48, 14th Armored Division, 68th Armored Infantry Battalion, 614-Inf-(68)-0.3 through 614-Inf-(68)-3.1, Boxes 13248 and 13249, Stack Area 270, Row 58, Compartment 30, Shelf 3, National Archives II Building, College Park, MD, Box 13248, 14th Armored Division, 614-Inf (68)-0.1 to 614-Inf (68)-0.9,

Folder 614-Inf (68)-0.7.

Keefer, Louis E., "The Army Specialized Training Program In World War II," http://www.pierce-evans.org/ASTP%20in%20WWII.htm (Jan. 1, 2014).

Kemp, Harry, "Lt. Harry Kemp Remembers," http://www.alien78.com/14th/harry1.htm, (Jan 20, 2014).

Korte, Jeff, "Eisenhower, Berlin and the National Redoubt," *Gateway: An Academic History Journal on the Web*, http://grad.usask.ca/gateway/archive22.html, (Jan. 26, 2014).

Lambert, Angela, *The Lost Life of Eva Braun*, (New York: MacMillan 2008).

Lankford, Jim, "Stalag VIIA: The Liberation," http://www.moosburg.org/info/stalag/14theng.html, (Jan. 20, 2014).

Lankford, Jim, "The 14th Armored Division and the Liberation of Stalag VIIA," *Army Historical Foundation*, https://armyhistory.org/09/the-14th-armored-division-and-the-liberation-of-stalag-viia/ (Jan. 20, 2014).

Levine, David, "Remembering Camp Shanks," *Hudson Valley Magazine,* http://www.hvmag.com/Hudson-Valley-Magazine/September-2010/Remembering-Camp-Shanks/ (Jan. 20, 2014).

"Liberty Ships and Victory Ships, America's Lifeline in War," *National Park Service,* http://www.nps.gov/nr/twhp/wwwlps/lessons/116liberty_victory_ships/116liberty_victory_ships.htm, (Jan. 28, 2014).

"Living Hell of Norway's 'Nazi' Children," *BBC News,* http://news.bbc.co.uk/2/hi/6432157.stm, (Mar. 16, 2014).

"Lorraine American Cemetery and Memorial," *American Battle Monuments Commission,* http://www.abmc.gov/cemeteries/cemeteries/lo.php (Jan. 20, 2014).

"Luster Pruett," *Baseball's Greatest Sacrifice,* http://www.baseballsgreatestsacrifice.com/biographies/pruett_luster.html, (Jan. 29, 2014).

"M-1944 and M-1945 Combat and Cargo Packs," Olive–Drab.com, http://olive-drab.com/od_soldiers_gear_ww2pack_m1944.php, (Jan. 3, 2015).

Madden, Lt. Graham and Kovanda, Pfc. Ralph, *Unit History: 68th Armored Infantry Battalion: From Port of Embarkation to V-E Day*, (Altötting: Gebr. Geiselberger, believed to be 1945).

"Military Awards," *Dept. of the Army*, http://armypubs.army.mil/epubs/pdf/r600_8_22.pdf (June 22, 2014).

"Morning Reports: Commonly Used Abbreviations," *80th Division Digital Archives Project*, http://www.80thdivision.com/WebArchives/abbreviations.htm (March 20, 2014).

Morse, Ralph, "George Lott, American Casualty of War", *Life Magazine January 29, 1945*, http://life.time.com/history/wwii-a-wounded-u-s-soldiers-odyssey-from-france-to-the-states-1944/#1, (Jan. 3, 2015).

"Nazi Past Haunts 'Aryan' Children," *BBC News*, http://news.bbc.co.uk/2/hi/world/europe/4080822.stm, (Jan. 26, 2014).

"Operational Reports and Supporting Documents, 68th Armored Infantry Battalion, 14th Armored Division, March 1945," *Record Group 4307, Records of the Adjutant General's Office*, 1917-, Entry 427 WWII Operation Reports, 1940-48, 14th Armored Division, 68th Armored Infantry Battalion, 614-Inf-(68)-0.3 through 614-Inf-(68)-3.1, Boxes 13248 and 13249, Stack Area 270, Row 58, Compartment 30, Shelf 3, National Archives II Building, College Park, MD, Box 13248, 14th Armored Division 614-Inf (68)-0.1 to 614-Inf (68)-0.9, Folder 614-Inf-(68)-0.3.0.

"Our History," *American Red Cross*, http://www.redcross.org/about-us/history, (Jan. 24, 2014).

"Overview of Global Issues–Peace, War & Conflict," *World Revolution.org*, http://www.worldrevolution.org/projects/globalissuesoverview/overview2/PeaceNew.htm, (March 16, 2014).

"Periodic Reports and File, 68th Armored Infantry Battalion, 14th Armored Division, December 1944," *Record Group 4307, Records of the Adjutant General's Office*, 1917-, Entry 427 WWII Operation Reports, 1940-48, 14th Armored Division, 68th Armored Infantry Battalion, 614-Inf-(68)-0.3 through 614-Inf-(68)-3.1, Boxes 13248 and 13249, Stack Area 270, Row 58, Compartment 30, Shelf 3, National Archives II Building, College Park, MD,

Box 13248, 14th Armored Division, 614-Inf (68)-0.1 to 614-Inf (68)-0.9, Folder 614-Inf (68)-0.9.

"Pfc. Herman Joseph Karnes," *FindaGrave.com*, http://www.findagrave.com/cgi-bin/fg.cgi?page=gr&GRid=68733091, (Jan. 29, 2014).

Pinkowski, T. Scott, "The Siegfried Line," *Lost Images of World War II*, http://lostimagesofww2.com/photos/places/siegfried-line.php, (Jan. 23, 2014).

Priolo, Gary P., "Service Ship Photo Archive," *NavSource Online*, http://www.navsource.org (Jan. 3, 2015).

"Ration D Bars," *Hershey Community Archives*, http://www.hersheyarchives.org/essay/details.aspx?EssayId=26 (Jan. 1, 2014).

"Records of U.S. Theaters of War, World War II," *National Archives*, http://www.archives.gov/research/guide-fed-records/groups/332.html#332.2, (Jan. 28, 2014).

Renouard, Jean-Pierre, *My Stripes Were Earned in Hell, A French Resistance Fighter's Memoir of Survival in a Nazi Prison Camp*, (New York: Rowman & Littlefield Publishers, Inc., 2012).

"S-3 Periodic Reports, 68th Armored Infantry Battalion, 14th Armored Division, Jan. 1945," *Record Group 4307, Records of the Adjutant General's Office*, 1917-, Entry 427 WWII Operation Reports, 1940-48, 14th Armored Division, 68th Armored Infantry Battalion, 614-Inf-(68)-0.3 through 614-Inf-(68)-3.1, Boxes 13248 and 13249, Stack Area 270, Row 58, Compartment 30, Shelf 3, National Archives II Building, College Park, MD, Box 13249, 14th Armored Division, 614-Inf (68)-1.13 to 614-Sig-0.2, Folder 614-Inf-(68)-3.1.

"S-3 Periodic Reports, 68th Armored Infantry Battalion, 14th Armored Division April 1945," *Record Group 4307, Records of the Adjutant General's Office*, 1917-, Entry 427 WWII Operation Reports, 1940-48, 14th Armored Division, 68th Armored Infantry Battalion, 614-Inf-(68)-0.3 through 614-Inf-(68)-3.1, Boxes 13248 and 13249, Stack Area 270, Row 58, Compartment 30, Shelf 3, National Archives II Building, College Park, MD, Box 13249, 14th Armored Division 614-Inf (68)-1.13 to 614-Sig-0.2,

Folder 614-Inf-(68)-3.1.

Sanner, Richard L., *Combat Medic Memoirs: Personal World War II Writings and Pictures*, (Clemson: Rennas Productions, 1995).

"Shiplife1.jpg," *Popular Military Magazine*, http://www.popularmilitary.com/magazine/shiplife1.jpg (Jan. 20, 2014).

"Signal Corps Photographic Center," *Army Pictorial Center*, http://www.armypictorialcenter.com (Jan. 20, 2014).

Smith, Robert L., *Medic, A WWII Combat Medic Remembers*, (Berkeley: Creative Arts Book Company 2001).

Stanton, Shelby C., *Order of Battle U.S. Army, World War II*, (Novato, CA: Presidio Press, 1984), 67-68, 268, 270.

Steinert, David, "World War II and the Combat Medic," *World War II Combat Medic*, http://www.mtaofnj.org/content/WWII%20Combat%20Medic%20-%20Dave%20Steinert/index.htm#World%20War%20II%20and%20the%20Combat%20Medic (Jan. 6, 2014).

Steinert, David, "Equipment of a WWII Combat Medic," *World War II Combat Medic*, http://www.mtaofnj.org/content/WWII%20Combat%20Medic%20-%20Dave%20Steinert/EquipmentOf-WWIICombatMedic.htm, (Jan. 29, 2014).

Stephenson, Gertrude, *Gone…But Not Forgotten*, (Evansville: Evansville Bindery, Inc. 2005).

Stephenson, Gertrude, *Heroes Among Us*, (Evansville: Evansville Bindery, Inc. 2005).

"Birthplace: John Milton Hay," *John Hay Center, Stevens Memorial Museum*, http://www.johnhaycenter.org/index.asp?mod=2 (Jan. 24, 2014).

Streeter, Timothy, "U.S. Army Field Rations: The 10-in-1", http://www.usarmymodels.com/ARTICLES/Rations/10in1rations.html, (Jan. 23, 2014).

Streeter, Timothy, "U.S. Army Field Rations," http://www.usarmymodels.com/ARTICLES/Rations/crations.html (Jan. 21, 2014).

"Take a Closer Look at Ration Books," *The National WWII Museum*, http://www.nationalww2museum.org/learn/education/for-students/ww2-history/take-a-closer-look/ration-books.html (Jan. 24, 2014).

"Tent, Shelter Half (Pup Tent)," *Olive-Drab.com*, http://olive- drab. com/od_soldiers_gear_shelter_half.php (Jan. 1, 2014)."The Nazi Party: The "Lebensborn" Program," *Jewish Virtual Library*, http:// www.jewishvirtuallibrary.org/jsource/Holocaust/Lebensborn. html, (Jan. 26, 2014). -

"U.S. Army Morning Reports (1912-1946), 68th Armored Infantry Battalion Morning Reports, October 1944," *National Archives*, (Microfilm Publication Box 758, reel 18.227, item numbers 25444 – 25474); Record Group 64, Records of the National Archives and Records Administration, National Archives at St. Louis, MO.

"U.S. Army Morning Reports (1912-1946), 68th Armored Infantry Battalion Morning Reports, November 1944." *National Archives*, (Microfilm Publication Box 548, reel 10.264, item numbers 16613 - 16688); Record Group 64, Records of the National Archives and Records Administration, National Archives at St. Louis, MO.

"U.S. Army Morning Reports (1912-1946), 68th Armored Infantry Battalion Morning Reports, December 1944," *National Archives*, (Microfilm Publication Box 413, reel 5.294, item numbers 10206 - 10217); Record Group 64, Records of the National Archives and Records Administration, National Archives at St. Louis, MO.

"U.S. Army Morning Reports (1912-1946), 68th Armored Infantry Battalion Morning Reports, February 1945," *National Archives*, (Microfilm Publication Box 519, reel 15.157, item numbers 19121 - 19157); Record Group 64, Records of the National Archives and Records Administration, National Archives at St. Louis, MO.

"U.S. Army Morning Reports (1912-1946), 68th Armored Infantry Battalion Morning Reports, March 1945," *National Archives*, (Microfilm Publication Box 460, reel 8.389, item numbers 13396 - 13438); Record Group 64, Records of the National Archives and Records Administration, National Archives at St. Louis, MO.

"U.S. Army Morning Reports (1912-1946), 68th Armored Infantry Battalion Morning Reports, April 1945," *National Archives,* (Microfilm Publication Box 708, reel 3.532, item numbers 23494 - 23523); Record Group 64, Records of the National Archives and Records Administration, National Archives at St. Louis, MO.

"U.S. Army Morning Reports (1912-1946), 68th Armored Infantry Battalion Morning Reports, May 1945," *National Archives,* (Microfilm Publication Box 525, reel 18.472, item numbers 14218 - 14231); Record Group 64, Records of the National Archives and Records Administration, National Archives at St. Louis, MO.

"Use of Contents of First–Aid Kits & Packets," *WW2 US Medical Research Centre,* http://www.med-dept.com/application.php, (Jan. 23, 2014).

"Vichy Leader Excuted for Treason," *History.com,* http://www.history.com/this-day-in-history/vichy-leader-executed-for-treason, (Jan. 29, 2014).

"V-Mail," National Postal Museum, http://www.postalmuseum.si.edu/exhibits/2d2a_vmail.html (Jan. 24, 2014).

"World War II in the San Francisco Bay Area," National Park Service, http://www.cr.nps.gov/nr/travel/wwiibayarea/qua.htm, (Feb. 9, 2014).

Winston, Keith, *V-Mail Letters of a World War II Combat Medic,* (Chapel Hill: Algonquin Books of Chapel Hill, 1985).

"WWII Shoepacs," *Olive-Drab.com,* http://olive-drab.com/od_soldiers_clothing_combat_ww2_shoepacs.php (Jan. 1, 2014).

Wyant, William, *Sandy Patch–a Biography of Lt. Gen. Alexander M. Patch,* (Praeger, 1991).

Yellen, Emily, *Our Mothers' War, American Women at Home and at the Front During World War II,* (New York: Free Press 2004).

ACKNOWLEDGMENTS

My gratitude begins with my mother, who planted the seed for this project in 1995, when she typed up Dad's journal of his year overseas and told me she hoped to make a book from it someday. I am so thankful that she saved all the journals and letters that make this memoir possible.

I have been blessed with finding the right people at the right time to research and proofread the manuscript. Erik Lohof edited for correct military terms and German city names, shared film footage, 14th Armored Division history, military organizational information and personal accounts of his father, Ray, who was in B Company, 68th Armored Infantry Battalion. Elizabeth Terry was essential in researching the Morning Reports housed at the National Archives in St. Louis. Jared Johnson researched and acquired Unit Histories at the National Archives in College Park. Julian Adoff created the maps. For assistance in locating other important historical documents I wish to thank the staff at the National Archives in St. Louis, Missouri and College Park, Maryland. Thanks also go to Wendy Elliot and Mikeal Wright of the Indiana University Alumni Association, Dawn Powell of the Washington County Historical Society, Elton Ross, Past President of the 14th Armored Division Association, Lynn Manship, and Carol Sue Weatherholt.

For sharing first person accounts and answering numerous questions, I wish to thank Buster Crockett, Edgar DeJean, Juanita Rodman, Julia Dyer, Eleanor Frew, and Carol Berkey.

I am grateful to Sharon Michaud for the first pass editing on the book and to Cindy Clague, Peggy Good, and Peter Dunn for reading the draft and providing me with feedback.

This book would not have been possible without the financial support of these generous benefactors: Leo Altmann, Eric Berkey, Evan Berkey, Carol Ann Bucksot, Cindy Clague, Peter Dunn, Eleanor Frew, Stephen Frew, Melissa Frew, Peggy Good, Dawn Graff, Wesley

Hendrix, Debra Janison, Bill and Evelyn Kroener, JD Ross Leahy, Erik Lohof, Greg Lowe, Mark and Lynn Manship, Sharon Michaud, Gail Napier, Diane O'Leary, Wayne Parker, Deborah Pattin, Sheri Wertheimer, and Ellie Wilson.

I wish to thank my editor, Lisa Ohlen Harris, for her tremendous attention to detail in making the manuscript a cohesive whole, her enthusiasm for the book and keeping each writer's voice true.

I am sincerely grateful for Patricia Marshall of Luminare Press for her skill and expertise in the layout and publishing of this book. Thank you to Claire Flint for her wonderful cover design.

Thank you to the family members who have provided information and photos, especially Eleanor Frew, Carol Berkey, Carol Ann Bucksot, Nina Seven, and Kim Compton.

I am so thankful for all the people I have met on this journey and am so appreciative of each person's support and enthusiasm for the project over the past five years.

I am extremely grateful for the support of my brothers, Evan and Eric, for providing letters, historical objects and recollections of our father. Many thanks to my son, Eric, for his encouragement and reading of the draft. And last, but not least, I thank my husband, Michael, for his continued support, editorial advice and patience.